AD 43

THE ROMAN INVASION OF BRITAIN

a reassessment

JOHN MANLEY

TEMPUS

To Mollie and Alec

It just occurred to me
that things aren't as they seem:
it's conspiracy
and we're living in a world of quicksand
castles on their keep
still waiting under siege
for the turning tide up
need some inspiration
time to hitch a ride
on the turning tide

'Turning Tide', from *Guerrilla* (1999)
by Super Furry Animals. Lyrics by Gruff Rhys

Cover: Aerial photo of the Chichester harbour. The location of Fishbourne Roman Palace is right at the top of the channel; the image also shows sailing ships moored off Dell Quay (right-hand side of the channel), and Chichester itself at top right. *Photograph John Manley*

First published 2002

PUBLISHED IN THE UNITED KINGDOM BY:

Tempus Publishing Ltd
The Mill, Brimscombe Port
Stroud, Gloucestershire GL5 2QG
www.tempus-publishing.com

PUBLISHED IN THE UNITED STATES OF AMERICA BY:

Tempus Publishing Inc.
2 Cumberland Street
Charleston, SC 29401
1-888-313-2665
www.tempuspublishing.com

British Library Cataloguing in Publication Data.
A catalogue record for this book is available from the British Library.

ISBN 0 7524 1959 5

Typesetting and origination by Tempus Publishing.
PRINTED AND BOUND IN GREAT BRITAIN

Contents

Acknowledgements

This book is in two very obvious ways a collective effort. Firstly it draws on much of the work by historians and archaeologists over the last 100 years and more. I have used their results, published in their own books and articles, and rearranged them to suit my arguments. Needless to say, if I have mis-quoted, misunderstood or even wilfully ignored some of the points they have made (and I am sure I have), then the blame can be fairly laid at my feet. Secondly, just before Christmas 2001, I posted the draft typescript of the book to a number of colleagues, hoping that the accompanying cheery letter announcing a 'Christmas Offer', coupled with the season of goodwill, would persuade as many of them as possible to take a red pen to my text and return it to me with all the obvious and the not-so-obvious errors underlined. They were incredibly generous with both their time and ink, and as a result have steered me away from some of the very large traps into which I could have fallen. That I still fell into many is no fault of theirs.

Many people have therefore, directly or indirectly, had a say in shaping this book. I would like to thank each and everyone of them personally. They include: David Kennedy, Nigel Nicolson, Barry Cunliffe, David and Joanna Bird, James Kenny, Ernest Black, Derek Turner, David Rudkin, Sally White, Gerald Grainge, Claire Beurion, Paul Bennett, John Smith, Tony Wilmott, Eberhard Sauer, Malcolm Lyne, John Creighton, Sarah Hanna, Paul Wilkinson and Philip de Jersey. In addition, Mike Fulford and Sheppard Frere kindly sent me a pre-publication copy of their recent article on the Invasion now published in *Britannia*, while Mark Hassall answered my email queries with commendable patience. Brian Philp was good enough to ask me to talk at a conference in Faversham, Kent in April 2001. I would also like to thank those individuals and institutions who gave me permission to reproduce their illustrations in this book. These include: English Heritage, the Society of Antiquaries of London, the British Museum, the Cambridge University Press, Pearson Education Ltd, the UK Hydrographic Office, David Rudling, Peter Drewett, Mark Gardiner, Martin Millett, Andy Freeman, Sue Rowland, David Taylor, and Barbara Alcock.

My remaining votes of thanks are rightfully reserved for my employers, the Sussex Archaeological Society, the organisation which provided me with the time and some of the funds to excavate at Fishbourne Roman Palace, near Chichester. Generous grant aid for the dig was also given by the British Academy, the Roman Research Trust, the Royal Archaeological Institute and West Sussex County Council. The excavations I co-directed at Fishbourne, helped by incredibly hard-working supervisors, such as Richard Jones and David Maynard, members of the Society and trainees, produced the results that were indirectly to lead to the writing of this book. In the final season (1999) I discovered the Super Furry Animals, and I am grateful to them for allowing me to quote from their lyrics. Barbara, Michael and Marita were a distant support, although I don't think they realised it. And lastly I would like to thank the Romans. They have done a lot for me, anyway, and without them this book would not have been possible.

The book is dedicated to the memory of Alec Down, who did so much for the archaeology of Chichester, and to Mollie Vernon-Cullen, who worked as a volunteer digger for both Alec and myself. I expect Mollie and Alec would have debated vigorously most of the contents. And the book would have been immeasurably better as a result. I hope a little of them lives on in the pages that follow.

John Manley
Sussex

List of illustrations

Foreword

In the summer of AD 43 the Roman army landed in southern Britain to begin a conquest that was to bring much of the island under Roman control. This much is beyond dispute and had we been writing a mere 20 years ago we might have gone on to say that the invasion force landed at Richborough in Kent and thence marched along the North Downs, fighting a two-day battle at the river Medway before moving on to cross the Thames, there to wait until the Emperor Claudius joined them for the assault on the native capital of Camulodunum (modern Colchester). It was a story told with comfortable assurance and one familiar to many a schoolchild.

But now many scholars are doubting the conventional wisdom. Perhaps, some argue, the army, or a large part of it, landed in the Solent and marched northwards along the east Hampshire Downs, just as another military force had done in AD 296 when the central government was intent on regaining Britain from the usurper Allectus. Such unconventional views have generated some agitated ripples on the otherwise placid pool of Romano-British studies! In some quarters the argument has taken on an amusing confrontational aspect with the 'men of Kent' defending themselves against the 'men of Sussex'. But behind all this lies a genuine academic debate; old certainties have been shaken and it is time to reassess the evidence.

Two things have brought all this about: a growing awareness among ancient historians of the complexities involved in interpreting Greek and Roman historical texts, and a rapidly increasing archaeological database allowing far more subtle interpretations of the state of southern Britain at the time of the Invasion to be offered. As perceptions change and evidence multiplies comfortable preconceptions must be challenged; that, after all, is what scholarship is about.

What John Manley has done in this book is to lead us stage by stage through the fascinating debate now raging around the events of those crucial first few weeks of the Invasion and to lay before us, in a proper critical way, the full range of evidence considered to be relevant. It is a journey of discovery, its tour leader sharing with us his own, sometimes irreverent, insights. For those used to accepting the authority of textbooks this will be an unnerving experience; this book is for those who want to know how professional archaeologists and historians go about their work and, detective-like, sift their clues.

And after all this where did the Roman army land? Was it Richborough or the Solent? . . . Well read on . . .

Barry Cunliffe
Oxford

A personal preamble

Today is Sunday 1 April 2001 and the time is approaching 9.00a.m. That last sentence is the very first sentence I have written for this book, which I know has to be finished by the end of the year, at least to first draft stage. I write at home in Sussex, usually for about one day per week. The county is important to me. It is where I have worked for the last eight years. The neighbouring counties, of Kent and Surrey and Hampshire, are also known to me, but still somehow 'other' or foreign. Because of where I work, who I know and where I write, I think I have some sort of Sussex bias. I will try and neutralise that during this writing, I will try to be objective. But, like you, I am only human and I do not think many humans are, were or can be objective. There is a nagging feeling then, that if I worked in Kent and knew different people this book would be somehow different. And, of course, if I was a woman, I probably wouldn't have written it at all.[1]

The focus of this book is pretty well defined. It concerns some of the events that took place in the south-east of Britain over a few months in the summer of AD 43. It concerns the arrival of around 40,000 soldiers of the Roman army and the consequent formal reintroduction of Roman rule into southern Britain. Geographically the focus of the book is tightly drawn also. I am interested in the campaigns of the army in the south-east, up to and including the crossing of the Thames. But I am not interested in military things *per se*, and maybe have a slight aversion to such matters – perhaps there lies another bias. I am less interested in the march on Camulodunum (Colchester) and less interested in the campaigns of Vespasian in central-southern Britain. Inevitably the book will be seen as one that debates the merits of the various proposed landing places of the Roman army in AD 43. And it certainly is about that in part. However, I hope to show that it is also a case-study in how archaeologists work, evaluate, conclude and defend their theories. But before we get into the detail, I want to ask a basic question: does anyone really care about this?

1 It was a long time ago: does it really matter?

Well, does it really matter? I think it does, on a number of levels. The first and most obvious one is that the Roman control which was initiated with Julius Caesar in 55 BC, but only consolidated with the arrival of Roman soldiers in AD 43, ushered in an historical period that we have come to call Roman Britain, and which endured for approximately 350 years. It is one of the key dates in British history, recognised by all sorts of writers as significant. Some, indeed, think that there are only two very significant dates in British history: 55 BC and 1066 (Sellar & Yeatman 1974, 9). The period of Roman Britain also represented a clear break with what had gone before (i.e. prehistory). It marked the end of prehistory and the beginning of ancient history. And, because of who the Romans were and at what they were efficient, it was marked in a very clear way by material changes in the way some people lived (e.g. new architectural forms, literacy, piped water, new styles of dress etc.). It also marked probably the first time when the southern part of this island was formally linked administratively to continental Europe, and ruled by a governor and his staff whose authority originated with the Emperor in Rome. This period is thus important and we need to understand as much about it as we can, and that includes its beginning, the very first footfall, the first day of Roman rule under the Emperor Claudius.[1]

Where the Romans landed also matters. It is important to know whether the army arrived united at one place or whether it arrived more or less simultaneously at separate landfalls. From such information we may be able to glean what the real, as opposed to perceived, objectives of the invasion[2] were. We may also be able to deduce what kinds of pre-conquest contact there were between south-east Britain and Gaul leading up to AD 43, whether there really were pro-Roman or anti-Roman factions,[3] and what level of knowledge the Romans possessed about the geography of the south-east, about sailing conditions in the Channel, about the strengths of indigenous fighting forces in the south-east (**1**).

On a very different level the subject matters to archaeologists and ancient historians. Indeed, those few months in the summer of AD 43 offer ambiguities and uncertainties of evidence of different kinds. These allow historians and archaeologists to engage in various changing interpretations built upon a fragmentary framework of 'established facts'. Archaeologists pore over pot-sherds, post-holes and ditches and try to read into them the unequivocal signs left by the invading army in AD 43. Historians pore over the surviving texts and inscriptions that are relevant to AD 43 and weigh up sentences and words for conclusive proof that the invading army came by this spot, heading in

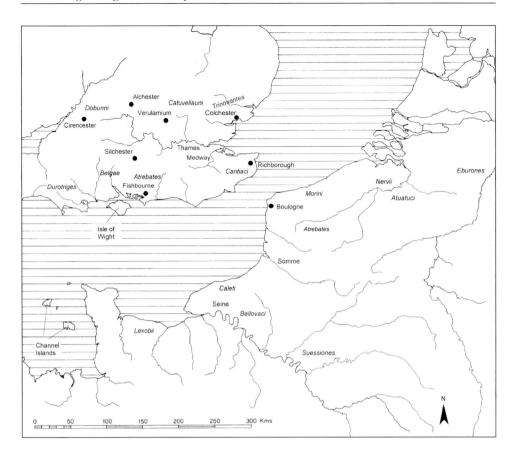

1   *Location map of south-east Britain and northern Gaul, indicating major sites and rivers mentioned in the text; selected tribal names are in italics*

that direction. Military historians, usually ex-military servicemen, have a field day drawing up landing arrangements for the ships, battle lines for the key engagements and deliberating tactics and overall strategy. As an example of the dangers in producing a coherent story from very few facts the interpretations of AD 43 are classic.

On a public, contemporary level, it matters. This book is being written following a very well-attended conference held to debate the issue in Chichester in October 1999. It has also been started six days before a second conference is held at Faversham in Kent. I am speaking at the latter but did not do so at the former. With my fellow excavation director, David Rudkin, and on behalf of the Sussex Archaeological Society, I completed a five-year programme of excavations in 1999 at Fishbourne Roman Palace, just outside Chichester. When, during the later phases of that excavation, it was thought that the discoveries could throw additional light on AD 43 there was a good deal of media interest, and I remember doing a live radio debate with Brian Philp on the so-called Sussex landing versus Kent landing controversy. As an indication of the strength of feeling on the subject, and the need to claim ownership of the invasion

2   *The Medway Monument; the church is on the other (western) side of the river.* Photograph John Manley

route, the modern monument set up on the banks of the river Medway in 1998 to commemorate the Roman river crossing is hard to beat.[4] Here is a monument (**2**) marking an historical event for which there is no archaeological evidence and only circumstantial historical evidence. But it is proof of contemporary passion.

That passion deserves explanation. Nigel Nicolson, owner of Sissinghurst Castle in Kent, erected the monument to the Roman crossing of the Medway; he is a man who thoroughly identifies with Kent. He also has a military background. But the passion for this particular historical event was instilled in him as a child when his father took him up onto Bluebell Hill, to look down to the banks of the Medway at Snodland, and indicated where the invading Roman army had crossed (**3**). This was an extremely significant moment in young Nigel's life; two very powerful emotions were set in train. The first concerned the identity and meaning given to a specific place in the landscape. No longer was this stretch of river a neutral current of water flowing through the North Downs. This was now a place imbued with a pivotal moment in Roman history. Whenever Nigel Nicolson subsequently crossed the Medway by car, coach or train he may have remembered, fleetingly and unconsciously, the Roman crossing too. And how many times has he crossed the Medway? Each crossing, each momentary recall, would have sedimented the event in memory. The second concerned the linkage that was established between the place of the Roman crossing and Nigel's relationship with his father. This was not some 'fact' that had been delivered to him impartially on a school outing; it was a personal knowledge imparted by his father. A sense of place, love for a father and knowledge of a Roman army crossing were carried forward by Nigel from that day onwards. I don't see how such a belief, so lovingly instilled, evoked and remembered over decades, can be surrendered readily by anyone in such circum-

3 The view from Bluebell Hill, looking west down into the valley of the Medway at the supposed site of the Roman crossing. The defending forces were supposed to be stationed on the hill on the far side. Photograph John Manley

stances. To do so would be to admit that some part of your own upbringing had been false, and that your father had been mistaken.

And so it is with many people who have developed a sense of local history through a sense of growing up and living in one place. To some in Kent the Roman invasion of AD 43 is one of the defining attributes of the county, along with St Augustine, Canterbury, hop gardens and the ferry ports. To some in East Sussex the Norman invasion of 1066 is likewise a defining characteristic, along with the South Downs, the Weald and the iron industry. I imagine that if some Kentish historian came out with a theory that William had actually landed at Faversham in 1066 there would be quite an uproar in this part of the south-east. I suppose all this points to the possibility that those who live closest to the scene of the events are even less likely to be objective than those from further afield. Indeed, they cannot be objective since the history they are studying is within them and has evolved and grown up with them. For some, then, who we are and where we are influences, perhaps dictates, what we think and what we write.

As a slight digression it is interesting to compare the public interest in where the Romans landed with the academic interest. I sense that for most academic archaeologists who write about the Romans or Roman Britain, the actual place where they landed holds relatively little interest. Indeed, one eminent professor of archaeology asked me if people were really still interested in that question. Most academic archaeologists are now keen to answer questions of process (e.g. the whole question of romanisation of the indigenous population) rather than specifics of when and where things took place. Not surprisingly, archaeology is better at providing data for the former than the latter.

I am also conscious of contemporary interest from the tourism industry. Some visitors from far afield are likely to be more attracted to locations which enjoy specific marketing labels tagged to the heritage. '1066 Country' here in East Sussex is an obvious one, and a very successful one too. Tourists, by and large, don't like uncertainty. They need to know when their aeroplane is departing, which hotels they are staying in, and when and where the history that they are supposed to be appreciating actually happened. In short they want to buy the tea-towel that says the Romans landed here (so they can say they were there as well) rather than the Romans *may* have landed here (and they were possibly holidaying in the wrong place). It is easy to lampoon and be patronising about history for tourists, but not so easy to deny that tourism is a big industry in Britain and that many people earn a comfortable and rewarding living from it.

Lastly, it matters to education and intellectual enquiry in its broadest sense. The study of Roman Britain has featured prominently in the National Curriculum in England for a number of years. Most schoolchildren[5] in England tend to learn about the Romans relatively early on in their school careers, and for the majority of them this is the only time at which they will formally study the Romans; a 'fact' learnt at this stage is likely to influence an individual's opinion for life. Contemporary education is more about problem-solving, stimulating powers of analysis and deduction, than accepting received wisdom unquestioningly. I remember, and still have, one of the first archaeological textbooks I bought, as an 18-year-old. It was *Britannia – a history of Roman Britain* by Sheppard Frere, first published in 1967.[6] I look now at that book beside me, and note that the pencil underlining I did then still survives. 'At Richborough, then, the army landed' (Frere 1967, 63); a short sentence and an unequivocal one, leaving no room for argument; case closed. The author was Professor of Archaeology of the Roman Empire at the University of Oxford; I was a grammar school product, brought up on a council estate on the outskirts of Bristol, and had never set foot on an excavation. I didn't feel I was in a position to argue with him. I am not sure I feel much different now. But personal insecurities aside, a flurry of recent papers in learned journals does seem to indicate that things might not be so cut and dried as seemed then. However, it has taken a long time to get from absolute certainty to debating probabilities and possibilities; a generation in fact. And that generation has grown up with the knowledge that the Romans definitely landed at Richborough. Such incontrovertible facts are repeated in books[7] and museum displays.[8] Now, I dare say that for all or most of these people suddenly learning that what was a given fact might be now a subject of debate will not turn their contemporary lives upside down, or drive them to drink or religion or worse. But it does seem a shame that those people, for the very brief period in their lives when they learnt about the Romans in Britain, were not afforded the opportunity to weigh up the evidence for themselves. After all, there isn't much of it, just three sides of A4 for the documentary evidence and a few excavations in ditches that produced some pottery.

So for all these reasons, for some people, admittedly a minority, it does matter and they do care. But before I begin to discuss the little evidence we have for the Roman invasion, for my own sake if not for yours, I wish to investigate an issue which I find stimulating. The first question is this: were the Romans really like us? And the second question is: if not, in what ways did they differ? You may regard this as an annoying digression and want to be convinced of the relevance of these questions for the subject matter of this book. It is a bit of an indulgence, and I must confess that I also hope that the Romans were not really like us – I don't want to believe that they were the same sort of people as we are, only with less sophisticated technology and less scruples about slavery. Please bear with me and I hope that, by the end of the book, you will have found the digression useful.

2 Were the Romans really like us?

Let me confess to something right at the start. I do not have the answer to this conundrum, but I do believe there is merit in at least posing the question. I am writing at a time of significant media interest in archaeology and history, and the Romans, as ever, provide a rich source of public appeal. Their usual portrayal in books or on film is as thinking, rational beings, whom we can empathise with, understand, and, if we are engineers, engage in a good conversation about the construction of, for example, buildings, roads, aqueducts and sewers. In short, the Romans were a lot like us. If we have a military background we can probably get on with them quite well too. Indeed, there are some who argue that whatever may have changed between the Romans and us (for example, they worshipped different gods than we do; we have the internal combustion engine – they didn't) some things have stayed constant. The Romans laid drains and we lay drains, and indeed they look similar and function in the same way. If we could speak the same language, could we have had a meaningful conversation with a Roman about a drain? And there are those who certainly think that soldiering is soldiering, whatever millennium we are talking about. They believe that Aulus Plautius'[1] tactics would have been obvious and understandable to a five-star US General, and vice versa. But are they right?

I am conscious of using the term 'Romans' as a shorthand and a little too loosely. Clearly what is implied by that term depends on the time and place in which it is being used. In the mid- to late first century AD, in south-east Britain for instance, depending on place Romans might mean legionary soldiers, auxiliary troops, traders, clients, freedmen, slaves, enfranchised indigenous individuals and the families and dependants of these people: ethnically a multi-racial society and linguistically polyglot. In essence, Romans means those people who are in some way part of the Roman cultural system and, superficially at least, subscribe to the ideas and beliefs of that culture; they need not necessarily be from Rome, or Italy, or have any form of Roman citizenship. They may also have been a minority in south-east Britain, at least in the decade immediately following the invasion.

But what is the problem with thinking that the Romans were a lot like us? Well, for those of us familiar with the difficulties of trying to reconstruct the lives of late prehistoric people in Britain, there appears to be something of a mental sea-change when the Romans arrived. In the middle of the twentieth century many archaeologists thought that, for prehistoric communities, it was possible to recover evidence of surviving material culture (in the form of pottery sherds, metal artefacts and plans of settlements for instance) and then, in exceptional circumstances, it was possible to reveal something about their 'economies' by the study of plant remains and animal bones. Their belief systems and ritual or religious behaviours were deemed to be beyond retrieval (Model 1). In the last two decades or so there has been almost a reversal of this position. This stems from a growing awareness that religion and ritual were absolutely central to the daily lives of prehistoric peoples. So central, in fact, that they may have governed the types of pottery they used, the shape of the houses they lived in, and the foodstuffs they ate. In other words, without some understanding of ritual beliefs, and how these affected daily behaviours, which in turn affected how things were made, used and subsequently found their way into the ground, archaeologists did not have much chance of really understanding late prehistoric communities (Model 2). As an archaeologist I feel happy with Model 2 with regard to prehistoric peoples, but am aware that many writers use Model 1 when it comes to the Romans, assuming that the Romans thought and acted in similar ways to ourselves. I am not suggesting here that there were no differences in cognitive processes between prehistory and the classical periods, but the transition at present appears far too abrupt.

A good recent example of the sort of implied congruence of thinking between ourselves and the Romans is a book on the building of a Roman Legionary Fortress (Shirley 2001). The book is an excellent one and goes into considerable detail, based largely on the author's work on the legionary fortress of Inchtuthil in Scotland, of the various stages involved in planning and constructing such a fortress – from site preparation and the erection of defences, to the construction of masonry buildings, streets, drains, water-supply, logistics of manpower and materials and the time it took to construct the fortress. The theoretical underpinning of the work is, however, essentially a twenty-first century one.

> The first step here is the theoretical reconstruction of the buildings . . . using archaeological remains . . . and informed pragmatism about the building process . . . all that can be suggested is a plausible way of constructing the buildings, consistent with the evidence, with traditional building practice, and with common sense. (Shirley 2001, 10).

One of the key phrases here is *common sense*; the implication is that the Romans thought like us, and that common sense was a shared common sense. I am not indicating here that you don't require a great deal of organisational ability to construct a legionary fortress; quite clearly the Romans possessed that. But might they have reached the same ends through quite different thought processes and planning procedures than the ones we possess? It is the recognition of that possibility that is missing from books like these.

There is plenty of surviving evidence, both in ancient texts and in material form, that the Romans were different from our twenty-first-century selves. Some of this evidence is pretty obvious. For instance the spectacles of animals and occasionally humans being put to death for entertainment in amphitheatres is abhorrent to our current moral codes, as is the concept of a society where human beings were bought and sold as slaves. Anyone who has walked around Pompeii and looked at the decorative schemes applied to the houses will know that the Roman sense of aesthetics must have been quite different from our own. In addition, it is always salutary to remember that all those grand stone public buildings, with their imposing columns, may well have been painted in colours that we would now consider garish. Differences probably existed in many, if not all, areas of life. Attitudes to family life were markedly different with, for instance, the integration of some slaves within the domestic household of larger and wealthier families. One of the difficulties faced by students of the Roman house is the problem of identifying where children slept and played, and indeed, where slaves slept. It is quite possible that, in some houses, favoured slaves slept in the bedrooms of their masters and mistresses. Of course, that there were manifest differences does not imply that the Romans *thought* differently from ourselves, or when faced with undertakings governed by the immutable laws of physics, such as how to get 900 ships or so across from Gaul to Britain, *acted* differently. In addition, we would be as strange to them as they might appear to us; after a little explanation they might have understood the rules of golf, but they would not necessarily have understood why anyone would want to play it.

So what evidence do we have for the contention that the Romans thought and acted differently from ourselves?[2] I am going to try to present this question in greater detail by drawing on the work of Florence Dupont (1989). In her book, translated into English with the rather bland title of *Daily Life in Ancient Rome*, there are some possible insights into how the Romans thought very differently. The book deals with the era of the Republic (especially the earlier Republic) and, partly because it is based on historical sources, focuses on narrow and aristocratic sections of society. For this reason it would be dangerous to assume that the customs and practices described correspond with the realities of daily life. Indeed the views in her book essentially portray the ideals of a Roman aristocratic romanticism and as such are almost a *caricature*; yet the concepts at least provide a little insight into the *theoretical* underpinnings of Roman lives.

According to Dupont, in the days of the early Roman Republic wars were fought by citizen armies who returned to their farms during the winter. A man who did not have land could not become a soldier. For the best possible relationship that a man could have with the soil was that of a ploughman.[3] Arable cultivation was almost seen as a form of religious observance, with the cultivator not only growing food for the household but becoming cultivated in the cultural sense. Livestock breeding, by contrast, was regarded as a slavish activity (Dupont 1989, 46).

The fact that without citizenship life was impossible enabled a particularly Roman view of slavery. Many freemen owned at least one slave, and slaves might be managers of estates or high-ranking government officials, as well as workers in the mines. A slave was in one sense a mere extension of the body of the citizen; yet masters and mistresses could be bound to slaves by a sort of grateful compassion. Slaves were, however, a pre-requisite for the aristocrat, and a man without a slave was as naked as a soldier without a weapon (Dupont 1989, 58).

For the Romans, religious observances dwelt in every daily activity. There were gods of war, gods of home life, gods of gardens, gods of forests; each god was linked to a particular human activity and each god had its own appropriate place. The Romans thus spent their lives moving between one religious space and the next, switching god and behaviour as they went. Each human activity was an act of worship to the deity that watched over it. On starting to plough, on sitting down at table, or at the outset of a military campaign, it was wise to make a sacrifice to the god in whose space one intended to take up temporary residence (Dupont 1989, 75). Gates and boundaries were places where Romans had to tread particularly carefully. The god Terminus stood guard at boundaries and needed to be honoured by specific rites, whereas Janus watched over gates. To cross boundaries safely one had to be free of hostile intent, and to pass through a gate was always dangerous (Dupont 1989, 85).

During the early Republic, when the majority of wars lasted one campaigning season, there was no standing army; most soldiers were freeborn citizens. In order to go to war the cause had to be just and honourable, so that a religious or moral sanction could be invoked, even if, in reality, the cause was fake or unjust. A good example of the 'Just War' was Caesar's campaign against Ariovistus in Gaul, and the pleading of the Aedui and Sequani which preceded it, imploring Caesar to intervene on their behalf (Caesar, BG, 1, 31). To move from peace to war, and to enter the territory of an enemy, was not only a potentially dangerous activity but also a ritually charged process. A good beginning had to be made to a military campaign, and the first actions performed and first words spoken were highly significant. It was essential to avoid unfortunate remarks and birds of ill omen, and instead seize upon any favourable sign that might appear. Indeed Romans had a horror of beginnings. Beginning an action was a decisive moment that set off a whole train of events, and every beginning had to start in the best possible circumstances associated with the most appropriate gestures and words. What happened afterwards was simply the result of a good or bad beginning.

The gods supplied the best guarantees; this is why half of Roman religion was devoted to the interpretation of portents. These came in three kinds: those requested of Jupiter, known as auspices; those that were observed but unsought; and extraordinary phenomena that forced themselves on people's attention (Dupont 1989, 181). The gods sent signs, such a birds flying past, a storm rumbling in the distance, or, as in Dio's treatment of the Roman invasion, a shooting star travelling from east to west. For military campaigns the augurs had developed a special procedure for examining the auspices, which involved sacred chickens. On the morning of a battle, they looked to see if the chickens were feeding properly, letting the food drop from their beaks. If they were, then the auspices were deemed favourable; if not, then battle was best avoided that day (Dupont 1989, 183). In addition, according to the Roman calendar, about one third of all days were considered unlucky, and certain days were deemed so unlucky that not only human action but any form of religious observation was out of the question (Dupont 1989, 196).

When on campaign the Roman army built marching camps, and, at the end of the campaigning season, more permanent forts. Most of these in Britain are of the classic sub-rectangular, playing-card shape, with an internal orthogonal grid of streets. These forts certainly supplied a vital utilitarian need in that soldiers could rest in complete safety. But they also symbolised the cultural order and regularity of the soldiers' life. The strict regulation of camp life, and the rites performed during its construction, made it a place of civilisation and separated it from the world of the barbarians.

The army was subject to the god Mars, but also to the exhortations of its generals. From its origins as a free citizen army in the Republic, armies of the Empire still needed to have confidence in the abilities of their generals, and one way of instilling such confidence was through oratory (Dupont 1989, 128). It is in this light that the speech delivered by Narcissus to the wavering armies of AD 43 prior to embarkation needs to be understood. It was a speech in a certain tradition. Its delivery by a freedman and not a general was legitimised by the invocation of the feast of Saturnalia. This took place every year on 17 December and was the one day in the year in which order was overturned, and slaves took the place of their masters.

Does this caricature bear any resemblance to Roman life as lived? Was their daily life, whether going about their business in the forum in Rome, or building a fortress for the legion at Inchtuthil, significantly different from that which we experience in the contemporary world? Different in the way in which ritual practices and sacrifices pervaded every activity they engaged upon, every location they visited during the day? Different in the ways they observed the environment around them? We are used to perceiving the environment in an historically peculiar, objective way, drawn from the influence on our education system of Descartes, who promoted the separation of body and mind, and the consequent privileging of abstract reason over the world, leading to the dichotomy between nature and nurture. There is plenty of evidence to suggest that this Western view is atypical of the human experience (Ingold 2000), and that, for many peoples, including the Romans, the perception of the environment, how landscape is infused with meaning, the importance of processes over outcomes, the indivisibility of body and mind, and the intentionality of 'natural' agencies were quite different from our own perceptions. So can we stand, therefore, on the coast of northern France, gazing out across the Channel, and think how the Romans, in ships of this or that sort, would have thought about sailing in numbers to the south coast of Britain? Can we make the same calculations as them, or did they think in fundamentally different ways?

A new generation of archaeologists studying Roman Britain is beginning to consider these questions. Much of this new thinking is informed by different theoretical perspectives, presented at annual gatherings of the Theoretical Roman Archaeology Conference, and published commendably promptly. Simon Clarke (2000) has studied the assemblages from the pits at the fort at Newstead in Scotland, and has argued that both pit-fills and occupation spreads may be the result of ritual behaviours (Clarke 2000, 26). By comparing the different distributions of artefact types a contrast was found between the deposition of personal objects, weapons and tools in pits (and the absence of nails) with the reverse patterning (i.e. hardly any personal objects and lots of nails) in the occupation debris spread on the surface of the site. Symbolically charged artefacts were removed from day-to-day living and deposited in pits. By implication the surface deposits comprising the occupation debris had been sanitised by their removal. He emphasises that to the Romans gods and ritual practices were not paranormal or supernatural, but part of everyday reality, as much as weather fronts and economic cycles are to us. He argues that there is no reason why our interpretation of Roman period behaviour should proceed under different rules to that of late European prehistory. After all, the population of soldiers and camp followers at Newstead was ethnically Germanic and Celtic, and only lightly Romanised. Similarly, David Dungworth (1998) has drawn attention to the possible ritual attributes of the humble nail, and has questioned the functional explanation of the burial of nearly a million nails (10 tonnes) from the fortress of Inchtuthil. He argues from ethnographic parallels, from the evidence of deliberate deposition of some artefacts on Roman sites and from the Roman practice of nailing of curse tablets that the ordinary nail could, in certain circumstances, be an object of ritual significance.

Some major new insights have been shed on the Roman army itself. In a fundamental challenge to the orthodoxy of the previous century, James (2001) has presented an alternative construction and the following paragraph summarises his viewpoints. The idea that 'the Roman army' was a monolithic machine, of trained automata, is a modern construct, which bears no relation to how the Romans thought and wrote about their soldiers. Since Roman soldiers could trace their ancestry back to the republican legionaries drawn from the wealthier free citizenry, the soldiers were not willing to be organised in a top-down hierarchy, but organised themselves from the bottom-upwards (i.e. the complete opposite of our own tradition). Soldiers thought of them-selves as belonging to body of *milites*, owing an oath of loyalty to the person of the Emperor. At least until the Late Empire, there was no level of military organisation above that of the provincial, and the Romans wrote of soldiers as a 'class of men' rather than an institution. Consequently, in the first century AD there was no such thing as the Roman army because the Romans had no such concept. In Roman accounts of their soldiers there are frequent references to the need to lead, win over, cajole and persuade the soldiers to do their duty. Such attitudes may lie behind the appeal of Narcissus to the troops in AD 43 and the failure of Caligula's mission to invade Britain in AD 40. An entirely new light has also been shone on the understanding that early imperial army units were quasi-monastic institutions, at least in barracks. James has pointed out that non-combatants (such as servants, slaves, grooms, and other depen-dants including children) were intimately integrated into the lives of soldiers and regiments, and some of these could reside within the ramparts of fortifications. The corollary was that soldiers were not just confined to the frontier zones, but were spread throughout the province on any number of surveillance, policing or administrative tasks and settled and mixed extensively with the local population. It follows from this that distinguishing a material culture that is inherently military from one that is civilian may be more difficult than previously imagined, since the domestic side of a soldier's life was probably effected through the same material culture as the locals, either within the walls of the fort or in nearby civilian settlements. The ethnic identities of the soldiers could clearly affect the 'classical' ideas of how Roman soldiers behaved.

Lastly, I will explore elsewhere in this book some of the conclusions reached by an earlier generation of British archaeologists, a number of whom, in the twentieth century, came from military families or had had direct experience of military life. Richard Hingley (1994; 2000) has persuasively argued that an earlier generation of scholars recreated the Romans, and particularly the invading Roman armies, to the more familiar template of the forces of the British Empire, expanding the territories, recognising the monarch, and bringing civilisation to all its subjects. By a form of contorted logic the Roman Empire provided an origin myth for the purpose and morals of the elite of the British Empire. Whether such an imitation was intentional or otherwise, knowing or unknowing, is beside the point. If true, then such a British Imperial paradigm for Roman armies will have recreated the Romans in our own likeness, and masked the differences between us and them.

As confessed at the outset to this chapter, I cannot answer the question I have raised here. Nevertheless I think that the question was worth posing. The Romans clearly had different belief systems, political processes, social practices, class distinc-tions,[4] aesthetic senses and material culture from ourselves. However, they lived in the same world, governed by the same physical laws, as we do. But did they *think* differently from us? And faced with a logistically complex undertaking, such as the invasion of an island, would they have thought about such a project differently, and therefore carried it out (or at least parts of it) in different ways, very different from the logical (to us) way we would approach such an undertaking?

It is time now to look in a little more detail at the kinds of evidence we have for reconstructing the events surrounding the first few months of the invasion in AD 43. This is the subject of the next chapter.

3 What kinds of evidence do we have for the Roman invasion of Britain?

It is as well to examine, before embarking on a study of the events of AD 43, the kinds of evidence that are used to reconstruct the narrative of the event. They broadly fall into four different categories: archaeological, historical, environmental and contemporary. I will examine these in detail in what follows.

Archaeological evidence

The kinds of archaeological evidence that have been used to substantiate the events of AD 43 comprise ditches, especially of a military nature, and the artefacts that are recovered from them; post-holes that make up the ground-plans of military buildings; and other isolated finds such as the Bredgar Hoard of Roman coins or the soldier's helmet from Chichester harbour. Taken together some of these are interpreted as providing evidence for military installations of the Claudian era, groups of which can sometimes be interpreted as forts or locations that may mark the line of the Roman advance.

It is worth stating the obvious, however: most archaeology is interpretation, only a small percentage is fact. If you locate a length of ditch, providing that the soils that fill the ditch are distinct enough from the soils into which the ditch is cut, you should be able to define the shape or profile of the ditch and its overall dimensions; so far, so good. You have found a ditch, you can call it that, although you do not know how those who dug it would have described it. Problems of interpretation then begin. You need to know what the ditch was dug for, how long it was left open, or whether the actual *process* of digging it was its purpose. The profile and dimensions may lead you to conclude that the ditch is military in nature; you also need to know whether it was associated with a bank of upcast earth on one side or another or both sides. For instance there is a supposed bank on the east side of the Claudian ditches (**4**) at Richborough (Bushe-Fox 1949, 12-13). But it is only a supposition; the bank is implied by posts that flank either side of the gateway passage. Such posts are supposed both to form the framework for the wooden entrance passage, and provide the barriers that would have retained the butt end of an earth bank behind. You then need to know how the ditch was filled in, whether by natural causes or artificial processes or a mixture of both. You need to examine the artefactual finds from the filling of the ditch and glean from them what you can about how, when and maybe why the ditch was filled.

4 *The Claudian Ditches at Richborough, looking north; the figure stands in the only known entrance across the ditches; the stone walls of the later Saxon shore fort are in the background.* Photograph John Manley

In similar vein, let's assume you find a piece of pottery in the ditch. You can conclude, safely enough, that it is pottery; again, so far, so good. Drawing further conclusions leads you inevitably into interpretation. You want to know about the shape of the original vessel, who made it, when and where. You want to know who owned it, how it got to the site, what kinds of daily uses it had, what it contained. You would like to know how it was valued, how people felt about the particular vessel. Finally you want to know how long it stayed as a serviceable entity, how it was discarded (accidentally? deliberately? formally during some ceremony?), how it was broken, and finally how it ended up in your ditch. In particular you are interested in where all the other bits of your vessel are. In other words, each fragment of pottery in your ditch has an unique biography, an unique story to tell, if only you could make it talk. Similarly, other types of artefact and ecofact from your ditch (copper alloy objects or animal bones, for instance) have their histories too.

Now the problem of drawing conclusions from the ditch example quoted above usually comes down to trying to answer two fundamental questions: dates (of digging and filling) and function. The latter may be easier. For example, a well is a well in many periods, being a square or circular hole in the ground for the purpose of getting access to drinking water. Even here, however, care needs to be exercised. How are you going to exclude the possibility that it might be a ritual shaft for communicating with the underworld, with water being a sacred entity rather than a utilitarian commodity? But back to the ditch: you might feel pretty confident that the straight feature you have excavated is indeed some sort of ditch, and, from its size and profile, military in nature. Dating the ditch from the pottery found in it, however, is problematic. You need to know not only the manufacture dates of all the sherds you recover, but also the deposition dates of the discarded or placed fragments in the ditch.[1] The length of time between manufacture and deposition is clearly crucial. Some Roman coins are known to have been in circulation for hundreds of years before entering the ground. In the case of pottery you may be able to get some idea by the size of the sherds present, and whether the breaks look sharp. Big sherds and sharp breaks might imply a relatively short period of time between manufacture and deposition (since the sherds would usually be more broken up and abraded if left lying around on the surface for any length of time), but it is an inexact science.

With regard to Roman pottery, the most dateable likely to be located on military sites of the invasion period is imported red fabric table and drinking ware, either from around Arezzo in central Italy (called Arretine ware[2]) or from factories in southern France (called samian ware). However, such pottery, in terms of manufacture, can only be dated, usually, to the reign of a particular Emperor, or, if stamped with a known potter's name, to the period when that potter was producing. No piece of Arretine or samian ware can be dated to a particular year of manufacture, AD 43 or otherwise. To return to our ditch example: in theory you should be able to date the closure or infilling of the ditch[3] by the date of the latest sherd deposition (i.e. by the date that the latest or youngest sherd was deposited in the ditch). Likewise, in theory, you should be able to date the digging of the ditch by the date of the earliest sherd deposition[4] (i.e. by the date that the earliest or oldest sherd was deposited in it). In practice, since deposition dates are extremely difficult to work out, you look at the assemblage of pottery as a whole and take a judgement from the manufacture dates of all the individual sherds. So, for instance, if the ditch is full of broken sherds of early Claudian date, with nothing earlier (and cut into a deposit full of Late Iron Age pottery), and sealed by a layer containing quantities of late Claudian pottery, with nothing later, then it might be reasonable to date the digging and filling of the ditch to the early Claudian period. However, even in such unusual circumstances the ditch could still not be tied down to a specific year, only to the early Claudian period, and that is not specific enough when trying to isolate those archaeological features that are definitely associated with the events of AD 43. There are also other obvious problematic areas. Even if you could conclude definitively that a ditch was dug in AD 43, it would be completely beyond the bounds of inference to state whether the ditch had been excavated by an army campaigning and marching east to west as opposed to west to east.

These then are the practical realities of trying to date securely a length of ditch in the early Roman period. Very occasionally, you may be extremely fortunate in finding other evidence that allows you to fix the date more securely. Waterlogged gateposts of an annexe to a Roman fort[5] at Alchester, north of Oxford, allowed tree-ring dating to determine that the timber had been felled for the construction in the autumn of AD 44 or spring AD 45 (Denison 2001, 6), indicating almost certainly that date for the construction of the annexe by the military.[6]

So far we have looked at the difficulties of interpreting a single length of ditch. Higher levels of uncertainty are associated when we try and link together many disparate features on an archaeological site, in order to make an overall statement about contemporary activities. Sometimes this is not so problematic, especially when there are clear stratigraphic links between separate features. For instance, a layer of stone rubble from the demolition of a building may overlie a ditch and the post-holes of a timber building that is located some way from the ditch. In other cases, such a clear stratigraphic link is missing, as is the case with the two ovens located at Richborough and thought to be contemporary with the Claudian ditches. These ovens are some way from the ditches and contemporaneity is based on the discovery of artefacts of similar date range in the two features (Bushe-Fox 1949, 17). Even higher levels of uncertainty are introduced when we try to interpret several different sites that we think may be contemporary.

Historical evidence

I have shown above that, for the first century AD in Britain, there are considerable problems in trying to make definitive statements purely from the archaeological evidence. The reality is that we debate degrees of uncertainty; archaeologists know this but the interested public may not. It is not surprising, therefore, that when a smattering of historical evidence exists for an event, archaeologists turn to it with delight and attempt to correlate it with the features and finds that they have excavated. The documentary texts, however fragmentary, might provide the glue that binds the whole edifice of archaeological interpretation together. This is especially true when the documentary evidence relates to a specific event, be it an invasion or the foundation of a town, rather than a process. For instance, there are references to the introduction of Christianity to Britain in the late Roman and post-Roman period, and it is possible to look at the spread of religious establishments across Britain. These separate foundations can be viewed and understood as manifestations of the process of a religious conversion, and the individual date of a single church is arguably less important than an overall understanding of the temporal progress and spatial extent of this conversion. However, this is not so with an event, such as the foundation of a town or the Roman invasion. Documentary evidence may exist which categorically states that such a foundation, or such an invasion, occurred in a particular year. The temptation for archaeologists to fit their data to the historical evidence has proved too strong in the past.

Indeed, the relationship between archaeological and historical data, and specifically the way archaeologists use historical data, has evolved over the last century, especially in those periods such as the Roman or Early Medieval, where archaeology is relatively plentiful and documentary evidence relatively scarce. The following example will, I hope, suffice. When Mortimer Wheeler conducted his famous excavations at the great hillfort of Maiden Castle (**5**) he uncovered a number of human skeletons in the east gateway of the site. Some of these unfortunate people had clearly met a violent death, and his photograph of a Roman ballista bolt embedded in a section of vertebrae remains to this day a

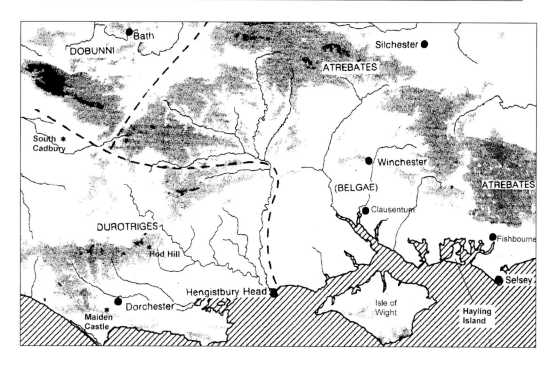

5   Location map of Fishbourne and Southampton harbours, and the Isle of Wight, with selected tribal names and significant sites

memorable image. Wheeler was a military man, who had no doubt that hillforts were primarily for defensive purposes. He obviously had knowledge of Suetonius' description of Vespasian's attacks on more than 20 settlements in the south-west during the invasion campaign, and interpreted the skeletons as evidence of a dramatic assault by the Romans on an indigenous population seeking refuge at Maiden Castle. His vivid description of the last hours of these people is as evocative now as it was when first published (Wheeler 1943). Later excavators of Maiden Castle have not been quite so sure about Wheeler's interpretation. A re-assessment of the cemetery indicated that only a small percentage of the individuals had met a violent death, that some of those deaths may have occurred elsewhere, and that all of them had been formally buried, suggesting a degree of preparation, care and ceremony that may sit uneasily with the concept of a war cemetery (Sharples 1991, 125). In a similar vein, the authors of the excavation report on another south-west hillfort, Cadbury (Barrett *et al.* 2000) described in detail a mass of human remains and artefacts, dating to the early Roman period, located again in the south-western gateway passage of the hillfort (**5**). The deposition of these assemblages was a complex one, involving at least seven different episodes and modes of deposition. An earlier generation of scholars might have interpreted such evidence as pointing clearly to the campaigns of Vespasian, or the disturbances surrounding the Boudiccan rebellion. These authors, however, writing in the late 1990s, positively eschew any attempt to link what they describe to fragmentary historical references relating to the years AD 43/4, 47 and 60/1. They recognise that the dating evidence does not allow the construction of a firm historical narrative, and they indicate that, in any case, the important questions to be answered, relevant to an understanding of human processes, are how and why, not *specifically* when (Barrett *et al.* 2000, 114-6). Unfortunately for them, the public still expects answers to what and when.

I want to stress that I am not saying that Wheeler's generation got it wrong and we are now getting it right. So much of archaeological interpretation is driven by the theoretical viewpoints which the excavator possesses, and through which the excavator views any archaeological site. These viewpoints, obviously, are a product of the excavator's education and upbringing, and are also a product of that particular age.[7] In that sense archaeological data, in themselves, are *texts* which can be read differently by individual archaeologists. Hodder has correctly pointed out that inter-pretation begins at the trowel's edge (1999, 92), and I have known some archaeolo-gists who seemed to have made up their minds about how an excavation would be interpreted before they set a foot on site. If Wheeler was alive and practising archae-ology in the early twenty-first century he would excavate differently, interpret differ-ently and write differently. Future generations of excavators will excavate, interpret and write differently from ourselves.

So where does all this lead us? I think it indicates that, for the Roman period at any rate, we should be extremely cautious about linking archaeological and histor-ical data, no matter how appealing the prospect. I will try and heed my own advice in this book. But I now want to turn to another aspect of the historical evidence, or rather the nature of historical evidence written in the Roman period about the invasion of Roman Britain. It has become a truism that history is written by the victors, and this is certainly true of historical writing on the Roman invasion. The fragmentary texts that have survived, by Cassius Dio, Tacitus, Suetonius and Josephus are all from authors who grew up in the Roman world and, although no doubt imbued with specific biases, they reflect Rome's view of the events surrounding the invasion. There are no texts written from the point of view of the vanquished, and the indigenous leaders and armies that resisted the invasion remain in the shadows; we know that they were there but we cannot really see them.

There are a number of additional difficulties with accepting at face value the texts that describe the Roman invasion. I list them here in numbered points, for the sake of clarity but at the sacrifice of elegance.

1   None of the historians describing the invasion was a contemporary of the event or, with the probable exception of Suetonius, had visited Britain. They were all using, to some extent, secondary sources, and this is particularly true of the main narrative of the invasion, that produced by the Greek historian Cassius Dio. In this sense, historical writing has its own stratigraphy,[8] and the value of a surviving text can only really be evaluated by uncovering the original sources, and evalu-ating those sources in turn. This recursive process is in some ways analogous to the hierarchy of interpretations of archaeological data (ditch to site to groups of sites) outlined above.

2   Each of the historians describing the invasion will have had his own reasons for writing and own biases. Josephus, for example, was clearly pro-Flavian dynasty and used sources which were sometimes anti the Julio-Claudians. Such biases are in some ways analogous to the theoretical viewpoints of archaeologists as outlined above. And, of course, the sources used by these historians will in turn have had their specific biases.

3   The references that have survived are not references from works that deal solely with the Roman invasion of Britain. The text from Cassius Dio is a part of one book, itself a part of a work comprising 80 books, which Dio wrote over a twelve-year period during his retirement. We place enormous value on the two pages of description in Dio because, apart from a few other scraps, that is all we have.[9] However, to him it was a very small and insignificant part of a much larger whole. He may have written it in a couple of hours during a morning's endeavour. We have spent more than a century trying to decipher a morning's work.

4   We tend to assume that modern historians are trying to be objective, and record events in a dispassionate way. They are, of course, not always successful. It is possible that objectivity meant something else for ancient historians. There are signs, in Dio's texts, of events that have a formulaic ring to them. For instance, we know that Romans had a dread of beginnings, and that if you set out on an undertaking without good auspices, without making the appropriate religious observances, the event could be doomed from the start (Dupont 1989, 181). Romans often looked for auspicious signs, and the shooting star mentioned by Dio can be interpreted in this light. Similarly, on the eve of embarkation across the Ocean, we might have expected an edifying speech of exhortation to some of the ranks (Dupont 1989, 128), and Narcissus, according to Dio, dutifully tries to supply one. Objectivity, therefore, is not a universal cross-cultural attribute of historians; objectivity is culturally constructed within a given place and time.

Environmental evidence

There is not a great deal of either archaeological or historical evidence for the Roman invasion of Britain, and both types of evidence are problematical, as we have seen. I now want to turn to what can be loosely described as the environmental evidence. In essence, this means trying to pull together what we know of the natural environment of the Channel and south-east Britain, since Roman soldiers and defending locals will have had to move through a real environment of seas, channels, rivers and countrysides.

The principal issue, which needs to be addressed, is the way in which the environment might have changed over the last 2000 years. For instance, have the tidal regimes in the English Channel altered over the last two millennia? Have wind speeds, frequencies and directions changed at all? What did the coastline of south-east Britain look like during the early Roman period? Has there been erosion of coastal land, and, in other places, accretion of land through silting? Consideration of some of these answers may lead us to a more informed appreciation of the difficulties and possibilities of the Roman naval crossing and subsequent landing.

Likewise, it will be useful to look at the evidence for sea-level and river-level changes, and try to estimate the heights and widths of key rivers like the Thames during the early Roman period. River crossings and battles form key elements in the descriptions of the invasion that have survived. There is also the crucial question of the extent of forest cover in the Weald. The Weald covers most of inland south-east England and our appreciation of its impenetrability, its densely wooded character, its cloying clays, stem largely from eighteenth- and nineteenth-century writers (Woodcock 1967, 163), some of whom described the difficulties of urbane London folk crossing the Weald to enjoy the delights of the coastal resorts. Was it so wooded in the early Roman period? Would a Roman army, mindful of the fate of Varus and his three legions in the forests of Germany in AD 9 (Tacitus, Ann, 1, 58), have considered crossing such a wooded area when alternatives were available?

Contemporary evidence

I am using the term contemporary evidence loosely. Let me explain what I mean. I am assuming that you, the reader, are, like me, a product of a modern, specifically Western, education system. We have all grown up with a certain world-view, one that takes 'progress' as given, one that separates the natural environment from the works of human beings, the sciences from the arts, one that has by and large marginalised collective religions and one that is now hi-tech and encourages us to perceive our reasoned actions in very common-sense ways and as the outcomes of logical thought processes (Ingold 2000). There is plenty of evidence (see elsewhere in this book) that other cultures, including the Romans, did not share this world-view.

However, trapped as we are in what historically is a very odd way of thinking, we are forced to try and interpret events from the distant past in ways that make sense to us. Indeed, we often try to impose *our* common-sense on *their* actions. This is what some people do with the Roman invasion of AD 43. Let me make an anecdotal digression to illustrate. Over the last several years I have regularly given talks about Iron Age hillforts, making the simple point that, despite the name given to this category of monument by archaeologists, not all of them may have been exclusively fortifications and that the earthworks around them, so automatically interpreted as defensive barriers, may have also defined places that were special for other non-utilitarian reasons, such as for ceremonies or rituals. I hasten to add that these ideas are not mine, but that I draw on the work of colleagues, which I have read. The audiences who receive these talks are largely made up of members of local archaeological or historical societies, and essentially comprise informed groups of people. Invariably the talks are well received and invariably the chairperson asks if there are questions of the speaker. Someone will usually raise a hand and ask how many people it would have taken to construct the ramparts. Another may follow, asking the location of the nearest water-sources. It is not the answers to these questions that are important, but the nature of the questions themselves. It is as if the audience cannot grasp such a construction as a hillfort being for any other reason than defensive, cannot accept an explanation unless it is couched in functional terms.[10] Indeed, some will bring up the example of Wheeler's excavation in the gateway at Maiden Castle as evidence that a more prosaic explanation might, after all, be correct. The point of this digression is not to talk about the meaning of hillforts, but simply to demonstrate two things: one, our inclination to interpret in common-sense, functional ways and two, the power and durability of an explanation (like the one Wheeler provided), once received and understood by us, to survive in the memory.

So contemporary evidence can be taken to mean our contemporary insights into the events of AD 43. These take the form of former soldiers writing about the invasion of AD 43 from the standpoint of their own experiences as soldiers (e.g. Peddie 1987). Such authorities assume that soldiering is a cross-cultural phenomenon unchanged by time: 'the same principles of war which were employed in the past, appear again and again throughout history . . . '.[11] Other authorities are former or current sailors, who use their expert knowledge of things maritime as a starting point to try and understand the mechanics of Roman ships and then to hypothesise about how and from where and to where a Roman fleet might have crossed the Channel. Such insights can be rewarding and powerful in their detail. However, they do rest on the premise that, in whatever era, soldiering is soldiering, or, for that matter, sailoring is sailoring; this premise needs to be explored rather than accepted without question. Can we really learn anything about the events of AD 43 from the observations of a nineteenth-century US general (as quoted in Frere and Fulford 2001, 46)? I am not convinced.

There is also an implicit assumption, by users of contemporary evidence, that the Romans were blessed with foresight and were invading a territory, detailed maps of which had miraculously fallen into their hands. In order to give themselves some intellectual grasp of Rome's territories, maps were produced, but on too large a scale to be of any use for an individual. When Augustus was transforming Rome as an imperial capital, he had a large map set up in the Porticus Octaviae in the Campus Martius to reassure the citizens of Rome. This displayed Rome at the physical centre of the world, at the mid-point between the frozen North and the burning South, the violent barbarians of the West and the spineless barbarians of the East. At the outer limit of the world, the Romans set a fabulous and divine stretch of water, an ocean that encircled the universe and could never be crossed (Dupont 1989, 86).

Decades of campaigning were not worked out in advance, so that the overall progress of conquest, from the south-east to the Fosse Way, subsequently to Wales and to the Pennines, finally to Scotland, was not a pre-ordained culmination of a plan dreamt up in Rome, but instead the outcome of hundreds of smaller decisions, and reactions and counter-reactions, taken by commanders over a period of 40 years. Similarly, the knowledge that the Romans possessed in AD 43 of the Channel and of the terrain in the south-east would have been gained from Caesar's field notebooks, from any itineraries deriving from such books which would have given approximate distances between places, from the knowledge of local traders plying the Channel crossings and from suppliant chiefs such as Verica. Some limited two-dimensional representations of the terrain of the south-east may have existed. Vegetius confirmed that itineraries were a usual form of military intelligence; with reference to military commanders:

> First he should have itineraries of all regions in which war is being waged written out in the fullest detail, so that he may learn the distances between places by the number of miles . . . the more conscientious generals reportedly had itineraries . . . not just annotated but illustrated as well. (Vegetius, EMS, 3)

So imagine that you have never seen a map of North Wales, and have never been there; someone describes the terrain of North Wales to you, giving details of major settlements, approximate walking times between them, names of major rivers, and the varying character of the terrain. This is what Aulus Plautius knew on the eve of the invasion; his soldiers and sailors, remember, knew far less. In general ordinary people in the ancient world frequently had little idea where they were on land (and were even worse off at sea) and depended heavily on local guides.

For the sake of completeness, it is necessary to take one last digression, this time into historiography to relate how different generations of scholars have traced the route of the Roman invasion of Britain. This is the subject matter of the next chapter.

4 Why was Richborough eventually chosen by modern historians?

As the study of Roman Britain develops in the twenty-first century it is easy for the current generation of young scholars to forget that the subject has a considerable history of research already. The flood of new books and articles, the development of new ways of looking at the data, mean that earlier generations of works, most out of print and many written in a form of dated English, are forgotten or ignored. Archaeologists can suffer from a form of collective amnesia[1] with regard to published works older than say 50 years or so. Anything before that tends to be dismissed as out of date and irrelevant to current research, unless the publication deals with actual data as opposed to interpretation, commentary or synthesis. It is worth pausing, therefore, to reflect that the Richborough hypothesis for the Roman landing was not one that was advocated so energetically in the nineteenth century. Fortunately, Hind (1989) has presented the principal conclusions of four nineteenth-century scholars and these are included in summary form in the Table on the next page.

Hind, I think, makes the very valid point that in the nineteenth century and earlier, scholars, in the absence of archaeological evidence, concentrated on trying to interpret the fragmentary historical evidence and came up with a variety of scenarios for the invasion, albeit some of them a little fanciful. Hübner's conclusions are particularly interesting, not least for being written by someone with an European, as opposed to an insular, perspective. The approach of looking at what Dio actually wrote, and trying to interpret it free of archaeological influences, was, in fact, re-invented by Hind in his paper in 1989. Between Hübner and Hind, of course, came the publications of Francis Haverfield and the Society of Antiquaries' excavations at Richborough; it was this combination of publication and excavation that firmly curtailed any further debate on the issue by apparently confirming that the Romans had landed at Richborough.

When considering the circumstances in which the 'Richborough hypothesis' became accepted fact I want to look briefly at the role of Francis Haverfield. Born in 1860, by 1892 he had been awarded a Senior Studentship at Christ Church, Oxford and he became the leading expert on Roman Britain. He died in 1919 after publishing a long list of books and articles, many of them on aspects of Roman Britain. Sir Ian Richmond and Sheppard Frere both hold him in high esteem, and the latter remarked in 1988 that Haverfield was the real founder of the study of the archaeology of Roman Britain (quoted in Hingley 2000, 12). Haverfield's *The Romanization of Britain* was published in the *Proceedings of the British Academy* in 1905 and separately as a short book. It was subsequently republished in 1912, 1915 and posthumously in 1923. There is little doubt that this work set the overall tone, if not the detail, of Romano-British studies for most of the twentieth century. Haverfield's many interests included frontier issues, and the organisa-

Author/ proponent	Date	Main conclusions	Publication
Camden	1789	Richborough very important in the time of the Romans; Roman ships arrived here as the 'most usual passage into Britain'	*Britannia*
G.B. Airy	1860	Landing on coast of Essex, near Southend; battle at river Lea; both Britons and Romans then crossed the Thames southwards; the Britons re-crossed it northwards; Plautius waited for Claudius	*Athenaeum*, June 28, 1860 and reprinted 1865
Dr Guest	1883	Plautius lands at Richborough, Dover and Hythe; marches to Silchester, then to Cirencester, battle at river Thames (Wallingford) then on to the river Lea to wait for Claudius	*Origines Celticae* ii
F.C.J. Spurrell	1888	Plautius landed in Hampshire, marched to Gloucestershire; from there to the river Lea and then crossed the Thames southbound at Tilbury	Paper delivered to the Archaeological Institute 1888
Hübner	1890	Favours Plautius landing in the Solent; marches inland to the Dobunni (equated with the Bodunni); garrison left at Gloucester and river battle in the west-country; Britons retreated eastwards to Thames and crossed it. Plautius waits at the Thames	*Römische Heerschaft in Westeuropa* (Berlin 1881, 1890)

tion of Roman frontiers, which repulsed the barbarian. At this time the image of the frontier was unsophisticated – it was seen as a distinct physical line, felt to separate civil-isation from barbarism (Hingley 2000, 43). Although the concept of client kingdoms outside the areas of formal Roman rule was appreciated at the time, such kingdoms do not figure prominently in the writings of Haverfield. For instance, while admitting that at Silchester there must have been 'some sort of Romanization long before AD 43' (Haverfield 1923, 74), this community (and others like it) was assumed to have 'Romanized themselves' by contact with the Roman world, but without the official settlement of Roman soldiers or citizens. With reference to the Iceni, they had submitted to Plautius 'without a struggle'; they then 'grew restive' and Ostorius had to 'read them a sharp lesson'; hardly a decade later 'heedless of what they had learned, they again rose in revolt. The whole land was aflame' (Haverfield 1924, 109).

In addition, Haverfield's Ford lectures, originally delivered in 1907, revised in 1913 or 1914, and eventually published posthumously in 1924 (Haverfield 1924), effectively ended the debate on where the Romans landed. While admitting that Cassius Dio was 'brief and vague' (Haverfield 1924, 101) he went on to write categorically:

> We may presume that they landed at the three ports of Richborough, Dover and Lympne. Thence, moving forward along the fertile and easy plains of north Kent and never losing touch with their base, they quickly forced the Medway, and pushed on to the Thames. (Haverfield 1924, 101-2)

In person Haverfield could be brusque and could easily brush the views of others aside. He certainly was contemptuous of other versions of where the Romans had landed.

> The whole theory of a landing in or about Hampshire rests ultimately on Camden's more than doubtful conjecture as to the Bodunni . . . We may dismiss it without more ado. (Haverfield 1924, 103).

As president or vice-president of several archaeological societies, including the Society of Antiquaries and the newly-formed Society for the Promotion of Roman Studies, Haverfield's views must have carried enormous weight.

Of course, Haverfield was writing on Roman Britain in the years leading up to the First World War. He had contemporary knowledge of the build up of German military power, its drive into Belgium and northern France in 1914 and the subsequent catastrophic war of attrition that took place advancing and retreating from fixed defensive lines. Indeed, his favourite pupil at Oxford, Leonard Cheesman, died in the Dardanelles, a loss which affected him deeply (Haverfield 1924, 31). It would have been entirely natural for Haverfield, aware of contemporary events around him and on the near continent, to envisage an AD 43 advance across the shortest sea-crossing and a defensive strategy based around fixed lines of defence, such as the Medway and the Thames. His conclusions, therefore, may have been influenced by the contemporary historical and geographical contexts in which he wrote. This is why the views of Hübner, freed from such a historical and geographical context, provide such a counterpoint. In addition, Haverfield's views on romanisation, and his unsophisticated perception of client-kings, seeing the Romans' arrival as a *good thing* in terms of progress and the imparting of higher culture to the indigenous populations, would not have been easily reconciled with a Roman invasion that sought to restore stability to a client kingdom ruled by a local elite.

Following Haverfield, later twentieth-century academic opinion reached a consensus of Roman landings at three different places on the East Kent coast. However, Verica and the Dobunni were not quite forgotten and contingents of the Roman army landing in Sussex or the Solent to restore Verica or secure the alliance of the Dobunni were championed by the O'Neils (1952) and by Hawkes (1961). But it was the publication of a paper by Hind in 1989, suggesting that the entire invasion force could have landed in the Fishbourne area, which marked a break with the twentieth-century orthodoxy.

I have already questioned the objectivity of archaeologists and historians with respect to the Roman invasion, and suggested that views are influenced by the geographical area in which people have worked. Another potential bias lies in the controlled access to publication channels that determine which ideas get onto the printed page. A related question that I also want to raise in this chapter is the issue of how some professional archaeologists' and historians' views are ignored even when they do get into print. This is clearly a sensitive issue because it implies that the power structures that exist within the British archaeological establishment at times, knowingly or unknowingly, censor information and how it emerges. What evidence do I have for such an allegation? One of the issues that always struck me as slightly odd was the way in which Hind's paper in the 1989 edition of *Britannia,* advocating a Roman landing on the south coast, caused very few ripples at the time of its publication. Now I may be seeing smoke here where no fires exist, and it is a credit to the editorial board of *Britannia* that it published the article when it did; but it caused, as far as I can tell, little debate,[2] and the silence was, in its way, just as damning as a critical review of the article would have been. So little impact did the article have that it was possible, in 1995, to publish an atlas indicating Richborough as the undisputed landing place (Scarre 1995), although others were a little more circumspect (Crummy 1997). In other words, the archaeological establishment, particularly that part of it involved in Romano-British archaeology, effectively sidelined Hind's ideas by its silence. Of course, I am not saying this was a deliberate conspiracy with an intended effect; I am saying that small decisions, taken individually for whatever purpose, had this cumulative and unintended effect.

The debate, however, was resurrected in the last few years of the twentieth century, resulting in two conferences, one in Sussex and the other in Kent, a number of articles and, of course, this book.[3] Pivotal in opening up the debate was the role of Barry Cunliffe, uniquely situated as an archaeologist who had edited the final Richborough volume, and who had excavated at Fishbourne Roman Palace. In his 1998 re-edition of his book on the Fishbourne excavations for the general reader he indicated that where previously he had espoused the Richborough hypothesis, he was now becoming increasingly persuaded by the arguments for a landing on the south coast (Cunliffe 1998, 21). At more or less the same time David Bird, another proponent of the south coast landings, was unable to get *Britannia* to publish his article, which provided additional information in support of a south coast landing, albeit with some significant variations from the route to the Thames championed by Hind; eventually Bird's paper was published in the *Oxford Journal of Archaeology*. *Britannia*'s subsequent publication of the paper by Frere and Fulford (2001), which simply restated the old arguments to support the Richborough hypothesis, without providing any new significant insights, could be interpreted by some as an attempt to 'close the door' on the debate.

None of this is, in a way, surprising. Archaeologists and historians are human too, and subject to the same frailties and intransigencies as the rest of us. Just because we aspire to seek the truth does not mean that we are always objective and detached. Like others, some of us have cherished ideas and theories that we have grown up with, repeated often, and are loathe to abandon, sometimes in the face of much contrary evidence. I remember going to a conference a few years ago, when the Sussex Archaeological Society and I were perceived by some to be championing the Fishbourne hypothesis as opposed to the Richborough hypothesis, and being greeted by an eminent archaeologist with the question 'still spreading the propaganda?' No offence was intended and none was taken but there is an easily and unconsciously crossed line between jocular put-down and more considered intransigence against the consideration of the views of others.

Having looked at the historiography of invasion research we can now turn to another strand of that genre, by briefly commenting on other sea-borne invasions or potential invasions of England. For ease of reference these are again summarised in a Table below:

Invasion	Date	Comment
Caesar	55 & 54 BC	Most of the fleet probably sailed from Boulogne; problems in both years with the beaching of ships on the Kent coast, possibly in the area of modern Deal; some ships blown back to coast of Gaul; see elsewhere in this book
Claudius	AD 43	See this book but note 'During the crossing they were for a time discouraged when they were driven back from their course' (Cassius Dio), and mention of the conquest of the Isle of Wight (Suetonius)
Constantius (C.) & Asclepiodotus (A.)	AD 296	Fleet split into two; C. sailed from Boulogne and A. from the Seine. The defending naval forces of Allectus were off the Isle of Wight but failed to spot A. because of fog; A. lands in the Solent area; C. reached London
William the Conqueror (W.)	1066	W. assembles fleet at Dives and in the Bay of the Seine; Harold, as a defensive measure, stations his fleet off the Isle of Wight; delay because of unfavourable winds; W. sails from Dives but is forced north-eastwards to the mouth of the Somme; late September sailing overnight leads to morning landing at Pevensey; possible that W. had originally intended to land in the Solent
The Armada (A.)	1588	A. sighted off the Isles of Scilly on 29 July. A. followed up the Channel; waited off the Isle of Wight; eventual plan was to anchor 'off Margate Cape' while the Duke of Parma and entourage sailed across in small ships; A. defeated at the Battle of Gravelines and forced to sail around the north of Scotland
Prince William (P.W.)	1688	Initial embarkation by PW from Dutch coast on the river Maas in late October; driven back by storm; 11 November fleet embarks north-westerly, then changes direction, heads south through the Channel and lands at Torbay on 15 November

Most of the details of the post-Claudian invasions have been taken from Grainge 2001 (Chapter XI, 125ff). Grainge makes the important point in respect of the 296 invasion that the Solent would have been an easier invasion landing place, since the tip of north-east Kent was by that time defended by the Saxon Shore Forts of Reculver, Richborough, Dover and Lympne, whereas the Solent was only defended by the fort at Portchester. In relation to the Norman Conquest, Grainge suggests that the original landfall that William wanted to make was possibly the Solent, but he was forced to sail in the end from the Somme. Embarkation points further to the north-east along the French coast were not available to him since they were outside his jurisdiction. With regard to the Armada, Bird (2000, 92) has argued that its commanders, in considering a Solent landing, realised that a prerequisite was occupation of the Isle of Wight, just as it had been important to Vespasian. Grainge (2001,140) indicates that Philip of Spain had recommended to the Armada commander to seize the Isle of Wight, but only if a rendezvous with the Duke of Parma proved impossible. In addition a council of captains off the Lizard decided to wait off the Isle of Wight to hear from Parma. These two decisions are clearly linked, which does tend to suggest that a Solent landing was considered, even if it was not the preferred option. Finally, with respect to Prince William, Grainge argues that the intended destination was probably a port on the east coast of England and that the initial tack to the north-west was not a feint; William was forced to turn south, and sail down the Channel, when the wind backed to the north.

I am not sure if there are many generalisations we can make of the maritime passages outlined above. Clearly wind direction and strength, and overall weather conditions, are critical to safe passage in sailing ships across the Channel, as evidenced by Caesar and the damage to some of his ships on the beach; by the Claudian crossing when ships were 'driven back from their course'; Allectus' failure to spot the invading fleet; William of Normandy's diverted passage to the Somme; and Prince William being driven back by a storm and his initial tack to the north-west. Waiting for the correct combination of weather, wind and tides, and the vagaries of those combinations, meant that neither embarkation on a specific date, nor landfall at a planned destination, could be guaranteed, and alternative landfalls might have been planned while en route. The third point to emphasise is the importance of political considerations for the invading force: William of Normandy embarked from the Somme because he did not have jurisdiction over lengths of the coast further to the north-east; the Armada attempted to sail right up the Channel because of the ill-fated plan to rendezvous with the Duke of Parma (as Grainge indicates, had the Armada attempted a landing in the Solent then things might have been different); and Prince William sailed from the Netherlands because of his hostility to Louis XIV. The final point concerns the prominence of the Isle of Wight in some of the accounts. It played a part in four of the six invasions outlined above and its role in protecting the Solent harbours (**5**) seems to have been vital from the time of Claudius through to the Armada and beyond.

So much for the brief overview of the maritime invasions of England; it is now time to re-trace our steps and look in considerably more detail at the background and evidence for the Claudian invasion of AD 43.

5 What happened between Caesar and Claudius?

I want to begin at the beginning, and, like most good stories, the beginning lies some considerable time before the main action. In the case of AD 43 it seems best to go back about a century and a half, even to before 55 BC, when one of the first named Romans, Julius Caesar, set foot on British soil. I think it is important that I try to reconstruct as much of the political situation in the south-east of Britain as possible, in the century and a half that led up to AD 43, in order that the invasion of AD 43 can be set in its proper historical context. By this method I hope to demonstrate what the motivations for the invasion of AD 43 may have been, and also to illustrate that the invasion was the predictable result of a policy of increasing romanisation of the indigenous leaders in the south-east. In order to do this I am relying heavily on a new interpretation of this period provided in John Creighton's book, *Coins and Power in Late Iron Age Britain*.

Before Caesar

Even before the arrival of Caesar there had been considerable contact between the communities on both sides of the Channel, and some of those contacts may have led to immigrants settling in the south-east. Around 100 BC there seems to have been increasing contact between Armorica and southern Britain, most notably demonstrated by the number of imports found during excavations at Hengistbury Head (**5**) in Dorset (Cunliffe 1987; Cunliffe & de Jersey 1997). These imports comprised amphorae full of Italian wine, raw glass, and a variety of pottery containers whose contents can only be guessed at. The sandstone headland at Hengistbury jutting out into the opening of the Solent made for a wonderfully protected harbour on its northern side, while the promontory itself was easily secured by the construction of a double dyke across its neck. There were other concentrations of imports, however, such as Poole Harbour and, further to the east, around Arundel in Sussex, as well as a little way inland near Pulborough. Presumably some of these imports were brought across by either traders or by emissaries of leaders perhaps providing gifts between different elite groups. (A third possibility is that some were the result of a mode of transfer that has been defined as acquisition, whereby individual artefacts drawn from a distant world which has mythical associations, are used by an indigenous elite to bring cosmological harmony to their own world – Helms 1993, 91ff.) In the case of trade what the ships returned to the Continent with is a matter of speculation, but it may have been resources particularly associated with Britain, such as those famously listed by Strabo (grain, cattle, gold, silver, iron, hides, slaves and dogs – Geog 1, 5, 2), tin, or, more locally, shale from Kimmeridge. These contacts seem to have been spread across northern Gaul from Armorica (roughly modern Brittany) eastwards. Clearly, the degree of contact implies a considerable amount of maritime activity in the Channel, and detailed familiarity with the conditions of the crossing between northern Gaul and the coast of southern Britain. This is a relevant point when we turn to the later events of AD 43. It is important to realise that knowledge of sailing conditions between Armorica and the Solent, and expertise in sailing laden boats, had been built up over a century and a half before AD 43.

Some indication of the sailing routes between Gaul and Britain can be obtained from Strabo (Geog), who was writing at the end of the first century BC.

> There are four crossings which men customarily use from the Continent to the island, from the Rhine, from the Seine, from the Loire and from the Garonne, but for those making the passage from places near the Rhine, the point of sailing is not from the mouths themselves but from the Morini. (IV, 5, 2)
>
> The crossing to Britain from the rivers of Gaul is 320 stades. People setting sail on an ebb tide in the evening land on the island about the eighth hour on the following day. (IV, 3, 4)
>
> Then (along the Seine) traffic is conveyed to the Ocean and to the Lexobii and Caleti; from these it is less than a day's run to Britain. (IV, 1, 14)

The locations of these trade and sailing routes are illustrated in (**6**).

Did these contacts and imports mean that new peoples also arrived in southern Britain? It is notoriously difficult to prove, from archaeological evidence alone, the arrival of new communities, especially in the prehistoric period. The problem lies largely in the difficulty of deciding whether the appearance of a new type of artefact or settlement type represents the arrival and acceptance of just new ideas or the arrival of new people with those ideas. However, there are increasing signs that new communities did indeed arrive, and settle in the south-east. The most well-known example is that of the Belgae, recorded by Caesar:

> The interior of Britain is inhabited by people who claim, on the strength of oral tradition, to be aboriginal; the coast, by immigrants *from Belgica*[1] who came to plunder and make war – nearly all of them retaining the names of the tribes from which they originated – and later settled down to till the soil. (Caesar, BG, 5.12)

The identity and location of these immigrants in Britain is now thought to have been in the Silchester-Winchester area of modern-day Hampshire. Here we find evidence in the form of names that link communities in this area with their homelands on the Continent. The Roman name for Silchester was *Calleva Atrebatum*, and the Atrebates was the name given to a people on both sides of the Channel. Similarly, the Roman name for Winchester was *Venta Belgarum*.

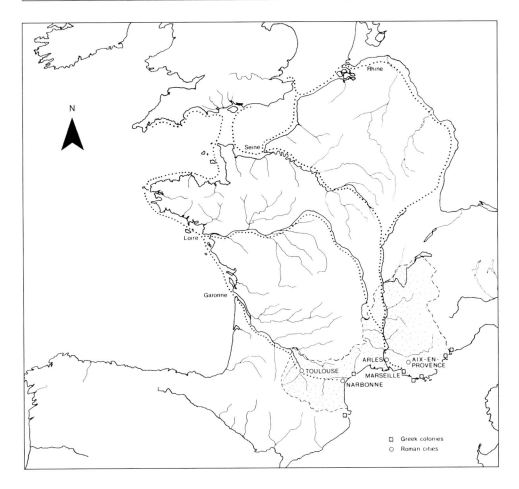

6 *Trade and sailing routes described by Strabo (after McGrail 1997); the shaded area (bottom right) indicates the extent of the Roman province of Gallia Transalpina, before the conquest of Gaul by Caesar*

There is also a growing body of archaeological evidence to suggest that communities were arriving from the Continent and settling. The early cremation graves at Owslebury in Hampshire (Collis 1968) present many novel features that could be regarded as intrusive. More recently, excavations at Westhampnett, just to the east of Chichester, have revealed probably the earliest cremation cemetery of the southern Iron Age. For a period of around 40 years, from approximately 90 to 50 BC, burials took place using a rite that was strongly influenced by contemporary traditions in Normandy or adjacent regions of France (Fitzpatrick 1997, 208). The ceramics, although of local manufacture, were based on types found in Normandy. This was also about the time when coinage was no longer just imported but began to be made in south-east Britain. Arguments derived from coinage are important, as will be seen below, in helping to throw light on the political structures of the south-east between the time of Caesar and Claudius. The large number of imported coins that have recently been found around Chichester could be taken to indicate the arrival of another new community in this area in the middle of the first century BC (Hamilton & Manley 1999, 22).

The biggest surprise and a significant addition to this type of evidence comes from the pre-Roman occupation of Silchester. Excavation in the 1980s revealed a planned late Iron Age street pattern, underlying the Roman timber and masonry basilicas. The excavators thought that this street pattern probably dated from the last two decades of the first century BC. Who were the people who lived here? According to the excavators, *Calleva Atrebatum* was probably a planted and planned settlement of colonists from north-west Gaul. It, and similar sites such as *Camulodunum* (Colchester) and *Verulamium* (St Albans), may mark a new phase in the Roman impact on south-east Britain (Fulford & Timby 2000, 564).

So there is plenty of evidence, some historical and some archaeological, for both the movement of objects and ideas and for small-scale movements of people between Gaul and the south-east from the period after 100 BC, and I think the archaeological evidence for contact is likely to grow as more excavations are conducted. How was this contact organised – are we dealing with essentially local initiatives, or something that was on a more regional and political footing? Probably a mixture of both, but there is a little evidence for the latter. Let's return to Caesar.

> The Suessiones . . . had an extensive and very fertile territory. They had been ruled within living memory by Diviciacus, the most powerful king in Gaul, who controlled not only a large part of the Belgic country, but Britain as well. (Caesar BG, 2, 4)

The Suessiones occupied a territory on the Aisne around Soissons. Taken together with the appearance of the name Atrebates on both sides of the Channel (**1**), this statement could be used to argue the case for unitary political structures that spanned the Channel at certain times between 100 BC and AD 43. Such structures would, of course, have been rather loosely organised but they could have been reinforced and maintained by the exchange of elite goods across the Channel, and occasionally by the immigration of whole communities. In addition, such structures could explain the fact that, according to Caesar (BG, 4, 20) in almost all the Gallic campaigns the Gauls had received reinforcements from the Britons. Some of these reinforcements could have involved large numbers of warriors. It is instructive to remember the numbers in the opposing forces described by Caesar. The Bellovaci, western neighbours of the Suessiones, could muster 100,000 warriors, while the Aquitani and the Cantabri could manage 50,000 men between them (BG, 3, 26). Earlier in the Gallic Wars, Ariovistus was reported as deploying 16,000 light infantry (Caesar BG, 1, 49). If warriors from the south-east were sailing across to the Continent to support Gallic tribes then, to have had any impact, they must have done so in large numbers.[2]

If some of these contacts, however, were more the result of local initiatives then we can imagine the nature of those contacts. They are likely to have been diplomatic contacts between elites across the Channel, which might have involved the drawing up of alliances, and the exchange of gifts and hostages. Such agreements might have paved the way for a limited exchange of exotic goods and services, and also for the occasional transfer of bands of warriors between neighbouring elite groups (Nash 1984, 93). When Caesar arrived in south-east Britain, therefore, in 55 BC, he was coming to a part of the island which had already had considerable contact with the Continent and where imports from the Roman world, including coinage, were not commonplace, but rather restricted to the elite groups.

Caesar's two expeditions to Britain

Caesar made two expeditions to Britain in 55 and 54 BC and it is useful to consider some aspects of them briefly, especially with regard to what they might tell us about the political situation in the south-east, and with respect to what parallels we can draw with the invasion of AD 43. Caesar sailed with the bulk of his troops in 54 BC from *Portus Itius* (Boulogne[3]) – the assumption is that he used the same port in 55 BC – and made the short sea crossing at night, beaching his ships both times possibly in the area of modern Deal.

The first expedition took place towards the end of the summer of 55 BC, and an officer Volusenus was sent ahead to carry out a reconnaissance. Once appraised of the imminent arrival of Caesar, some of the tribes in the south-east sent hostages to him. In due course Caesar set sail with about 80 ships, sufficient for two legions.[4] An additional 18 ships sailed from slightly further up the coast, carrying the cavalry. Caesar sailed at midnight and was off the coast of the south-east, probably near Dover, at nine the next morning. The transports carrying the cavalry, however, were carried back to the coast of Gaul by a storm. Caesar had great difficulty getting ashore, because of the defending British forces and because of his men's unfamiliarity with fighting in shallow water. Eventually, the landing was successful and the British sued for peace, sending hostages to Caesar. Disaster then struck as some of Caesar's anchored ships were damaged in a storm and the British renewed hostilities. Eventually another battle took place, with the Romans victorious and the Britons again sued for peace, sending even more hostages. However, Caesar, without cavalry and knowing of the damaged state of some of his ships, decided to return to the Continent. This account of the first encounter mentioned no names of chiefs or tribes, nor any placenames; however, it is presumed that most, if not all, of the action took place in the area of present-day Kent.

The second expedition was a much larger affair. Two thousand cavalry and five legions embarked, many in specially-constructed ships, made lower and wider to cope with loading and unloading of cargo, horses and men; 800 ships were involved. Caesar decided to take with him, as hostages, many of the tribal leaders in Gaul, as a safeguard to prevent hostilities breaking out while he was away. He set sail about sunset, and after being carried by the tide to the north of his intended destination, managed to row back and make an unopposed landing about midday, again presumably somewhere near modern Deal. After making a night march, crossing a river and taking a fortification (Bigbury in Kent?) to which the Britons had retreated, another storm caused havoc with Caesar's ships, wrecking about 40 of them. Caesar then returned to the beachhead and enclosed all the ships behind one line of fortifications. By then the Britons had regrouped and appointed Cassivellaunus as their leader. There then followed a number of skirmishes, with the Romans experiencing the novel difficulty of fighting warriors who rode to battle on chariots, but eventually the Romans were victorious. Caesar then led his army to the Thames, to cross over to the north and into the territory of Cassivellaunus. The Thames was crossed at one fordable point (west of London?) and the opposing forces repulsed.

Once north of the Thames, Trinovantian envoys asked Caesar to return their young prince, Mandubracius, who had fled to the Continent to put himself under Caesar's protection. Caesar, in return, demanded 40 hostages and grain for his troops. Other tribes then submitted, and Caesar made a successful attack on the stronghold of Cassivellaunus, assumed to be near Wheathampstead in Hertfordshire. Cassivellaunus eventually sued for peace, offering Caesar hostages. Caesar made the return voyage to Gaul in two trips, because he took with him a large number of prisoners. He pointed out that not a single ship with troops on board was lost in either expedition.

One or two general comments can be made concerning the accounts of these two expeditions. One is that the sea-crossings, while problematic because of the tides and winds, were not dangerous in the sense of very rough seas. The real dangers were an opposed landing (in 55 BC), and the threat of storms (in both 55 and 54 BC) either damaging vessels at anchor or wrecking ships if they were beached in places without good protection from the weather. Since Caesar disembarked on both occasions on the coast of north-east Kent it has to be asked why he did not locate Richborough or the Wantsum Channel (separating the Isle of Thanet from mainland Kent) as in little over 100 years (i.e. in AD 43) these places are claimed as excellent harbourages. The usual, if contrived, argument is that in Caesar's day the Wantsum was not sufficiently formed by natural agencies to accommodate a large number of ships, but it apparently was by AD 43. The second point is the role played by hostages. The word hostage is mentioned at least 13 times in the two chapters that describe Caesar's two expeditions to Britain. However, again as we shall see, these hostages (and they could be handed over in considerable numbers) were not hostages in the more modern usage of the word, of people held in captivity against their will and returned eventually at a price, but people who may have been willingly given and have willingly gone themselves, in order to promote a rather longer term relationship with the Roman world.

Between Caesar and Claudius

Much of our evidence for the beginning of recorded history in Britain derives from the introduction of coinage, particularly in the south-east. I have shown above how, pre-Caesar, imported coin may have been used in gift exchange to reinforce alliances between communities on both sides of the Channel. The first coins to appear in any significant number in Britain were imported gold coins, known by numismatists and archaeologists as comprising groups of coins called Gallo-Belgic A and Gallo-Belgic B. These were imported from the mid-second century BC onwards. The image on the majority of the coins from north-west Europe was derived from the gold staters of Philip II of Macedon (359-336 BC), depicting the head of Apollo on one side and a two-horse chariot on the other. When communities in north-west Gaul began to mint their own coin they derived the imagery from coins from the Greek world, coins that had probably come into their possession through exchanges between elites, or from warriors who had gone to fight for Greek leaders and returned with the coins. The imagery that they used, the head/horse, was associated with authority and kingship (Creighton 2000, 54).

In the first half of the first century BC, when coins began to be minted in Britain, the same imagery was knowingly used, since the exchange of coin was meant to communicate messages of authority. Creighton (2000, 36-7) demonstrates that the head and horse imagery on the British coins becomes gradually more abstract. He argues persuasively that this is not the result of slavish, and occasionally incompetent copying, leading to gradually debased images, but instead that there were subtle and deliberate variations on the underlying imagery, variations that would have had meaning and have been immediately understood by those subsequently handling and exchanging the coin. Coinage was, therefore, pre-Caesar, being knowingly used in the south-east as a medium for communicating and establishing authority, using consciously chosen imagery ultimately derived from the Mediterranean world.

Around the time of Caesar two new series of coins emerged in the south-east, known to numismatists now as British Q and British L. These coin types do not appear to derive from earlier series in Britain, but instead have their origin in continental proto-types known as Gallo-Belgic F. Two very significant features associated with the British coins suggest that they were being used in novel ways. Although the head/horse derived imagery still continued, the two new series seem to have been associated, geographically and temporally, with emerging dynasties of rulers who controlled approximate territories; British Q was associated with a southern kingdom and British L with an eastern one.[5] In addition, some of the imagery was now further altered to accommodate the use of Latin names of the rulers. In the Q series we see the name COMMIOS, whilst a successor coin has the name TINCOMARUS, with the addition on some issues of COMMIOS F (son of Commius – Creighton 2000, 64).

So what can we deduce from this relatively sudden change in the type of coins in circulation, and the first appearance of rulers' names on them? An argument can be put forward to demonstrate that Caesar's sudden appearance in the south-east should not just be perceived as a temporary diversion for a great Roman general in the process of conquering Gaul, but instead a determined effort to establish dynasties in the two most powerful tribes of the south-east who would owe their loyalty to Rome. How might this have been effected? One of the ways might have been through the influx of gold and other gifts to the south-east from Caesar. Caesar was not short of gold, having taken a considerable quantity from defeated Gallic tribes. Subsidies to potential allies, perhaps in return for hostages, had always been part of Roman foreign policy:

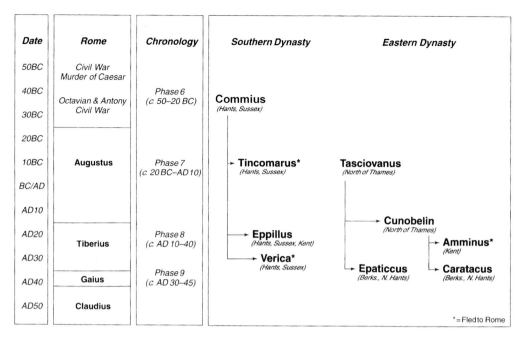

Date	Rome	Chronology	Southern Dynasty	Eastern Dynasty
50BC	Civil War Murder of Caesar			
40BC	Octavian & Antony Civil War	Phase 6 (c. 50–20 BC)	**Commius** *(Hants, Sussex)*	
30BC				
20BC				
10BC	**Augustus**	Phase 7 (c. 20 BC–AD 10)	→ **Tincomarus*** *(Hants, Sussex)*	**Tasciovanus** *(North of Thames)*
BC/AD				
AD10				
AD20	**Tiberius**	Phase 8 (c. AD 10–40)	→ **Eppillus** *(Hants, Sussex, Kent)*	→ **Cunobelin** *(North of Thames)*
AD30			→ **Verica*** *(Hants, Sussex)*	→ **Amminus*** *(Kent)*
AD40	**Gaius**	Phase 9 (c. AD 30–45)		→ **Epaticcus** *(Berks., N. Hants)* → **Caratacus** *(Berks., N. Hants)*
AD50	**Claudius**			

*= Fled to Rome

7 *The dynasties of south-east Britain in the Late Iron Age.* After Creighton 2000; courtesy Cambridge University Press

> Caesar began by recalling the favours that he himself and the Senate had conferred on Ariovistus – how he had been honoured with the title of 'King' and 'Friend', and had received handsome presents . . . (Caesar BG, 1, 43).

Subsidies could be given for a variety of reasons: to ensure loyalty to Rome; to bolster the declining fortunes of a ruler; to provide expenses so that a ruler could ward off the aggressive intentions of a neighbour. It may well be that the influx of gold bullion into the south-east was used to issue new series of coins (Q and L), replacing earlier varieties. These new coins would proclaim in novel ways the identities and loyalties of indigenous rulers. It is plausible, therefore, that Commius could have been set up as a client-king in the south, with possibly Mandubracius as a client-king in the east (Creighton 2000, 70). The practice of establishing client-kings, outside the areas under the direct control of Rome, but friendly and loyal to Rome, was a standard device of Roman foreign policy. These two rulers now exercised their authority over all of the south-east on behalf of Rome (**7 & 8**). In effect, the south-east of Britain was brought under significant Roman control by the events of 55 and 54 BC, almost a century before the direct control introduced in AD 43.

In south-east Britain between Caesar and Claudius the names of successive rulers in the two dynasties become apparent. North of the Thames the first ruler to have his name inscribed on coinage is Tasciovanus. Epaticcus and Cunobelin claimed to be his sons, and in turn literary sources suggest that Amminus, Togodumnus and

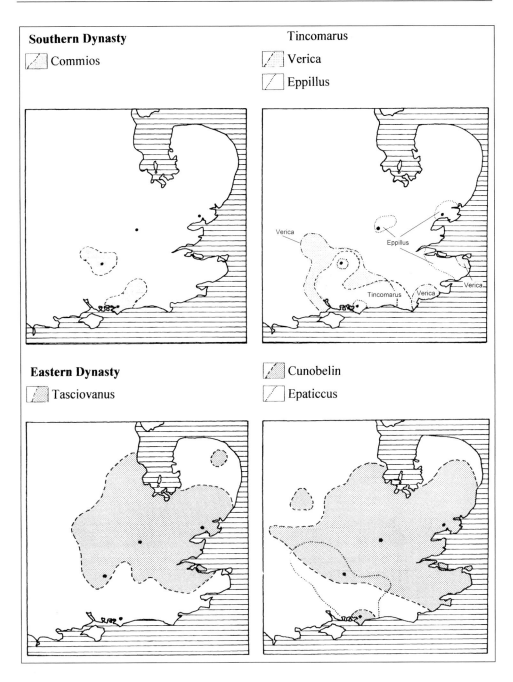

8 *Coin distributions in the southern and eastern kingdoms in the Late Iron Age. The contours show where more than 0.5 coins per 20 mile square have been found.* After Creighton 2000; courtesy Cambridge University Press

Caratacus were sons of Cunobelin (Creighton 2000, 74). While distribution maps of the coinage of the eastern dynasty indicate that the home territory was confined originally to modern Hertfordshire and Essex, by AD 40 it had spread significantly south of the Thames. The first ruler of the southern dynasty appears to have been Commius, who also had several 'sons', Tincomarus, Eppillus and Verica, who issued coins over the south and sometimes in Kent. Our definition of the term 'son' in these shadowy historical contexts must of necessity be loose; it may not necessarily imply a blood-relationship. The named rulers of these two dynasties and geographical distributions of their coins are given in **7 & 8**. Using the different coin distributions of all the various tribes of the south-east, and the meagre literary sources, it is possible to reconstruct a pseudo-historical narrative of the rise and fall of certain individuals, expansion and contraction of tribal territories, and whether tribes at different times were pro- or anti-Roman. An example of this genre is provided by Webster (1980, 41-75). However, it is important to note that such narratives are backed by very flimsy evidence (Creighton 2000, 79) and it is difficult to substantiate whether they reflect Late Iron Age political realities. That is not to say that political rivalries between elites did not occur; it is to say that the evidence to chart these changes in any detail is simply not there.

What does seem apparent, again relying on information from the coinage, is that some of these indigenous rulers were inextricably linked with Rome. The evidence concerns a radical change of imagery used by some of the rulers. For instance, Tincomarus' first issues were identical with those of Commius and continued the basic head/horse derivations. However, his subsequent coins began to illustrate unambiguous classical images drawn from Rome itself. The images used by Tincomarus and other rulers in the south-east included a variety of mythological beasts (sphinxes, gorgons, Pegasus) as well as altars, temples, vine leaves, ships' prows and sacrificial bulls. How and why did these images, indicating such a break with previous coin imagery, start to appear and what did they mean? The answer, briefly summarised here but more eloquently put at length by Creighton, is that rulers such as Tincomarus, future client-kings, may have spent much of their youth as 'hostages' growing up in Rome. Remember Caesar's repeated indication that hostage taking and giving (and hostages in considerable numbers) was part and parcel of Roman foreign policy. It is conceivable that Tincomarus spent his youth in Rome, growing up in aristocratic circles, learning Roman culture, even gaining experience in the Roman army, before returning to Britain sometime in the 20s BC to succeed Commius. The use of classical imagery on coins then becomes explicable as the newly arrived client-king, almost entirely educated at Rome, uses the kind of imagery he saw in Rome on his coins in south-east Britain.

Indigenous rulers in the south-east may have also used other devices and selected trappings of Roman culture to demonstrate their allegiance to Rome, and to differentiate themselves from other rulers in Britain. Such mechanisms may have included the use of Latin on coins, the use of portrait imagery of the rulers themselves on local coinage, the exchange and import of specifically Roman elite items such as chain mail, gold ribbon and folding stools (symbols of authority in the Roman senate), the adoption of specific Roman rituals, the use of orthogonal street systems in settlements (e.g. Silchester), the use of rectangular buildings, the construction of large dyke systems to mark out areas of territory (e.g. the dykes around Chichester, Silchester, Verulamium and Colchester), and the consumption of special types of food (e.g. oysters). In particular, the Late Iron Age temple on Hayling Island (**5**), some 11km to the west of Fishbourne and Chichester, may have been established as the shrine of the rulers of the southern, Atrebatic dynasty (Creighton 2000, 196).

At some point between AD 40 and AD 43 three events conspired to provide, finally, the circumstances for a second invasion of Britain. First Cunobelin died; secondly the Emperor Gaius Caligula was assassinated and succeeded by Claudius, and thirdly a certain Berikos (Verica) journeyed to Rome following civil discord in the south-east. It was by now probably custom and practice for rulers in the south-east to consult formally with Rome about who should succeed the ruler of a client-kingdom. It may well be, therefore, that there was political unrest among the elite in the south-east about who should succeed Cunobelin, and perhaps someone inimical and unacceptable to Rome or Verica was being proposed. It may be in this context that we can imagine Verica's journey to Rome. The subsequent invasion under Claudius may have been, initially, an annexation of the territory ruled by Cunobelin, rather than an invasion of Britain itself.

Before leaving the archaeological evidence it is worth contrasting the two key areas in southern Britain associated with the Roman Invasion – north-east Kent and the area around Chichester in Sussex. Iron Age coinage is one area of direct compar-ison (de Jersey 1999). A recent study of exotic[6] Celtic coinage in Britain drew attention to concentrations of exotic imports in these two areas (de Jersey 1999, 203). In north-east Kent there is a marked concentration of Massiliot imitations, which seem to have been the inspiration for locally produced derivative Thurrock potin coinage, the first of a series of cast bronze coinages produced in Kent from the late second century BC (Holman 2000, 220). A recent study of coin finds by metal-detectorists in Kent is rapidly changing previous impressions of this region. Iron Age base metal coins in east Kent are now found as frequently and as widely dispersed as most Roman coinage prior to AD 260 (Holman 2000, 231). This strongly suggests that base metal coinage was in everyday use. The impression hitherto created of the relative isolation of east Kent has also been modified by the large number of imported base metal Gaulish coins found there which might suggest thriving cross-Channel contacts. In the Chichester area the concentration of exotic imports implies some sort of major development in the mid- to late first century BC (**9**). Indeed, it has been tentatively suggested that these coins might be the numismatic evidence for the settlement of the Belgae in this area as recorded by Caesar (Cunliffe & de Jersey 1997, 106). The concentration of exotics is restricted to the Chichester area, in contrast to the general spread of Armorican issues which are found predominantly in a triangle formed by Chesil Beach and Chichester as the western and eastern limits of its base, with the lower reaches of the Severn forming the northern apex (de Jersey 1999, 201). The ultimate impression in regard to the exotic coins is that most of them, whatever their origin, were imported through Belgic Gaul and not Armorica.

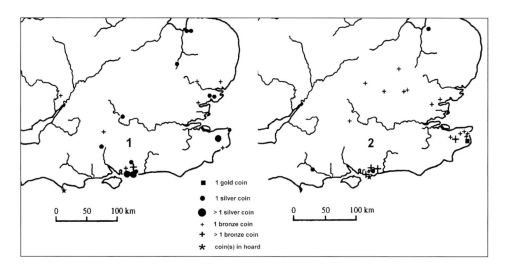

1 gold coin

1 silver coin

> 1 silver coin

1 bronze coin

> 1 bronze coin

coin(s) in hoard

9 *Distribution of exotic Iron Age coins from east central Gaul (map 1) and from west central Gaul (map 2).* After De Jersey 1999

The 150 or so Armorican coins found in Britain seem likely to have arrived on the southern coast of Britain a short time before, and perhaps during a decade or two after, the Gallic War (Cunliffe & de Jersey 1997, 89). The distribution of indigenous coins with possible Armorican influence is markedly concentrated in the Hayling Island and Chichester area. The preponderance of motifs which may have been copied are from tribes on the eastern boundary of Armorica and may indicate cross-channel contact with the Cotentin peninsula and the region to the immediate east. Such contacts may ultimately have been disrupted by the aftermath of the Armorican revolt in 56 BC, the reorganisation of communications in northern Gaul and the possible development of the port of Boulogne as a centre of Roman shipping. These developments led to a new axis of exchange and trade between Belgica and eastern Britain (Cunliffe & de Jersey 1997, 57). Certainly, this early numismatic flourish of the Chichester area seems to have dissipated at the end of the first millennium BC when the local coinage is subsumed within the general Atrebatic issues.

In Rome between Caesar and Claudius, of course, a series of seismic political events had reduced the old Republican order to rubble, clearing the way for the establishment of the principate, under the first Emperor Augustus. Despite the murder of Caesar and the chaos of the ensuing Civil Wars there is some evidence to support the contention that the re-invasion of Britain was never completely abandoned as a project. In 34 BC Octavian (later Augustus) contemplated another invasion of Britain (Cassius Dio, RH, 49.38). He needed a military success to offset the reputation of his chief rival, Antony, and he wanted to emulate the exploits of his adopted father, Caesar. However, dangerous revolts in Pannonia, Dalmatia and northern Italy prevented him from executing the plan. The idea was revived twice more in the following decade after he had assumed sole power.

[27 BC] He also set out to make an expedition into Britain, but on coming to the provinces of Gaul lingered there. For the Britons seemed likely to make terms with him, and the affairs of the Gauls were still unsettled . . .

[26 BC] Augustus was planning an expedition into Britain, since the people there would not come to terms, but he was detained by the revolt of the Salassi . . .

(Cassius Dio, RH, 53.22 &25)

It is clear, then, that invasion of Britain was relatively high on the agenda of Augustus, even if it never succeeded in quite getting to the top. This may simply be because Augustus realised that political domination could be achieved through the offices of client-kingship. In an Ode, written probably not before 15 BC, Horace lists Britons who 'pay attention to' the Emperor. It was about this time that Tincomarus began striking coinage with overt classical imagery and, as we have seen above, this implied a very close relationship between the Atrebatic household and Rome. Likewise, whatever the difficulties Augustus was experiencing with the indigenous rulers of Britain, these seem to have been relatively quickly settled, without the need for formal intervention:

> Some of the dynasts of Britain, having arranged friendship with Caesar Augustus and by paying court, had set up dedications on the Capitol and made all but one with the Romans the whole island.
> (Strabo, Geog, 4,5,3, completed *c.*AD 18)

However, difficulties in the local politics of the south-east did force supplicants to Rome on a number of occasions. At least two, Dubnovellaunus and Tincomarus, had fled to Rome before the death of Augustus in AD 14. They were recorded in documents detailing the accomplishments of Augustus, written by Augustus himself, and subsequently inscribed in stone and known as the Res Gestae (RG, 32).

The expansionist policies of the early Empire, which clearly included Britain, were reversed abruptly after the infamous loss of Varus' three legions in the forests of northern Germany in AD 9. For a quarter of a century an invasion of Britain was discounted; indeed, there must, at times, have seemed hardly any need. Tacitus (Ann 2,24) records that in AD 16 some Roman soldiers were cast ashore in south-east Britain and were promptly returned to the Continent by the local ruler.

The penultimate attempt at invasion occurred under Gaius Caligula (AD 37-41) in AD 40. Whilst on inconsequential exercises in Gaul and Germany, he received the surrender of Adminius son of Cunobelin:

> All that he accomplished was to receive the surrender of Adminius, son of Cunobelin king of the Britons, who had been banished by his father and had deserted to the Romans with a small force.
> (Suetonius, VC, Caligula, 44.2)

The historians who recorded this event treated it as a farce, with Caligula having assembled the troops and siege engines on the coast of Gaul, suddenly ordering them to pick up sea-shells and send them to the Senate as the spoils of war (Suetonius, VC, Caligula, 46). The only concrete legacy of the failed expedition was the erection of a lighthouse, as a monument of victory, at Boulogne. It is feasible, however, that the real reason for the non-event was the refusal of the troops to follow Caligula across the Channel.[7] It is entirely possible, therefore, that much military and naval planning and movement of personnel had been done by Caligula and that these preparations[8] were still available to Aulus Plautius three years later (Salway 1981, 61).

The Claudian invasion was, in reality, the last in a line of interventions, both actual and planned, that spanned the period between 55 BC and AD 43. Whatever other motivations were made explicit for the invasion, there must always have been an underlying sense of historical destiny felt by both Claudius and the senior military staff. When they sailed from the coast of Gaul they were following in the wake of the divine Julius Caesar, attempting to achieve what the mighty Augustus had failed to do, and righting the embarrassments of the mad Caligula. These were heady sentiments, and for some they may have proved impossible to ignore.

But, for the time being, we must ignore them in favour of looking at the specific evidence for what happened next. And to do that we must drag ourselves away from the busy and noisy scenes of embarkation in northern Gaul, and instead return to Dio's quiet study; there the retired professional politician and amateur historian, more than 150 years after the event, is struggling with his various notes to make sense of the episode of Claudius' personal intervention in Britain.

6 What can Roman historians tell us?

I suppose, if I am honest, that I have not been looking forward to writing this chapter. Even that first sentence, in the writing, felt a little laboured. And besides, today is Saturday 26 May and as I gaze out of my window I can see blue skies, gently swaying branches, hear birdsong, and almost see the comfortable mid-morning warmth announcing the start of an English summer. It's tempting to stop with the next full stop. But, of course, I will not. I am uncomfortable to the extent that I am not an historian, and the ways of historians are foreign to me, both contemporary historians and Roman historians. I blame my education (who doesn't?), where history seemed to me to be an endless succession of mad, bad and occasionally good kings and queens, eventually leading to numbing discussions of the British Constitution. The peasants (and people like me) only got a look in when they were revolting, fighting, burning something or each other, starving and/or marching on London. Their daily lives formed a silent backdrop for others. I gave it all up as quickly as I could. Professionally, as an archaeologist, if I have to understand some 'history' to make 'sense' of the site I am excavating, then I get an historian to 'do the history' for me, just as I would employ a pottery specialist to look at, and report on, the sherds I had excavated.

I do know that modern historians, while supposedly writing objective accounts of particular periods, will have particular biases. Whether they admit to them is another matter. Archaeologists, too, often have biases; these are sometimes grandly labelled 'theoretical standpoints' or somesuch; or, more incomprehensibly, they label themselves with such esoteric terms as 'processualists' or (with an eye to chronology that is habitual) 'post-processualists' or 'post-modernists'. Whether they admit to such labels is also another matter. But what of Roman historians? Were they similar to contemporary historians? Did they attempt to write 'objective' history? Did they admit to their biases? Did they appreciate that they had biases in the first instance? And who were they writing for? These are difficult questions to answer, but in asking them we at least raise the subject of potential differences between contemporary and Roman historians.

Apart from fragments of texts, nearly all Roman historical works composed before the middle of the first century BC are lost. Most of our extant sources for the Republican period (such as Livy, Cassius Dio, Plutarch) are based on these early lost works. These early writers based their observations on a variety of sources, including legends, the archives of prominent families and the official and corrupt annals of the Pontifex Maximus. The material contained a basic core of fact but was often embroidered with speculation and pure fiction. Moreover, the Roman annalists were often drawn from the aristocratic senatorial order, and their writings tended to reflect the aspirations of their own political class. In addition, they often sought to portray to the 'educated' Greek world the might and the right of Rome in worldly affairs (Lewis & Reinhold 1966, 5). The annalistic method of recording Roman history was abandoned in the second century BC, as the writings of Aulus Gellius testify; he compiled at least 97 books for his Roman history, and this set the model for later histories (e.g. Livy, Cassius Dio).

By the time of Caesar and Cicero, educated Romans were aware of the prevalence of historical inaccuracies in the works of earlier schools of historians, although it was not thought a useful exercise to attempt to correct them. However, Roman historians were also subject to other influences, not least their adherence to the principles and methods of Hellenistic Greek historians. Among the Greeks, history was regarded not as a social science but as a branch of literature. Thus Greek historians and their Roman counterparts were primarily literary artists, not scholars; their efforts were dominated not by an objective methodology but by canons of artistic form (Lewis & Reinhold 1966, 7). Therefore little need was felt, even by the great Roman historians such as Livy and Tacitus, when they were not dealing with contemporary events, to base their observations on primary sources. In addition, style usually triumphed over substance, so that historical documents were paraphrased, and speeches attributed to historical personages, which, while they may well have been delivered, were in their details and wording the creations of later writers. There was also an emphasis on patriotism, on the importance of the individual and a concomitant subordination or neglect of underlying historical forces.

With the emergence of the Empire the constraints on freedom of expression grew. Real and active political oratory declined and was replaced by the rhetorical excursions in the work of historians. There was an increasing tendency to write about the Emperor, his family, his court and Rome itself, to cater for the public taste for gossip and scandal. What little contemporary history was being written was compromised by the need to court favour with the current ruling dynasty. At the start of his *Annales* Tacitus notes how contemporary writers were afraid to write the truth in the reigns of Tiberius, Gaius, Claudius and Nero, and that after these Emperors were dead, they over-indulged their hostility.

It is as heir to this tradition of historiography that we have to place Cassius Dio and his *Roman History*. A very small section of his text, which is translated below in its entirety, is the key piece of historical evidence for the Roman invasion of Britain in AD 43. In its English translation it amounts to little more than 1300 words. I imagine it took him a morning to write, if that, in his study. But it is practically all the documentary evidence we have to recreate one of the most significant events in our history. Who was he, this Cassius Dio, whose work, by a quirk of preservation, has come to be so significant? Cassius Dio Cocceianus was a native of Bithynia (modern north-west Turkey), the son of a Roman senator, and, like his father, became a senator himself. He lived from approximately AD 155 to 230. During a long public career, which included the consulship, he devoted 10 years to collecting information and a further 12 years to composing his *Roman History*, from its legendary beginnings to AD 229.

He wrote in Greek – his native language. His vast *Roman History* was written down in 80 books, and he must have averaged about one book every two months. His work is of uneven quality and illustrates shared features with other Roman historiography: its annalistic method; its lavish use of rhetoric and fictitious speeches; its dramatised presentations and its reliance on secondary sources (Lewis & Reinhold 1966, 30). The work is also marked by a strong and unsurprising bias in favour of the imperial system, and by a blurring of details that often leaves an impression of vagueness. We can safely assume that he had never been to Britain. Before we look in detail at what Cassius Dio wrote about AD 43, it is useful to investigate what sort of sources, and specifically secondary sources, he had scattered on his study table that morning. And, in order that you, the reader, know the secondary sources that I have scattered on my settee this morning, the following summary is taken from Black (2001).

Black (2001) makes some essential points about Cassius Dio, by way of introduction: that, although a contemporary of the Severan campaigns in Britain, he was unable to distinguish between what was trivial or uncorroborated and what was significant and verifiable; that his usefulness for events in the first century AD is not rated very highly, particularly because of the adverse comparison with the more accurate works of Tacitus; that it would be a mistake to think Dio used the lost book of Tacitus as his principal source for AD 43, and simply garbled what he found there; that Dio, instead, probably used the works of earlier historians, either contemporary with Claudius and Nero, or, more likely of the Flavian dynasty; that Dio is, however, our major literary source for the events of AD 43.

Black goes on to compare the description of the Boudiccan rebellion in Tacitus and Dio, and particularly examines the reporting of unfavourable omens by both writers. He demonstrates that Tacitus uses the same list of omens as Dio (foreign gibberish in the senate-house; lamentations from the theatre; some dwellings underwater in the Thames; the sea between Gaul and Britain is blood-red at full-tide) but adds a new one (the statue of Victory at Colchester falling face-down) and is more specific about the dwellings in the Thames (he refers to a ruin of a colony (Colchester) in the Thames estuary). Black argues from this that both Dio and Tacitus were using a list of omens from an earlier historian, but that Tacitus has also used a second, early source. Because it is Tacitus who misplaces Colchester on the Thames, this seems to rule out the possibility that Dio has simply garbled a list he found in Tacitus.

Dio probably used historians contemporary with the Flavian dynasty. This would account for the pro-Flavian flavour of his account of the invasion of Britain (e.g. the primacy of the role of Vespasian) and the slight anti-Claudian bias reflected by the emphasis on the brevity of the Emperor's stay in Britain (16 days). One of these writers was Cluvius Rufus, who hailed from Campania and may have held the consulship before AD 41. Tacitus describes him as having no experience of warfare and this is probably reflected in his writings. There are many elements in Dio's treatment of the Boudiccan rebellion that could have come from the *History* of Cluvius Rufus. One is particularly notable. Before the decisive battle, Dio has Suetonius Paulinus, the governor of Roman Britain, deliver three speeches to three separate divisions of his army. This artificial triad of speeches recalls the three attributed to Chaerea by Josephus as he egged on his co-conspirators before they assassinated Gaius. The theatricality of these three speeches and the division of the army into three could therefore be a formulaic literary device, and might well have been the product of someone like Cluvius Rufus. Black points out that it is important to be aware of the licence that an historian like Cluvius Rufus[1] allowed himself in inventing material to enhance the rhetorical appeal of his work. This licence was perhaps embedded in and added to in the work of Dio.

It is now time to read the account left to us by Dio of the events of AD 43, which is reproduced in its entirety below. It is worth remembering that the original work was in Greek and this is a translation.[2] There will, inevitably, always be nuances of translation that are argued over by classicists, but the basic outline is clear:

> While these events were taking place in the city, Aulus Plautius, a most distinguished senator, led an expedition to Britain. For a certain Berikos, who had been expelled from the island during internal disturbances, had persuaded Claudius to send a force there. So it came about that Plautius was appointed commander, but he had great difficulty in getting his army away from Gaul. The troops were disaffected at the thought of campaigning beyond the inhabited world, so to speak, and they would not obey his orders, until Narcissus, who had been sent out by Claudius, climbed onto Plautius' tribunal and wished to make a speech. Then they became much angrier at this and would not allow him to say a word, but suddenly they raised the well-known cry, 'Io Saturnalia' (for at the festival of Saturn slaves celebrate, changing dress with their masters). Immediately, they willingly followed Plautius (their proper commander), but this was the reason why they made a later start than intended. They were divided into three squadrons, to avoid having an opposed landing, which might hold up a single force. During the crossing they were for a time discouraged when they were driven back from their course. But they took heart from a shooting star which flashed over from east to west, which was the direction they were making for. They put into the island, meeting no opposition. The Britons, relying on information they had received, did not expect them to arrive and they had not mustered their forces. Not even subsequently did the Britons come to close quarters with the Roman army, but they melted into the marshes and forests, hoping that they would wear them down in fruitless effort, so that they would sail back after an abortive mission, as had happened in the case of Julius Caesar.
>
> Plautius experienced a deal of trouble in searching out their forces, but when he did find them he defeated first Caratacus, and then Togodumnus,[3] both of them sons of Cunobelinus, who was himself by this time dead. The Britons were not free and independent, but the various tribal groups were under different kings. After the flight of the above-mentioned princes Plautius secured the voluntary alliance of a group of the Bodunni, a people dominated by the princes of the Catuvellauni, namely Caratacus and Togodumnus. He left a garrison there and moved forward.

Then he came to a river which the barbarians thought the Romans would not be able to cross without a bridge, and consequently they were encamped upon its bank opposite in a rather careless fashion. Plautius sent across the German auxiliaries, who were quite used to swimming easily even in full armour across the swiftest currents. These fell upon the enemy unexpectedly, but they did not shoot mainly at the men; rather they set about wounding the horses which drew the chariots and, when these were thrown into confusion, the mounted warriors were endangered too. Plautius then sent across Flavius Vespasianus (the man who later gained the imperial power), with his brother Sabinus who had a subordinate commission on his staff. They too got across the river somehow and killed many of the barbarians who were not expecting them. The rest, however, did not take to flight, but on the next day they joined issue with them again. The battle was indecisive, until Gn. Hosidius Geta, who had just missed being taken prisoner, defeated them so soundly that he exceptionally was granted ornamenta triumphalia, though he had not been consul.

From there the Britons retreated to the River Thames in the area where it empties into the Ocean and at flood-tide forms a lake. They crossed it without difficulty, as they had accurate knowledge of the firm ground and the places where movement was possible. But the Romans in attempting to follow them went astray in the area. However, the Germans again swam across, and another group crossed a little way up-stream by a bridge. Then they attacked the barbarians from several sides at once and cut down many of them. But they pursued the rest somewhat incautiously and fell into marshes from which it was difficult to extricate themselves and they lost a large number of men.

Togodumnus had died about this time, but the Britons, far from yielding, joined together all the more firmly to avenge his death. Because of this, and because of the losses encountered at the Thames, Plautius took alarm and advanced no further. Instead he proceeded to guard what had already been won and sent for Claudius; this is what he had been ordered to do, if there was any particularly stubborn resistance. Indeed extensive preparations had already been made in advance by way of gathering together various types of equipment, including elephants, to back up the invasion force.

When the despatch reached him Claudius entrusted affairs at home, and these included command of the troops in Italy, to Lucius Vitellius, his colleague in the consulship, whom he had caused to hold the office like himself for a whole six-month period. The emperor himself set off on the expedition. He first sailed down the river to Ostia, and from there he sailed along the coast to Massalia. Thence he travelled partly by land and partly along the rivers until he reached the Ocean. He crossed into Britain and joined the troops who were awaiting him by the Thames. Taking the legions with him he crossed that river and, engaging the enemy who had gathered together to block his advance, he defeated them in battle and captured Camulodunum, which had been the capital of Cunobelinus. After this he won over many peoples, some by diplomacy, some by force of arms. And he was saluted as imperator several times, contrary to precedent, for no man may receive this title more than once for the same war-campaign. He confiscated the weapons of these peoples and handed the tribes over to Plautius, and left him with orders to subdue the remaining regions. Claudius himself made all speed to Rome, despatching ahead of him the news of his victory through the persons of his sons-in-law, Magnus and Silanus. When the Senate learned of his achievement they hailed him with the title Britannicus and granted him the celebration of a triumph. They also voted that there should be an annual festival in commemoration and that two triumphal arches should be erected, one in the city and the other in Gaul at the point where he had crossed over into Britain. They granted his son the same title so that in a certain way it became his proper name, and his wife, Messalina, was granted the same privilege of taking a front seat in the theatres that Livia had had, as well as the right of using the two-wheeled carriage in the streets of Rome.

Parts of Britain were then captured, as has been described. Later, when the consuls were Titus Statilius and Gaius Crispus (the latter for the second time) Claudius reached Rome after an absence of six months, of which he had spent only 16 days in Britain. He celebrated his triumph (AD 44), following precedent in everything, including climbing the steps of the Capitol on his knees, supported on either side by his sons-in-law. He distributed the ornamenta triumphalia to those senators who had accompanied him, not only to those of consular rank. Such lavishness was liable to appear in him on other occasions too, on the slightest excuse. He gave Rufrius Pollio, the praetorian prefect, a statue, and a seat in the Senate whenever he entered their meetings along with the emperor . . . He also distinguished Laco, a former prefect of the Vigiles and then procurator of the Gauls, in the same fashion and in addition gave him the rank of an ex-consul. He then held the triumphal celebration, assuming a kind of consular power for the occasion . . . All this was done because of the successes in Britain and, in order that other peoples too might come to terms more easily, it was voted that all the agreements, which Claudius or his legates might make with any peoples should have legal force, just as if made by the Senate and people of Rome.
(Cassius Dio)

Since this is the key text for AD 43 it seems best to produce a commentary on this translation. The fundamental point to make at the outset is that the text is extremely deficient in terms of placenames. There is no indication where the invading forces sailed from or where they disembarked. The first paragraphs deal with the Channel crossing.

While these events were taking place in the city, Aulus Plautius, a most distinguished senator, led an expedition to Britain. Aulus Plautius was the first governor of Roman Britain (AD 43-7). Note that there is no mention of Sentius Saturninus, who is referred to as accompanying Plautius by the fourth-century writer Eutropius. *For a certain Berikos, who had been expelled from the island during internal disturbances, had persuaded Claudius to send a force there.* This is a critical sentence. Everyone assumes, with good reason, that Berikos was Verica, chief of the Atrebates, whose 'capital' was in the Chichester region. Note that he had petitioned Claudius because of internal disturbances in Britain, not necessarily because the Atrebatic territories had been overrun by the Catuvellauni. The petition of Verica may have been the trigger for the invasion, and perhaps the official reason given for Rome's direct intervention. Certainly Verica would have wanted the invading force to stabilise the Atrebatic territories and probably restore him to power, as the first objective of intervention, even if, ultimately, Camulodunum (Colchester) was the goal.

So it came about that Plautius was appointed commander, but he had great difficulty in getting his army away from Gaul. The troops were disaffected at the thought of campaigning beyond the inhabited world, so to speak, and they would not obey his orders, until Narcissus, who had been sent out by Claudius, climbed onto Plautius' tribunal and wished to make a speech. Then they became much angrier at this and would not allow him to say a word, but suddenly they raised the well-known cry, 'Io Saturnalia', (for at the festival of Saturn slaves celebrate, changing dress with their masters). Immediately, they willingly followed Plautius (their proper commander), but this was the reason why they made a later start than intended. There are several points to make about this passage. One is that, as an army made up of free citizens, the soldiers could exercise some free will in not obeying immediately the commands of their officers. The second is the emphasis on the enormity of the task ahead, and the dangers of going beyond the known limits of the world. The third is the role of Narcissus, a freedman of Claudius, which could be read as putting Claudius in a bad light. Why was not the Emperor himself exhorting the troops on the coast of Gaul? The fourth is the notion that it was this equivocation that delayed the crossing rather than unfavourable winds. The fifth is really a practical one. How many soldiers would have been able to hear Narcissus speak from Plautius' tribunal? Presumably just a tiny fraction of the nearly 20,000 legionaries assembled on the coast, although a slightly larger fraction might have been able to see him. His audience must have been, in effect, a small group of the most senior officers (or a small section of the mutinous soldiers). There must have been some system for relaying, via junior officers, to the majority of the encamped men what was being said from the General's tribunal, and who was saying it.[4]

They were divided into three squadrons, to avoid having an opposed[5] landing, which might hold up a single force. Much has been written about the division into three squadrons, but as noted above, this may have been a literary device. Certainly an invading army will have wanted to avoid both an opposed and a hindered landing. Caesar had experienced just how difficult it was to fight in the shallows immediately on beaching the ships. Plautius' objectives will have been to secure an unhindered landing, to set up an organised camp and to secure food from the surrounding area. The beaching or anchoring of several hundred ships and the unloading of men, horses, equipment and supplies would have created enough logistical difficulties, without an opposing enemy to worry about.

During the crossing they were for a time discouraged when they were driven back from their course. This may imply that either the winds changed while they were sailing, or more likely that the tide changed direction and carried them away from their destination.

But they took heart from a shooting star, which flashed over from east to west, which was the direction they were making for. The shooting star confirms that the crossing was made during the night, to ensure that the landing could be made the next morning. Was the shooting star just a literary device and the portrayal of a favourable omen? Its direction has been taken to indicate that the ships had to sail to the west to reach their destination. It has been pointed out that sailing from Boulogne to Richborough the direction would be south-to-north and not fit the direction implied by the star.

They put into the island, meeting no opposition. The Britons, relying on information they had received, did not expect them to arrive and they had not mustered their forces. The landing, unlike that of Caesar, was unopposed. The Britons, apparently, had been misled. Had they been misled deliberately?

Not even subsequently did the Britons come to close quarters with the Roman army, but they melted into the marshes and forests, hoping that they would wear them down in fruitless effort, so that they would sail back after an abortive mission, as had happened in the case of Julius Caesar. The final sentence in this paragraph indicates that the Britons did not want, for whatever reason, to engage the Roman army in a pitched battle. Speculation on where the forests and marshes that they melted into were located is fruitless. No doubt much of the Weald of southern Britain was forested, and all river banks, most of the coastal areas and much open terrain would have been marshy and ill-drained.

Plautius experienced a deal of trouble in searching out their forces, but when he did find them he defeated first Caratacus, and then Togodumnus, both of them sons of Cunobelinus, who was himself by this time dead. This is important information. Cunobelin, chief of the Catuvellauni who were based north of the Thames, has died. It is his sons who offer the first armed resistance to the Romans, but only after Plautius has spent some time in seeking them out. This confirms that the original landing was unopposed, and that Plautius was some way inland by the time he met Caratacus.

The Britons were not free and independent, but the various tribal groups were under different kings. Again, this is an important statement that sheds light on the political situation prior to AD 43. It suggests that some leaders (Cunobelin; Verica before his journey to Rome) had been able to extend their authority over neighbouring kingdoms.[6]

After the flight of the above-mentioned princes Plautius secured the voluntary alliance of a group of the Bodunni, a people dominated by the princes of the Catuvellauni, namely Caratacus and Togodumnus. He left a garrison there and moved forward. A half century of argument lies behind the latter sentence, with respect to the original Greek and whether it ought to be translated as 'there' or 'thereupon', i.e. whether a place is referred to, or simply the next event in an unfolding story. No-one now, I think, disputes the fact that the Bodunni mentioned by Dio are the Dobunni, with their tribal territory in the south-west of Britain, around the Bristol-Gloucester area. The significance for our story is that Plautius secured an alliance with them, probably as a result of their sending emissaries to him, once the defeats of Cunobelin's sons indicated the likely outcome of the campaign. Some have argued that Plautius may have actually established a garrison in the territory of the Dobunni, possibly at Cirencester (Hind 1989, 16). However, the dispute over whether an outlying garrison was established in the south-west is really irrelevant to our story. The real relevance is that the Dobunni were far more likely to send emissaries to Plautius if he was within campaigning distance of their kingdom (i.e. if he was operating in south-central Britain). If he was still in Kent, east of the Medway, then a mission to propose an alliance would not have been so necessary.

The following paragraphs (below) deal with the first river battle. It is prudent to point out at this juncture that much effort has been expended in trying to identify the location of this particular river. As we have seen above, there are fervent supporters of the hypothesis that this river was the Medway in Kent. My point is not to prove or disprove that this was the case, but simply to indicate that dangerous river crossings, especially wide river crossings, would have generally been avoided by a campaigning Roman army, even though such crossings were well practised by the soldiers in training. River-crossings were places where the discipline of a line of march could be disrupted, and where concentration on the tricky task of getting men, horses and supplies across the river compromised the alertness of the soldiers to enemy attack or ambush, hence creating a risk to security.

Then he came to a river, which the barbarians thought the Romans would not be able to cross without a bridge, and consequently they were encamped upon its bank opposite in a rather careless fashion. Plautius sent across the German auxiliaries, who were quite used to swimming easily even in full armour across the swiftest currents. These fell upon the enemy unexpectedly, but they did not shoot mainly at the men; rather they set about wounding the horses which drew the chariots and, when these were thrown into confusion, the mounted warriors were endangered too. The battle described in the preceding section has been conventionally placed on the river Medway in Kent, although exactly where on the Medway is problematic. Plautius sent across the Batavian[7] cohorts, who probably swam across the river upstream (in a narrower section and out of sight of the defending army), only then to steal up on the horses of the enemy and seek to hamstring as many animals as they could. There must have been a considerable number of horses, and these would have been used not only to pull the chariots of some of the warrior-defenders, but also were there as a means of flight if the Romans gained the upper hand in battle.

Plautius then sent across Flavius Vespasianus (the man who later gained the imperial power) with his brother Sabinus who had a subordinate commission on his staff. They too got across the river somehow and killed many of the barbarians who were not expecting them. Cassius Dio now introduces Vespasian, and his elder brother Sabinus, as we have seen probably because Dio was drawing on the works of earlier historians who were favourable to the Flavian dynasty. How did they cross the river? Presumably they had located a ford, or they had constructed a bridge, perhaps during the chaos that surrounded the intervention led by the Batavians. Frere & Fulford (2001, 47) argue that Vespasian and Sabinus were the commanding officers of two of the four legions under Plautius' command. If so, it can be assumed that a large number of men, perhaps running to several thousands, crossed with these two commanders.

The rest, however, did not take to flight, but on the next day they joined issue with them again. Clearly, despite the attacks of Vespasian, Sabinus and the Batavians, the defenders were not overcome on the first day and hostilities were resumed the following day. This is unusual in itself, as a two-day pitched battle in antiquity was not commonplace.

The battle was indecisive, until Gn. Hosidius Geta, who had just missed being taken prisoner, defeated them so soundly that he exceptionally was granted ornamenta triumphalia, though he had not been consul. The second day of fighting perhaps again involved the legions of Vespasian and Sabinus, and may have again been proving indecisive. At that point reinforcements in the guise of a third legion under Hosidius Geta were called up, and his final intervention proved the turning point. Geta was of praetorian rank and was awarded the consulship in AD 45 (Frere & Fulford 2001).

The subsequent paragraph of Dio records the retreat of the indigenous forces from the first river battle, and names the first specific place-name, the river Thames. *From there the Britons retreated to the River Thames in the area where it empties into the Ocean and at flood-tide forms a lake.* On the face of it, this statement seems to refer to the estuary mouth of the Thames, or at the very least a section of the river near its mouth where at full-tide the river was very wide. However, it is perfectly possible that people perceived the 'emptying into the ocean' as that section of the river below which you could not cross without a boat. In this respect the 'lake' of Dio could refer to the Tidal Pool of London, east of Tower Bridge.

They crossed it without difficulty, as they had accurate knowledge of the firm ground and the places where movement was possible. But the Romans in attempting to follow them went astray in the area. The Romans would have been intent on pursuing the defeated enemy as hard and as far as possible, since it was during such a rout that most casualties could be cost-effectively inflicted on the retreating forces.[8] But local knowledge of the paths through the marshes, mud-flats and across the fords seems to have been decisive in hampering the pursuers. *However, the Germans again swam across, and another group crossed a little way up-stream by a bridge.* Apparently, the Batavians were called into action again, and swam across a section of the river, while larger numbers of the army crossed by a bridge a little way up-river. It appears from the text that geographically these three incidents (the crossing of the defeated enemy, the Batavians' pursuit and the bridge-crossing) were not far apart. However, the reality may have been that the incidents could have been spread out along a 50km stretch of the Thames, if the retreat was near modern Gravesend, the Batavians swam across further up-river and the bridge existed, or was constructed, somewhere in the centre or to the west of modern London.

Then they attacked the barbarians from several sides at once and cut down many of them. But they pursued the rest somewhat incautiously and fell into marshes from which it was difficult to extricate themselves and they lost a large number of men. The attack from several sides, when it came, proved successful, but again the Romans made the error of pursuing the enemy into difficult terrain where their heavy armour and lack of knowledge of paths and firm ground put them at a disadvantage.

Before outlining the gist of the following paragraphs, it is appropriate to comment on the preceding one, and particularly in respect of the engagements at the two rivers. There are clearly similarities between the two river engagements, not least in the role of the Batavians and the crossing of additional forces at a different location.

Black (1998) has argued that such are the similarities that there may, in reality, have only been one battle. Dio may have used two different sources to compile this section of his history. One source could have been the lost books of the *Annales* of Tacitus, which described the unnamed battle and included a pro-Flavian emphasis on senatorial personalities. The other source (for the Thames engagement) could have been a pre-Flavian one, perhaps a copy of the very despatch sent by Plautius to summon the Emperor Claudius (Black 1998, 307). Intriguing though this possibility is, the two engagements are fundamentally different in that the first is a real battle with the outcome undecided until late on the second day, while the Thames crossing is, in effect, the continuation of the flight from the first battle. The following paragraphs deal with Plautius' decision to wait for Claudius by the Thames.

Togodumnus had died about this time, but the Britons, far from yielding, joined together all the more firmly to avenge his death. Togodumnus was one of the sons of Cunobelin and may have died at this time as a result of injuries sustained in the initial battle, or at the engagements at the rivers.

Because of this, and because of the losses encountered at the Thames, Plautius took alarm and advanced no further. Instead he proceeded to guard what had already been won and sent for Claudius; this is what he had been ordered to do, if there was any particularly stubborn resistance. This is one of the few episodes in the narrative on which practically all commentators are agreed. Plautius could have continued with the four legions across the Thames and on towards Colchester. Instead, as had been pre-arranged, once most of the serious opposition had been defeated, and victory was assured, a message was sent to Claudius so that he could arrive in person to lead the final stages of an assault that was in reality a formality. It is interesting to speculate what Plautius did with the troops under his command, during the long wait for Claudius. I will look a little closer at the possibilities once the actual months for the different episodes of the AD 43 campaign have been discussed.

Indeed extensive preparations had already been made in advance by way of gathering together various types of equipment, including elephants, to back up the invasion force. This sentence is ambiguous in the sense that it does not indicate whether it was Plautius who had carried out the extensive preparations, or whether such exotic creatures as the elephants were going to be brought across the Channel with Claudius. On balance, the latter seems unlikely and it can be safely assumed that all the preparations, from large details such as the elephants to smaller details, were carried out by Plautius. My guess is that both sides of the Thames had been secured and the elephants were stationed on the north bank before Claudius set foot in Britain. Nothing would have been left to chance, and all that remained was for Claudius to accompany his men and these animals to Colchester. It is worth speculating on the significance of the elephants. Were they a deliberate attempt to evoke the memory of previous successful campaigns? After all, Claudius himself was an historian. At various times since 280 BC Roman armies had been faced with elephants, and they had occasionally used them themselves. Their trumpeting and scent could spook the enemy horses, and intimidate the opposition, and they could also serve as pack animals (Crummy 1997, 32). How many Claudius had is a matter of conjecture – I suspect 10 or less.[9] Their part in this campaign was surely symbolic, and the symbol would have been understood in Rome, where in art triumphal chariots were shown drawn by elephants.

The final paragraphs of Dio's account deal with the arrival and departure of Claudius from Britain. Claudius enjoyed a remarkably short sojourn in Britain, a total of just 16 days. *When the despatch reached him Claudius entrusted affairs at home, and these included command of the troops in Italy, to Lucius Vitellius, his colleague in the consulship, whom he had caused to hold the office like himself for a whole six-month period. The emperor himself set off on the expedition. He first sailed down the river to Ostia, and from there he sailed along the coast to Massalia. Thence he travelled partly by land and partly along the rivers until he reached the Ocean. He crossed into Britain and joined the troops who were awaiting him by the Thames.* These sentences are important, for from them we can begin to get some insight into when in AD 43 Claudius actually arrived in Britain, and from that we can deduce something about the timing of the earlier arrival of Aulus Plautius. According to Dio (see below), Claudius was away from Rome for six months, returning to Rome in AD 44. This means that he can not have left Rome before early July of the previous year. Clearly Plautius would have had to invade, reach the Thames, and send for Claudius all prior to the Emperor's departure from Rome.[10] The optimum period for the Romans to launch an invasion would have been immediately prior to the harvest, when the Britons would be under pressure to fight an early battle and prevent the dispersal of warriors back to the fields. Plautius, like Caesar, may have intended to sail in mid-June, to maximise the hours of daylight, but both were delayed (Caesar by contrary winds and Plautius by the reluctance of his soldiers to sail). A crossing for Plautius some time in late June or early July is about the closest we can approximate, and perhaps by late July Plautius would have summoned Claudius and waited by the Thames. The Emperor could have reached Boulogne (from where he embarked) by late August[11] and campaigned in Britain in the first half of September.[12] He may have wanted to return to the Continent before the autumn equinox when sailing conditions deteriorated (Black 2001), or simply he may have wanted to maximise the time he could take slowly processing back to Rome, enjoying a fêted return at numerous towns along the way.

Taking the legions with him he crossed that river and, engaging the enemy who had gathered together to block his advance, he defeated them in battle and captured Camulodunum, which had been the capital of Cunobelin. Only one sentence summarises Claudius' assault on Colchester. Clearly, in order to win the award of a Roman triumph, he had to defeat the enemy in battle. Naturally enough, in this carefully orchestrated sequence, Claudius is depicted as crossing a dangerous natural obstacle (the Thames), engaging the enemy who had gathered to block his advance, defeating them and capturing the key prize, Colchester. Compared with the previous river engagements and battles this final sequence is bereft of topographic or tactical detail. This could be because Dio is using sources that were unfavourable to the Julio-Claudians. More likely, however, is that this final battle was a minor, stage-managed affair; it is doubtful if Claudius or his elephants ever witnessed battle in Britain at close quarters.

After this he won over many peoples, some by diplomacy, some by force of arms. And he was saluted as imperator several times, contrary to precedent, for no man may receive this title more than once for the same war campaign. He confiscated the weapons of these peoples and handed the tribes over to Plautius, and left him with orders to subdue the remaining regions. These sentences superficially indicate that after the fall of Colchester, Claudius consolidated the Roman gains, and set the scene for the future conquest of the rest of the island. In reality, much of this must be propaganda. We can assume, I think, that Plautius had already done a lot of the groundwork, particularly in respect of lining up a number of tribal leaders who would be ready to conclude a treaty with Rome, once Colchester had fallen. In addition, there will have been a symbolic handing over of some weapons from these leaders. Plautius is reduced to the role of a subordinate officer receiving orders from a wise and far-sighted commanding officer. The sentences above do not cite who these tribes were, and we can assume that this section of the text reflects elaborate window dressing, carefully arranged at the time for consumption in Rome itself.

Claudius himself made all speed to Rome, despatching ahead of him the news of his victory through the persons of his sons-in-law, Magnus and Silanus. While the sons-in-law of Claudius did make all speed to Rome, Claudius clearly did not, since he did not return to Rome until early in AD 44. The purpose of sending the sons-in-law ahead would have been to alert all the places at which Claudius would stop on his way back to Rome, in order that he could be received, as was his due, as a returning triumphant general, and to inform the Senate itself so that appropriate honours and festivities could be arranged.

When the Senate learned of his achievement they hailed him with the title Britannicus and granted him the celebration of a triumph. They also voted that there should be an annual festival in commemoration and that two triumphal arches should be erected, one in the city and the other in Gaul at the point where he had crossed over into Britain. They granted his son the same title so that in a certain way it became his proper name, and his wife, Messalina, was granted the same privilege of taking a front seat in the theatres that Livia had had, as well as the right of using the two-wheeled carriage in the streets of Rome. These last few sentences list some of the honours that were designed for Claudius, the Conqueror of Britain. They included the title of Britannicus, and the award of a full military triumph,[13] as well as honours for his son,[14] and wife Messalina.[15] An annual festival would ensure that the achievements of Claudius were not allowed to be forgotten, and the two triumphal arches,[16] especially the one in Rome, would constitute a concrete reminder of Claudius' success.

Parts of Britain were then captured, as has been described. Later, when the consuls were Titus Statilius and Gaius Crispus (the latter for the second time) Claudius reached Rome after an absence of six months, of which he had spent only 16 days in Britain. He celebrated his triumph (AD 44), following precedent in everything, including climbing the steps of the Capitol on his knees, supported on either side by his sons-in-law. He distributed the ornamenta triumphalia to those senators who had accompanied him, not only to those of consular rank. Such lavishness was liable to appear in him on other occasions too, on the slightest excuse. He gave Rufrius Pollio, the praetorian prefect, a statue, and a seat in the Senate whenever he entered their meetings along with the emperor . . . He also distinguished Laco, a former prefect of the Vigiles and then procurator of the Gauls, in the same fashion and in addition gave him the rank of an ex-consul. He then held the triumphal celebration, assuming a kind of consular power for the occasion . . . All this was done because of the successes in Britain and, in order that other peoples too might come to terms more easily, it was voted that all the agreements, which Claudius or his legates might make with any peoples should have legal force, just as if made by the Senate and people of Rome. This final paragraph seems to reflect an anti-Claudian secondary source used by Dio. The tenor of the paragraph attempts to belittle the achievements of Claudius, juxtaposing the long absence from Rome (six months) with the very short campaign (16 days), which Claudius was supposed to have led. There then follow a few sentences which contrive to paint Claudius as profligate and excessive, awarding both himself and others honours that did not seem proportional to the military conquest that Claudius claimed for himself. The thrust of this final paragraph is to suggest that Claudius' military success was really a stage-managed affair.

So much for the morning's work by Cassius Dio. There are other surviving fragmentary texts with relevance to AD 43 and it is time to look at these in turn. First, there is one paragraph from Tacitus. Tacitus was a native of northern Italy or Gaul and was born around AD 56. He began his political career under Vespasian and married the daughter of Agricola, the campaigning governor[17] of Roman Britain, in AD 77. Like Dio, he too used secondary sources such as the lost works of Fabius Rusticus, the Elder Pliny and Cluvius Rufus. Very rarely does he refer to conflicts between his sources, instead selecting and combining the evidence, and seemingly regarding controversy as unfit for a scholarly history.[18] His sympathies were pro-Republican (Hammond & Scullard 1970, 1034). He wrote one of his first works, the biography of Agricola, in AD 97 or 98; Agricola had died a few years earlier. Despite the close relationship that Tacitus had enjoyed with his father-in-law the biography is remarkably short on geographical detail: although Agricola goes on several expeditions in Britain, not once is his base there mentioned. There is no mention of the chief Roman towns of London or Verulamium. In addition, Tacitus still held the false belief that Britain was much nearer Spain than it actually is, and that Ireland lay between them (Mattingly 1970, 18). It must, I think, be assumed that such geographical precision would not be of interest to the educated elite in Rome and that, therefore, there was no need to include it in a work, the purpose of which was to eulogise Agricola himself. As Mattingly remarked (1970, 19), any province, any enemy, any campaign would serve equally well to illustrate the hero's virtues. Here is what Tacitus has to say in the abbreviated account in his *Agricola*.

The deified Claudius was the instigator of the renewed task. Legions and auxiliary troops were conveyed across to Britain. The role of Claudius is reduced to that of an instigator, who simply renews a task. *Taken into partnership, so to speak, in the venture was Vespasian, and this was the first step towards the fortune that was soon to greet him. Peoples were subdued, kings captured and Vespasian was fatefully thrown into the limelight.* By contrast, there is much more emphasis on the role of Vespasian, who is confirmed as having a starring role in the invasion. *The first of the consular governors to be put in charge of the province was A. Plautius and the next, Ostorius Scapula. Both were distinguished war commanders. The nearest part of Britain was gradually reduced to the status of a province. A colony of veterans was planted there as well.* The colony of veterans is, of course, the colony established at Colchester. *Several tribal areas were granted to Togidubnus[19] to be his realm, and he has remained consistently loyal down to our own time.* This is the only literary mention of Togidubnus, a client king of the Atrebates. As we have seen above,

Togidubnus may have been educated in Rome, and was, conceivably, the son of Verica. According to Tacitus he was granted other tribal areas, which meant that he could have controlled a substantial area of south and south-western Britain, quite possibly including the area around Bath and Cirencester. The remark about consistent loyalty must be a reference to the steadfastness of Togidubnus during periods of unrest against Roman rule, such as the Boudiccan rebellion. That Togidubnus was loyal down to our time is a tantalising phrase. Can this be taken literally, as meaning Togidubnus was still alive in AD 97, in which case he must have been a very old man of around 80 years, or does it simply mean that he was loyal until the accession of Vespasian (AD 69) or the current Emperor Nerva (AD 96)? *Thus exemplifying that old and long-hallowed principle in the policy of the Roman people, which employs even kings as its tools in maintaining mastery over its subjects (Tacitus, Agric, 13-14).* This last sentence is both a reference to the practice of client kingship, and the concomitant potential for exploitation in such an arrangement, and the fact that such mechanisms had been used by the Roman people for a considerable period of time.

Flavius Josephus was born in AD 37 or 38, and was a Jewish priest of aristocratic descent and a Pharisee. Though a zealous defender of Jewish culture and religion, his political sympathies were pro-Roman. A visit to Rome around AD 64 must have impressed on him the futility of resistance to Roman domination. In 67, a year after the commencement of the Jewish rebellion, he was commander of the besieged Jews in Jotapata and captured, but saved his life by prophesying that Vespasian would become emperor. When this prediction came true two years later he was released, but remained with Titus, Vespasian's son, until the capture of Jerusalem. He then settled in Rome where he received Roman citizenship. His first work was a history of the Jewish rebellion, written originally in Aramaic and translated into Greek; it contains one sentence that is relevant to our concerns in this book. Unsurprisingly, the statement is very pro-Vespasian and denigrates the actual contribution of Claudius.

> Vespasian had added to the Empire by force of arms Britannia, although till then it had been a hidden land, and hence he provided for Nero's father, Claudius, a triumph that cost him no personal sweat. (Josephus, BJ, 3, 4)

Suetonius was born in about AD 70 and was a native of Hippo Regius (Annaba in Algeria). He may have taught literature and practised law in Rome, before securing a succession of administrative posts at the imperial court; these included director of the imperial libraries and keeper of the emperor's correspondence. He served at the court under Trajan and Hadrian, and may have actually visited Britain under Hadrian, but he fell from favour in AD 122 after he was accused of being disrespectful to the empress Sabina. He seems to have lived at least until after AD 130.

Suetonius wrote the *Lives of the Caesars*, which comprised biographies of 12 'Caesars' from Julius Caesar to Domitian, who was assassinated in AD 96. With him we have moved away from the eulogistic treatment that Tacitus employed in his biography of Agricola, to a more objective and disenchanted approach. Suetonius' accounts provide information both for and against individual subjects, with the occasional weighing up of conflicting statements, but usually without any moralising interpretation by the author. Like earlier authors, however, the citing of secondary sources does not seem to matter. It seems that when writing about Augustus he had ready access to the archives in the imperial court, but for later lives this was not the case. The implication is that he was dismissed by Hadrian after he had completed the life of Augustus. Two of Suetonius' lives contain vital additional information for the invasion of Roman Britain. From the *Life of Claudius*:

> He [i.e. Claudius] undertook in all one expedition and that one of no great extent. When he was granted triumphal ornaments by decree of the Senate, he thought that the title was not weighty enough to grace the imperial majesty and craved the distinction of a proper triumph. He chose Britain as the most likely source of one; it had not been touched by anyone since the time of the Divine Julius and was at that time creating disturbances over some deserters who had not been returned by the Romans.

These sentences again reflect sources hostile to Claudius and again belittle the achievements of Claudius. The invasion of Britain is described as a simple pretext to enable the Emperor to claim a legitimate triumph, and at the same time link his exploits with those of Julius Caesar. The mention of deserters is presumably a reference to Adminius, a son of Cunobelin, who was banished by his father for an unknown offence and fled to the Continent and to the protection of the emperor Gaius (Caligula) with a small band of followers (Suetonius, *Caligula*, 44). *On his way there by ship from Ostia he was twice almost drowned in storms blowing from the north-west, off the coast of Liguria and near the Stoechades islands.* It is worth noting here that the travelling entourage of Claudius must have been considerable. Emperors travelled with large retinues of servants, officials, the apparatus of government, a large part of the Praetorian Guard, German bodyguards, plus, in the case of Claudius, leading senators whom he could not trust to leave behind in Rome. *Therefore, he journeyed all the way from Marseilles to Gesoriacum* [Boulogne] *by land, crossed from there and within a very few days received part of the island into submission without any battle or bloodshed.* Despite the heroics of the emperor's journey, the seemingly peripheral involvement of Claudius in the actual invasion of Britain is underlined here by the reference to the absence of battle or bloodshed. Indeed these two episodes (the difficulties of the journey and the ease of the actual conquest) contrast so much that the former may have been exaggerated to make the entire episode more dramatic and dangerous. *Six months after leaving the city he was back in Rome and held a magnificently appointed triumph.* (Suetonius, VC, Divus Claudius, 17)

From the Life of Vespasian:

> In Claudius' principate he (i.e. Vespasian) was despatched to Germany as legionary legate through Narcissus' influence. From there he was transferred into Britain, and there he came to blows thirty times with the enemy. He reduced two very strong tribes and more than twenty native townships, as well as the island of Wight which lies alongside Britain.

As we have already seen, the future emperor Vespasian was heavily involved in the events of AD 43 and here we have some more specific information. The 20 townships that Vespasian is supposed to have attacked are assumed to be in southern and south-west Britain and are usually assumed to be attacks on native hillforts, which may have been refortified to withstand a Roman attack. Circumstantial evidence for such attacks has been recognised by some in the cemetery at the eastern gate of Maiden Castle, and in the discovery of ballista bolts in the hillfort of Hod Hill (**5**) (both in modern Dorset). The two tribes are not named, but if the location of Vespasian's activities in Dorset is correct, then one must have been the Durotriges. The mention of the Isle of Wight is interesting, not least because it adds another geographical location, which helps at least to position unequivocally some of the invasion action. . . . *partly under the leadership of the consular legate, Aulus Plautius, partly under the overall command of Claudius himself.* Now, this latter clause is worth commenting on. How did Vespasian get to soldier both for Plautius and for Claudius? Plautius managed to arrive at the Thames fairly quickly, and as noted above, Vespasian seems to have been with him all the way, whether the Roman army had marched along the North Kent coast, or around the western end of the Weald. There the army waited for Claudius to arrive. In order for Vespasian to fight under Claudius' command, he would have had to have done so either accompanying Claudius as he travelled from a port of arrival to the Thames, or to have accompanied the Emperor to the north of the Thames.[20] He could certainly have done the latter. If he had done the former, that would have meant reaching the port at which Claudius was to arrive.[21] It is unlikely that he would have retraced his steps to the port at which the main army had arrived, since a detachment would have been left there, not just to secure and establish a major base at that place, but also in anticipation of the arrival of the Emperor. It is possible, therefore, that Vespasian marched from the Thames back to the Kent coast, subduing the Cantiaci at the same time, and waited at Richborough for the arrival of Claudius.[22] *For this he received 'triumphal ornaments' and, very soon after, two priesthoods, and the consulship besides, which he held for the final two months of the year.* (Suetonius, VC, Divus Vespasianus, 4)

The only other classical literary source for the invasion of Britain is a brief notice of the campaign which appears in the Breviarum of the fourth-century writer, Eutropius.

> Claudius waged war on the Britons, [a country] where no Roman had set
> foot since the days of C. Caesar, and when it had been vanquished by Cn.
> Sentius and A. Plautius, distinguished members of noble families, he held
> a magnificent triumph (Eutropius, B, 7.13.2)

Eutropius was an historian who took part in Julian's Persian campaign in AD 363, and was *magister memoriae* of the Emperor Valens (AD 364-78). He published a survey of Roman history in 10 books. Beginning with Romulus he reached Caesar's death by Book 6 and dealt with the Empire in Books 7 to 10; he used a variety of sources including Livy and Suetonius. The work is short but well-balanced and apparently impartial. But who was Sentius, what was his role in the events of AD 43, and why did no other classical writer mention him?

Sentius appears to be one Cn. Sentius Saturninus. A wax-tablet from Pompeii records a contract (*vadimonium*) made in Rome in the Forum of Augustus in front of the triumphal statue of Cn. Sentius Saturninus, and this suggests that he was one of the senators present on the British expedition who were awarded *ornamenta triumphalia* by Claudius (Black 2000, 1). In 1961 Hawkes (1961, 65) argued that Sentius landed with a part of the army in Sussex to prepare for the creation of the client kingdom of Togidubnus, while the majority of the forces landed in Kent. In 1981 Birley (1981, 360-1) suggested that Sentius may have been Plautius' deputy. In 2000 Black (2000, 4) essentially reverses the position adopted by Hawkes, suggesting that there may have been two invasion forces; the major force may have been commanded by Plautius and landed in Sussex; the smaller force may have been commanded by Sentius and landed at Richborough, probably to secure the port itself and north Kent so that Claudius could take the short sea crossing and meet up with Plautius at the Thames. Black cites a two-pronged campaign in AD 6 when Cn. Sentius' grandfather, C. Sentius, led a force from Upper Germany to rendezvous with an army commanded by Tiberius who had advanced from Carnuntum. Black goes on to remark about the statement in Dio that the invasion force of four legions was divided into three divisions, finding the mathematics of such a division puzzling. He argues that it is possible that Dio was only describing the major part of the invasion, i.e. that led by Plautius with three legions through Sussex, while the remaining one legion could have been led by Sentius through Richborough. So why does no other classical writer mention the two-pronged nature of the invasion, or indeed name Sentius in this context? It may be because Dio garbled his sources, or simply could not find all the notes he had made from the works of earlier historians. Tacitus was keen to make prominent the role of Vespasian, while Suetonius and Josephus were anti-Claudian. A mixture of oversight and antipathy to Claudius could therefore have conspired to overlook the role of Sentius (Black 2000, 6). Eutropius, by contrast, removed in time from the events he was describing, made more accurate notes and did not suffer from an anti-Claudian bias.[23]

So much for the writings of the historians; the texts are frustratingly short, the detail often absent, the meaning occasionally equivocal, and they amount to about 1800 words in total in their English translations. The historians themselves, as we have seen, used and confused details from secondary sources, and were often partial to placing bias and undue emphasis on some events or characters at the expense of others. In addition, current scholars can debate the exact meaning of a phrase of Greek or Latin. It is from such unpromising material that one of the major events in the history of Britain has to be reconstructed; it's not a great place to start, but it is all that we have.

I think, however, that the historical texts we have for the Claudian invasion can be read on another, more fundamental level, and read in a way that links them to similar stories in many non-Western societies (Helms 1993). This reading portrays the invasion of Roman Britain as an 'epic adventure' involving the exploits of a divine and wise culture hero (i.e. Claudius), travelling and overcoming hazards (e.g. shipwrecks; long overland journey) to a distant power-filled place (i.e. Britain), which carried dangerous but also ancestral connotations (i.e. associated with exploits of Caesar), acquiring valued resources beneficial for society back home (i.e. the province of Britain and all that went with it) and returning home with exalted status to be marked in specific, tangible ways (e.g. triumphs and triumphal arches; issue of coinage). In many traditional societies the concept of geographical distance can often be correlated with cosmological distance. For people in Rome, Britain would have been a remote, fearful and spiritually-charged place, separated as it was from Gaul by the waters of the Ocean. The journey of Claudius would link a physical passage with a sacred passage, meaning that his journey could be perceived as a re-creation of the ancestral journey of Caesar. Because physical travel can be physically and dynamically experienced it is particularly attractive to kings or chiefs since it presents personal challenges that can be overcome in the flesh. Elements in the texts that have survived, therefore, such as the disaffection of the troops, the contested river crossings, the near-shipwrecks that Claudius suffered, can all be understood as emphasising the physical trials of the adventure, while things like the shooting star and the use of the extraordinary (elephants) underline divine assistance and human efforts taken to overcome them. To what extent these more funda-mental motives and correlations were understood by the individuals at the time, or by the historians, is an interesting question.

Finally, there are two epigraphic sources that shed a little further light on the events of AD 43. One of these inscriptions is from the Arch of Claudius in Rome (that mentioned by Dio), and is also illustrated on Claudian gold coins, which commemorate the invasion. The inscription is not clear in all respects, but the content does provide additional detail:

> To the emperor Tiberius Claudius [son of Drusus] Caesar
> Aug[ustus Germani]cus
> Pontifex [Maximus, holding Tribunician] Power for the eleventh time
> Consul for the fifth time, saluted imperator [twenty two times, censor, father] of his country.
> The Senate and P[eople of] Rome (set this up) because
> [he received the submission of]? eleven kings? of the Britons
> [subdued] without any loss and because he was the first
> [to reduce] barbarian peoples [situated across the Ocean]
> under the sway [of the Roman people].
> (*C.I.L.* vi.920 + *C.I.L.* iii.5.7061 = *ILS 217*)

The inscription on the arch is dated to AD 52, but the reference to the submission of (11?) British princes submitting without loss must refer to Claudius' 16-day expedition to Britain, and the orchestrated and pre-arranged surrender of a number of local princes to him while he was in Colchester. The phrase 'without loss' could have informed Suetonius' phrase of 'submission without any battle or bloodshed'.

The second inscription is on a slab of Purbeck marble found at Chichester and dating to the Flavian period or earlier:

> A temple to Neptune and to Minerva
> and for the safety of the Divine House (of the emperor)
> by the authority of Ti. Claudius Togidubnus.
> [Great King] in Britain, (erected by)
> The Guild of fabri and its members at their own cost.
> [Pud?]ens son of Pudentinus, donated the site. (*R.I.B.*, I, 91)

This refers to the client-king Togidubnus, mentioned by Tacitus as being 'consistently loyal down to our time'. The *fabri* could be *ferrarii* or *aerarii*, blacksmiths or bronzesmiths, but the most common *fabri* worked in timber; it was certainly *fabri* who repaired the storm-damaged ships of Caesar (Hind 1989, 5, note 27).

Failing the discovery, perhaps in some Florentine attic, of a transcription of the lost books of Tacitus' *Annales*, that is all ancient historians are going to tell us about AD 43. I wish that more of them had visited Roman Britain. It would have made the next chapter much easier to write.

7 What do we know about the environment in AD 43?

I have a feeling this chapter will be quite short. I want to try and pull together every-thing that we know (or we think we know) about the environment in AD 43. By environment I mean the general vegetation patterns in south-east Britain; the water-levels and widths of major rivers; the climate and weather patterns; the tidal ranges and sea-level in the Channel. I know that the prime concerns of Plautius in the very first hours of the invasion will have been to manage as orderly a crossing of the Channel as possible, seek a safe (both for ships and men) and unopposed landing, get the soldiers, animals and equipment ashore without too many problems, deploy, camp, water and feed. Plautius would have wanted the same sort of information we now seek, to ensure that the initial landing, and subsequent march in search of the enemy, was carried out with as little hindrance from environmental factors as possible.

Fortunately for Plautius he was in a better position to assess these factors than we are. He was on the ground, on the north coast of Gaul, and could see what the weather was like, and receive and read all sorts of reports and accounts from a variety of sources not available to us. For much of our understanding we have to rely on what palaeo-environmentalists can deduce from the exercise of their science. As it happens, this is not very much, which is unfortunate, for this is where practical archaeological activity has to rely on the hard sciences for some of its information. Estimations of absolute sea-levels around the coasts of south-east of Britain at any one time in the past rely on data derived from cores driven into peat at various places around the coastline of the UK, which have been used to chart and date various marine transgressions, and the absolute height of them, since the Mesolithic period onwards. There are, in addition, occasional finds of fragments of ships or boats, or elements of trackways, quays or jetties, which can tell us where water was at a certain point in the past. Such evidence for south-east Britain is complicated by the fact that the absolute height of the land has subsided over the millennia since the last ice age. For vegetation, the main source of evidence is equally problematic. We have to rely, usually, on the analysis of pollen from dated peat cores, which can indicate something about the surrounding environment. Care has to be exercised in the interpretation of such data because some pollens survive better than others, some travel further than others, and some plant species produce more pollen than others. Occasionally, carbonised or waterlogged seed, plant or wood remains will be found on archaeo-logical sites, which can be indicative of the neighbouring locality. It is essentially from these types of evidence that we seek to reconstruct the environment of AD 43.

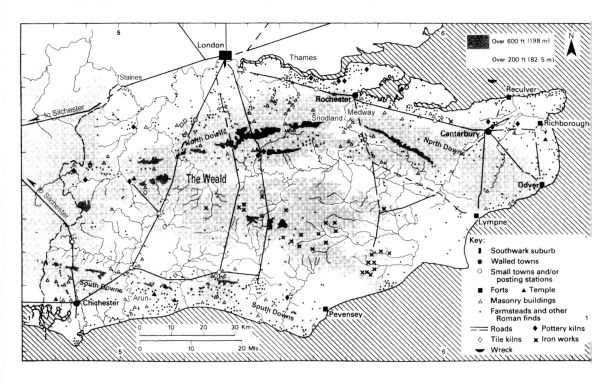

10   *Map of south-east Britain during the Roman period, showing the major rivers, the North and South Downs, the Weald and selected sites and the Roman road network. After Drewett et al. 1988; courtesy Pearson Education Ltd*

The general topography of south-east Britain was probably much as it is now, a central wooded interior (today's Weald), bordered by chalk hills to the north and south, with coastal plains, broken by rivers, bordering the sea (**10**). The climate too, despite being warmer in the preceding Neolithic and Bronze Ages, by the Roman period appears to have been fairly similar to the climate we enjoy today. So much for generalities; it gets a little bit more tricky when we want to be more specific. For instance, we know that the Weald was very wooded in the eighteenth century, and that its waterlogged clay soils were a nightmare to cross by horse-drawn carriage for those early London holiday-makers heading for the newly-fashionable resorts of Brighton or Worthing (Woodcock 1967). But was it such a forbidding place in AD 43? And, if so, would the invading Roman soldiers, mindful of the loss of Varus' legions in the forest of Germany in AD 9, have wanted to avoid it, not just for eminently practical reasons such as the difficulty of marching through uneven, wooded and muddy terrain, and the threat of ambush, but for premonitions ultimately based on cosmological beliefs, associating dark forests with malevolent spirits and the underworld (**11**)? What we can say, of course, is that the Weald was not an unknown place to indigenous communities (Gardiner 1990). It had been a place of seasonal camps for hunters and gatherers as far back as the Mesolithic period, and in the Late Iron Age there were a number of hillforts in the Weald, assumed to be located there, at least in part, for the working and smelting of iron ore. For local people, therefore, it was a known place, criss-crossed by well-worn paths and trackways.

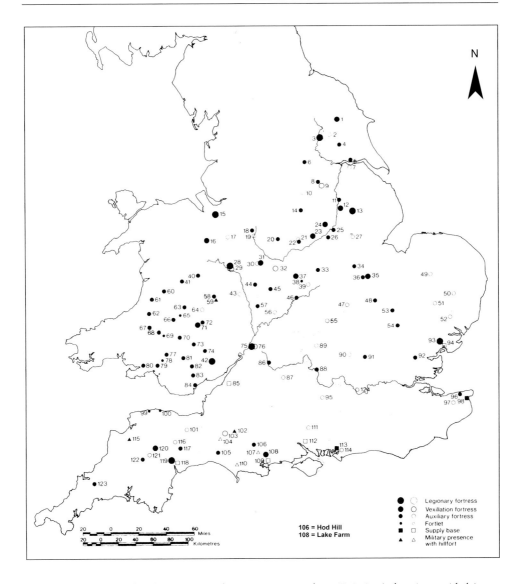

11 *Location map of early Roman military sites in southern Britain (a key is provided in Appendix 2); the lack of military sites in the south-east is striking.*
After Millett 1990; courtesy Cambridge University Press

Hard evidence for the past environment of the Weald, like the south-east generally, however, is difficult to come by. What few pollen analyses have been done in Sussex have concentrated on the heathlands, on the greensand in the west and on the river valley peats and inorganic sediments to the east; Surrey and Kent are even less well served (Gardiner 1990, 39). In the Mesolithic period small-scale clearances of woodland in the Weald may have been carried out by burning, in order to attract game to the clearings to graze. On the greensand, studies at Rackham (West Sussex) have shown that a local clearance of vegetation did not take place until the late Neolithic, with more general clearance later still, perhaps in the Bronze Age (Dimbleby & Bradley 1975). The unintended effect of even local clearance of woodland was probably to encourage rainwater run–off, taking soils with it, and the, sometimes rapid, accumulation of colluvial deposits in the valley bottoms. Additional Wealden evidence in the form of polished stone axes (Neolithic), Bronze Age barrows in Ashdown Forest and in Ewhurst, and occasional finds of cereal pollen (e.g. at Mayfield – Scaife & Burrin 1983) suggests a picture of scattered farmsteads being established in areas of localised clearance. The Iron Age hillforts generally date to the end of that period, which might be taken to indicate that woodland regenerated in the Late Bronze Age as the climate worsened. However, there is still, even in the Iron Age, evidence for agricultural activities in the Weald (e.g. enclosure and field systems on Ashdown Forest and pollen evidence for arable cultivation at High Rocks – Gardiner 1990, 43).

In the Roman period activity in the Weald is inevitably dominated by the iron industry, with the suggestion that the eastern part of the Weald may have formed part of an Imperial Estate, while the more western ironworks around Crawley may have been the product of private enterprise. Generally in the south–east Roman settlement appears to have been peripheral to the Weald – on the greensand, the chalk downs or the coastal plain; however, Roman roads, such as Stane Street, crossed the Weald after the conquest. In the ensuing Anglo-Saxon period the Weald seems to have reverted to dense woodland, as is indicated by sparse documentary evidence (Gardiner 1990, 47).

So where does all this leave us? I am afraid with a rather too generalised picture. It is clearly possible to demonstrate that the Weald was a much-frequented and used place from the Mesolithic period onwards, that there must have been numerous localised clearances, some abandoned and recovered with vegetation, some maintained in an open state by successive generations and communities. A decrease in the number of clearances during the Late Bronze Age and a subsequent increase in the Late Iron Age still begs the question of just how wooded the Weald was in the summer of AD 43. On balance I would guess still a much-wooded place – with oak, ash, beech, hornbeam, birch, hazel, hawthorn and elder (oak being by far the most common) – but the truth is we just don't know for certain. The greensand hills fringing the Weald would have supported dense stands of birch. And what of the coastal plain, and especially those grass-covered chalk Downs with which we are now so familiar? The latter, I think, must have been more wooded than today, with a mixture of beech and oak, although still with extensive areas cleared for agriculture, as is indicated by the relative density of prehistoric monuments and field systems, while the coastal plain was probably the least wooded, and perhaps the most densely inhabited, of these environmental zones.

What about sea-levels generally, and the river-systems of the south-east? The general consensus seems to be that sea-levels had risen to approximately their present height around 1000 BC (Robinson 1999, 8). A more recent and detailed study of Langstone Harbour, to the west of Chichester, suggested that the sea-levels in the mid-first century AD were some 1m below current sea-levels. A relatively rapid rise in sea-level between 100 BC and AD 100 may have made many south-coast inlets and estuaries much more navigable.[1] The coastline of the south-east in AD 43 would therefore have been much

12 *The river Thames at Staines, west of London. Such stretches of river have been controlled and channelled over the centuries.* Photograph John Manley

more indented than today, with rivers reaching the Channel in wide tidal estuaries which penetrated several kilometres inland. It is really only in the last 2000 years that gradual infilling of these estuary mouths, aided by the formation of shingle spits across them, has taken place. Rivers themselves, unconstrained by modern flood-banks, would have had a tendency to flow in more than one channel, especially on the flat areas of coastal plain. In the first century AD the river Thames, for example, flowed up to 700m south of the present Southwark waterfront along a network of intersecting channels between islands of higher ground and mudflats. The discovery of first-century waterfronts on the north bank illustrates that they lay about 100m north of the current channel, and a series of later waterfronts show the gradual advance of the north bank to its present position. The river was tidal in the mid-first century AD with a range of at least 1.5m, and it may have been up to 1km wide (including areas of marshland) at high tide. At low tide it was about 275m wide at its narrowest point, compared with 200m today (Dark K&P 1997, 26). We can imagine from this, therefore, that most rivers would have formed significantly greater obstacles to the march of an army than can be imagined from looking at those rivers in their contemporary state. Most rivers in the south-east in AD 43, especially near the coast, would have been wider, formed by more than one channel, and bordered by significant expanses of mudflats and marsh (**12**).

Some of these points are illustrated by consideration of the location of Richborough (**13**), much changed today from how it appeared in the Roman period. At that time Thanet was an island, separated from the mainland by an arm of the sea known as the Wantsum Channel, possibly as much as 4.5km broad in places, but only

13 *Richborough from the air looking south; note the river Stour to the east (left) and the Claudian ditches in the bottom right-hand corner of the enclosure formed by the walls of the Saxon Shore Fort.* Courtesy of National Monuments Record, English Heritage, Crown copyright

1.6km wide at its narrowest (Johnson 1999, 3). Into this flowed the river Stour, which was tidal and navigable at least as far as Canterbury (**14**). It remains uncertain how much of the Wantsum was completely open water in the Roman period; much of it may have been marine marshlands, and it is possible that it was fordable in places, notably on the road between Upstreet and Sarre. Richborough, at the southern end of the Wantsum Channel, was sited on what appears to have been an island. It is probable, however, that marshland had already choked the channel between this small island and the mainland, and remains of a well-laid road have been found crossing this point at Fleet, just over 1km west of the Roman site.

The topographic location at Richborough, however, is complicated by the presence of a shingle bank between Ebbsfleet, on Thanet, and Stonar, just to the north of Sandwich (**14**). The presence of this bank of shingle eventually forced the river Stour to seek a course to the sea at Pegwell Bay via a substantial southern loop which took it through Sandwich and thus past the eastern ridge of Richborough fort, removing part of it in the process. Although this shingle was forming in the Roman period, it is likely that the Wantsum Channel was still open until after the end of the sixth century, and that at Richborough there lay a naturally protected lagoon harbour, into which there were probably entrances at both the north end (near Ebbsfleet) and the southern end (near Sandwich). The formation of the shingle bank was probably the main reason for the eventual total silting of the Wantsum Channel. By the seventh century Sandwich had become the major port for the area, but, despite marsh formation, the river Stour was still navigable, whatever its course, as far as Canterbury until the fifteenth century.

Most of the last two paragraphs have been taken from the excellent English Heritage guidebook to Richborough, and I hope that (**14**) illustrates the locations of

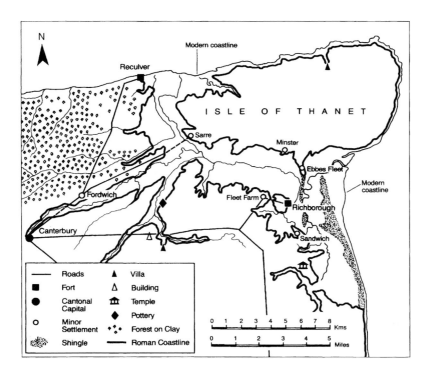

14   *Location map of Richborough, Reculver and the Wantsum Channel.*
     After Johnson 1999; courtesy of English Heritage

the principal places and features well enough. Clearly, the very long shingle bar that extends northwards from Deal was formed in more recent times and eventually allowed the complete in-filling of the eastern end of the Wantsum Channel and the formation of the present coastline. Before leaving this brief discussion of Richborough I want to ask three questions:

1   If we accept the orthodox view of the Roman invasion, current for most of the last century, then we have to accept that this small island was the place chosen to land 40,000 men, and that several hundred ships navigated access through the shingle bars into the protected harbour at the eastern end of the Wantsum. Was this island a good place to disembark such a number of troops? The island was just about big enough to hold the number of men, (although the Wantsum may not have had adequate anchorage – see Fulford 2000, 43) and I suppose being a small island it was easy to defend[2] and the water surrounding it prevented easy access. However, it also hindered easy egress, since the army engineers would have had to construct a road between Richborough and the mainland. The execution of this task and the subsequent march of the army across this narrow depression would not have been easy if the army had met immediate opposition (which we now know, thanks to Dio, it did not, although Plautius cannot have enjoyed such certainty).

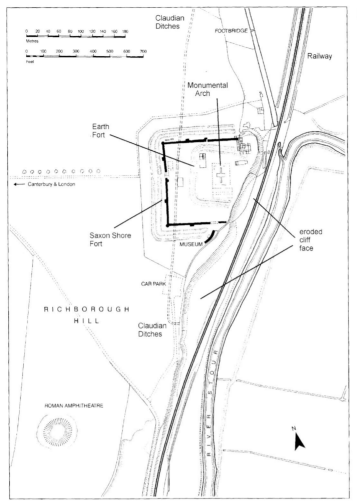

15 *Overall plan of Richborough, showing Claudian ditches and later stone-walled fort. After Johnson 1999; courtesy of English Heritage*

2 Quite clearly there has been significant erosion at Richborough since the construction of the north-south parallel ditches, which are the earliest demonstrable Roman features on the site (**15**). But how much land has really been lost? It appears that the main instrument of erosion would have been the Wantsum itself, (and later the river Stour) and this has been forced closer and closer to the site by the elongation of the shingle spit south of Ebbsfleet. A look at the plan of the later stone-walled fort at Richborough (**15**; erected probably before AD 286), indicates that in the south-east corner of the site, the land must have stretched at least 100m further to the east. If we assume that beyond the eastern wall of the stone fort there existed ground gradually sloping eastwards to the Wantsum then the extent of dry land would have been greater still.

3 The third question has already been alluded to earlier in this book. Why did Caesar not judge Richborough, or at the very least somewhere along the Wantsum, to be a safe landing place, and why did he choose (in both expeditions)

16 *Tidal streams in the Channel three hours before (top) and three hours after (bottom) high water at Dover; a longer and bolder arrow indicates a stronger tidal stream.*
Reproduced from Admiralty Tidal Stream Atlas by permission of the Controller of Her Majesty's Stationery Office and the UK Hydrographic Office – www.ukho.gov.uk

to beach his ships in much more vulnerable locations to the south of the Wantsum? I wish I knew the answer. If Richborough and the Wantsum Channel were not chosen was it because some other natural agency rendered them less accessible in 55 and 54 BC?

Finally we have to turn to consideration of the climate, and the currents and tides which would have affected the Channel crossing. Again it is very difficult to be specific but the consensus seems to be that from 1000 BC onwards, climate and tidal regimes were broadly comparable to today (McGrail 1987, 259). A brief description of the contemporary situation, therefore, will shed some light on the conditions of AD 43. The predominant winds in the Channel region are between south-west and north-west throughout the year, and this generates a slight surface current averaging some 6 nautical miles (nm) a day in a north-east direction. Superimposed on this horizontal movement are the regular ebbs and flows of the tidal stream generated by astronomical forces and moderated locally by topography and weather. In mid-Channel the set of this stream is east-west at speeds of 1 to 3 knots (kn). During each tidal cycle of $12\frac{1}{2}$ hours the mid-Channel stream flows east for 6.25 hours and west for $6\frac{1}{4}$ hours (**16**), resulting in a theoretical net displacement of zero in a 12.5 hour period. Cross-Channel boats will, however, generally experience some net displacement to the east over the 12.5 hour period. Tidal ranges (the vertical distance between high water and low water) and the absolute height of tides vary at different landing places. Around the southern coast of Britain the tidal range can vary from *c.*14m at spring tides and 6m at neap tides in the river Severn, to 2m at springs and 0.6m at neaps off the Dorset and Hampshire coasts (McGrail 1987, 265-6). The winds, as has been noted, are predominantly from between the south-west and north-west. However, in the case of a cyclonic depression moving north-east the sailor can experience winds from almost any direction, depending on the position of the vessel relative to the centre of the depression (McGrail 1987, 260). There are also seasonal differences in the Channel in that a greater variety of orientations of winds occurs in Spring, while in Summer winds come predominantly from the west. The wind's strength and direction can be modified by local topographical effects. For instance the harbours of the Solent are protected by the mass of the Isle of Wight, while the Wantsum Channel was protected from the north-east winds by the Isle of Thanet. In addition, land and sea breezes modify the overall pattern, with a tendency for there to be landward breezes during the night and seaward breezes developing in the morning and continuing into the afternoon, especially in settled summer conditions. This has a significant effect near the coastline.

But let us return to Plautius, standing on the coast of northern Gaul, sometime in the late spring or early summer of AD 43. He knew enough from his mariners to be able to assess the tell-tale signs of wind strengths, clearing skies or spreading cloud formations to estimate the wind and weather to come. His ships were being over-hauled, and last minute preparations effected, in a wide estuary mouth not far from where he was standing. He was sure that a night crossing would be best, so that they could land in daylight. He would have to sail in the afternoon, so the current assisted his vessels as they sailed away from Gaul, and he wanted a clear night sky to navigate by the stars. He knew the directions and speeds of tidal streams in the sea that separated Britain from his army, and had calculated that, in sailing for 12 hours or so, the tidal directions would even themselves out and that he would approach the coast of Britain when the incoming tide was at its highest in order to disembark his soldiers as close to dry land as possible. He was aware some of his soldiers were a little restless about crossing the sea into the unknown. But he, Plautius, knew that he was about to complete a project initiated by the divine Julius nearly a century previously; he was certain that he had the backing of the Emperor Claudius and that honours awaited him back in Rome if successful; he had witnessed that the omens from sacrifices were good; but above all, he knew where on the coastline of Britain he was heading for, and how to get there.

8 What else can we deduce from our own experiences about the events of AD 43?

I can hardly start this chapter by not telling the unchallengeable truth. Today is Sunday 24 June, almost the longest day of the year, and a bright blue sky, cotton wool clouds and enveloping warmth remind me that just for a few days every year this country has one of the most amenable climates around. Maybe it was just on such a day, nearly 2000 years ago, that Plautius gave the signal to sail; if so he would have had to endure a relatively short interlude of darkness at sea – perhaps six to seven hours at most.

In this chapter I want to consider what we know of the men who came with Plautius; in what sort of ships they sailed; how they navigated; their seafaring knowledge; what the unopposed landing would have been like and what they did when they landed. Some of this information is drawn from historical information, and some is supposition and inference, derived from contemporary experience of conditions under sail, or contemporary experience of warfare, and enthusiasts' wearing of replica Roman armour.[1] It is not my intention, nor is it my inclination, to provide a detailed introduction to the Roman army; others are much better equipped to do that. It is right to remember at the outset, however, that Plautius was not exactly sailing into unknown seas when he embarked; occasional crossings in sailing craft had been made as early as the Neolithic period, and by the Early Bronze Age contacts between places such as Armorica and central southern Britain were frequent and fruitful (Needham 2000, 151). Much nearer to our time of interest, de Jersey (1993, 333) has made a convincing case for pre-Gallic War maritime trade from Armorica, via Guernsey, to the south coast of Britain. He concludes that this trade may well have been controlled by the Veneti, as recorded by Caesar (BG, 3.8). And, of course, there was considerable maritime traffic between Gaul and southern Britain between Caesar and Claudius.

The Army

So who came with Plautius? Everyone seems to be agreed that the backbone of the invasion force comprised four legions – II Augusta; IX Hispana; XIV Gemina and XX Valeria (Webster 1980, 85; Peddie 1987, 180; Salway 1982, 73); we deduce this from circumstantial evidence: for example, epigraphic sources in Britain, such as inscriptions on the tombstones of soldiers. However it is worth remembering that the evidence is only really conclusive in respect of the II Augusta (Webster 1980, 179, fn 12). Most historians concur that, by the first century AD, the nominal strength of a full legion was of the order of 4800 to 5000 men – (10 cohorts of 6 centuries of 80 men plus cavalry and officers) (Webster 1980, 80; Gilliver 2000, 20). A small cavalry unit of 120 men was included in the centuries; the purpose of the cavalry was mainly to scout, carry messages and pursue defeated forces. Although the actual numbers in a legion could vary considerably at times from the theoretical complement, it can be assumed that for the invasion of AD 43 the legions were near full strength.[2]

Why were these particular four legions chosen? In part the answer lies in events that took place in military zones of the Empire in the preceding year. In AD 42, a year after the accession of Claudius, Camillus Scribonianus, the governor of Dalmatia,[3] rebelled against the new Emperor (Black 2000, 2). Plautius, at the time, was probably governor of the neighbouring province of Pannonia, and it may be that he was awarded the command of the British campaign for his loyalty to Claudius.[4] However, it is possible that the original plan to invade Britain with legions drawn from Germany had been formulated by Claudius' predecessor, Gaius. The latter was on campaign in Germany in 39-40, when a British chief, Adminius, reached him after being expelled by his father Cunobelin. Gaius went on to construct a lighthouse at Boulogne,[5] which may have been an indication of future plans, rather than the commemoration of a mere propaganda victory (**34**). (Indeed, Fulford (2000, 45) argues that the strategic decision to invade Britain may have been taken at this time, with the tactical decision to invade taken no later than September or October AD 42.) Sulpicius Galba was in charge of the army in Upper Germany in 40-2, a period which spanned both the last year of Gaius and the first of Claudius, while his counterpart in Lower Germany, P. Gabinius, recovered the last of Varus' lost eagles (Dio, Roman History, 60.8.7). The legions, therefore, were all drawn from these campaigns – one accompanied Plautius from Pannonia[6] (IX Hispana), two came from Galba's command (II Augusta; XIV Gemina) and one from Lower Germany (XX Valeria); these four legions comprised experienced troops.[7] All legionaries were Roman citizens, and these troops must have been largely drawn from Italy or Gallia Narbonensis, the most Romanised part of Gaul. Two new legions raised by Gaius were assigned to each of the German commands, presumably to free the experienced legions for Britain.

Since Adminius was expelled by Cunobelin from Kent (and fled to plead with Gaius), it has been assumed by some that parts of Kent would have been hostile to Rome (Black 2000, 3); Gaius then made for the Gallic coast, possibly with the real intention of invading Britain and restoring Adminius. Of course Dio states that Verica came to Claudius and beseeched him to intervene in the island's affairs. Since Claudius required the same military reputation that Gaius had sought, it may well be that Claudius simply took over a preconceived campaign formulated by advisors of the former Emperor. Claudius might have launched the invasion irrespective of the entreaties of Verica. If the lighthouse constructed by Gaius was a serious undertaking this would imply that Gaius had planned to sail from Boulogne, as indeed did Claudius. It is conceivable that three legions sailed with Plautius (perhaps this finds an echo in Dio's three squadrons) while a legion waited at Boulogne in order to accompany Claudius.

So much for the legionary soldiers, but what about the auxiliaries? A Roman army on campaign always included a complement of allies (Gilliver 1999, 22), and the allied contingent was usually the same size, if not larger, than the legionary component. These auxiliaries were recruited for specialist purposes, which included cavalry, archery and the use of the sling, or particular knowledge of a certain topography. The Batavians (drawn from a Germanic people living between the Old Rhine and the Waal) were famous for their expertise in water-borne assaults and were used in AD 43. Auxiliary units could be either 500 (quingenary) or 1000 (milliary) strong, but in practice actual numbers differed from the 'paper-strength' of such units. In addition, local units could be recruited on an ad-hoc basis while on campaign, and these could be commanded by local leaders.

As well as probably eight Batavian cohorts (4000 men), two Thracian documents are also documented from the evidence of very early tombstones in Colchester and Gloucester, namely Ala I Thracum and Coh VI Thracum respectively.[8] The only two other known units are those mentioned on two tombstones at Cirencester and one at Bath. The former two record the presence of the Ala Indiana[9] and the Ala Thracum, while the Bath stone mentions the Ala Vettonum.[10] Men who fought alongside the citizen army of legionaries were granted Roman citizenship on their discharge from service, and many lived out the remaining part of their lives in the countries they had campaigned in. Most commentators agree that, if the assumptions about which legions were present are correct, the size of the invasion force was about 40,000 men, split fairly evenly between legionaries and auxiliary troops (e.g. Webster 1980, 85; Fulford 2000, 42). Fulford argues (2000, 45) that only about half of this force would be active in the field in any one year, with the other half deployed on holding lines of communication, the organisation of supplies and the repair and provisioning of equipment. Perhaps included in this overall figure was a collection of people known as *immunes*, privileged soldiers who by virtue of particular skills (such as literacy or numeracy) were excused drudge jobs such as cleaning equipment or latrine digging. Other support personnel included such diverse professions as medical staff, architects, shipwrights, smiths, charcoal-burners, clerks, heralds and trumpeters. In addition, any campaigning army attracted a number of camp-followers, including servants, merchants, diviners and prostitutes. There could be a considerable number of these, as many civilians attached themselves voluntarily to a campaign in the hope of profiting from plunder, or other opportunities presented. Each legion may have had some 400–600 servants (Gilliver 1999, 29). According to Tacitus some of this group were despicable, being more ill-behaved than slaves, and sometimes more savage than the soldiers themselves.

Claudius, of course, did not sail to Britain just with a contingent of soldiers. He was also accompanied by a large group of advisors, including some distinguished senators who could have formed a war council (Webster 1980, 88). Some of these advisors, however, were likely to have been individuals who had demonstrated republican sympathies in the aftermath of Gaius' assassination, and these were people Claudius would not have wanted to leave in Rome during his long absence from the capital. High ranking officials who accompanied Claudius included Rufrius Pollio, commander of the Praetorian Guard; Valerius Asiaticus, who had been the first Gaul to become a Consul; M. Vinicius, who had been involved in the plot to assassinate Gaius in 41; A. Didius Gallus, who later became a governor of Britain; L. Sulpicius Galba, who became emperor in AD 68 and M. Licinius Crassus Frugi, who was married to Claudius' eldest daughter. The four principal military commanders, as we have already seen, were Titus Flavius Vespasianus,[11] the future emperor, his brother, Flavius Sabinus, Cnaeus Hosidius Geta, a legionary commander from a military family (the Hosidii) near Histonum, a town on the Adriatic coast of southern Italy and perhaps Cn. Sentius Saturninus, one of the senators awarded *ornamenta triumphalia* by Claudius.

Crossing the Channel

How did all these men, and their equipment, horses and elephants, get across the Channel? I am lucky to have access to a recent PhD thesis by Gerald Grainge (2001), from which much of the following is taken. Grainge suggests, drawing on the detail of Caesar's campaigns, that two types of ship would have been used – the warship and the basic transport ship (**17**). The warships were built locally, but to a Mediterranean design, and, although masted, would have relied on oars for propulsion in battle; they may have been equipped with a ram. Their purpose in the expedition to Britain would have been to transport the general staff and the senior officers. They would also have been an impressive sight, capable of intimidating an enemy. The much more numerous transports (carrying soldiers, animals, equipment and provisions), however, were built locally and to a local design. These ships may have had both sail (with a mast forward of amidships) and oars as well, and have been wider, with a lower freeboard, and flatter-bottomed, enabling them to be beached without damage.

Assessing the speed of these two vessel types is very problematic, since we only possess the most general information on the details of the construction of the ships (e.g. the archaeological evidence leaves considerable room for debate as to the type of sails that would have been rigged on Romano-Celtic sea-going vessels – Grainge 2001, 45). The speed of the vessels is dependent not only on the skills and strengths of the sailors, but also on the tides, swells and currents running in the Channel during the crossing, and the directions of winds and the performance of vessels when tacking into the wind. Experiments with a reconstructed Athenian trireme indicated that she was capable of up to eight knots under oars for short periods, but that the normal speed of the vessel over longer distances was probably significantly less. Höckmann suggests that the two-banked Roman *liburna* would not have exceeded five knots (1986, 394). When it comes to the transports, evidence for speed can be drawn from the example of the early second-century AD boat discovered at Blackfriars in London, from which the excavator determined that a theoretical maximum speed was between seven and nine knots (Marsden 1994, 197-8). However, Grainge (2001, 53-4) argues that in acceptable conditions of wind and weather this type of vessel was unlikely to achieve anything like these speeds. Instead, suggesting that the invasion force would not have set out in a wind more than the equivalent of a Force 4, he indicates that the likely maximum speed in a beam wind would have been five knots at the outside, and downwind it would have been even slower, of the order of three to four knots. He then goes on to suggest that the average speed of the entire fleet would have been the speed of the transports, and concludes that the average water speed of the invasion force of AD 43 was three knots.[12]

17   *Roman warships as depicted on Trajan's Column, Rome (completed c. AD 114).*
Photograph (by David Rudkin) of a partial cast in Fishbourne Roman Palace Museum

After type and speed of vessel we have to consider just how many vessels there were; again, calculating this is rather an inexact procedure, since any overall estimate hides a series of assumptions that cannot be proven. We can compare three different estimates. Grainge (2001, 85ff) assumes that the complete invasion force amounted to some 35,000 to 40,000 men. He goes on to assume that, fully equipped as these soldiers were, each vessel probably held some 60 to 70 men. Cavalry contingents would have required one transport for each 10 to 15 horses. The number of warships is estimated to be about 20 per cent of the fleet. These figures point to a requirement of 580 to 830 transports, together with 145 to 210 warships, and if the invasion fleet crossed at the same time then the total fleet would be some 725 to 1040 ships. Comparative figures are provided by Peddie (1987). He calculates the invasion force at 45,375 men, and in addition some 14,750 animals (including transport animals), which would require some 933 transports; this figure excludes warships (Peddie 1987, 40, Table II). For the record, Fulford (2000, 43) suggests a fleet of about 900 ships in total.

Now that we have an approximate estimate for the numbers of men, animals and ships involved, we can begin to imagine the organisational complexity of ensuring that the fleet embarked safely, enjoyed a safe passage, and disembarked in an orderly and secure manner. From what Dio tells us we can infer that the invasion force crossed the Channel at night. It can therefore be safely assumed that the strategy was to embark in the daylight of the previous day, and to arrive off the coast of Britain as early as possible on the following day, so that the maximum number of daylight hours could be given to the tasks of disembarkation. In 54 BC Caesar had approximately 626 transports. These ships were driven on to the shore bow-first, and probably needed to be spaced at 10m, or even as much as 30m, intervals. At 10m intervals, if all the transports came ashore at once, a front of $3\frac{1}{3}$ nautical miles[13] would have been required, while 10 nautical miles would be needed if a 30m spacing was adhered to. There is a possibility, therefore, that the army may have disembarked in phases in AD 43, or at separate landfalls. Clearly, much the same lengths of shorelines would have been required in loading men, equipment and animals on embarkation. Once away from the embarkation port, time would be needed to muster the ships into formation, to ensure, amongst other things, that contingents from the same legions sailed in close proximity and disembarked at more or less the same time. Grainge (2001, 103) has the interesting suggestion that Dio's reference 'to cross in threes' may have been a reference to the fact that the invasion force could have sailed on three separate days (although this could have jeopardised the entire undertaking if the weather changed abruptly between, say, the first and second sailings). Three separate sailings, however, would have reduced the scale of the naval operation at any one time, and with ships returning to Gaul, would also have lessened the requirement for ships to one third of the numbers quoted above.

Wherever the Romans sailed from, and wherever they landed, the general nautical consensus is that they would have sailed on an ebb tide, to take advantage of seaward currents, and landed with an incoming tide, so as to beach ships as far up the shore as possible.[14] McGrail (1997) carried out a comparison of five cross-Channel sea routes and four intermediate coastal routes probably used in antiquity (1997, 272, Table 10.1.1). Taking a number of factors together, such as the probability of not leaving due to no wind, the probability of favourable winds during the passage and the theoretical distance of being out of sight of land, McGrail scored the short crossings (Boulogne to north-east Kent) as having a reliability factor of above 97, compared with only 71 for the crossing from the Seine to the Solent. I have remarked above that in a crossing of some $12\frac{1}{2}$ hours the net effect of the tides from the Seine to the Solent would be to cancel each other out. While the distance from the Seine to the Solent is 80 nautical miles, that from Cherbourg to the Solent is 58 nautical miles and could be achieved in $12\frac{1}{2}$ hours by sailing at 4.64 knots. The nautical distance from Boulogne to Richborough is much shorter. Grainge, himself a sailor, records a passage on 24 August 1991, leaving Boulogne for Ramsgate in a lively south-westerly.[15] No formal navigation was required as the South Foreland was visible throughout. The passage was a fast one, taking only $6\frac{1}{2}$ hours with an average speed of 5.5 knots to cover the 36 nautical miles.

At this point a confession is in order. I am not a sailor; others, such as Gerald Grainge are. I can only imagine what a 'lively south-westerly' would be like (a bit blustery I expect) and I have not had first hand experience of the fearsome sub-surface currents between the Cotentin peninsula and the Channel Islands.[16] Grainge (2001, 86) does comment on the difficulty of trying to manoeuvre that large number of ships through the narrow approach channel into Richborough, or the narrow entrance to Chichester harbour, particularly if the landings were opposed. In fact, if opposition was met it would have been impossible for the warships to manoeuvre to cover the landing effectively. Grainge sees in such difficulties both the reasons for why Caesar landed on an open shore, and for why Plautius may have sailed in three phases, landing at the same place successively.

What must it have been like, when the first Roman footfalls splashed down into the mud and water of the landing place?

The landing

It must have been an extraordinarily difficult logistical operation. Remember the number of vessels taking part (nearly 1000), the number of men (around 40,000), the horses and the equipment, and the methods of communicating between ships and men, using basic visual and aural signalling methods (flags? burning torches and lamps (at night) and runners). There is a real case here for thinking that Dio's three sections of the fleet may have been heading for three different landing places, albeit such places need not have been necessarily far apart. If landing took place simultaneously in three separate places, then the degree of difficulty, and significantly the time taken, could have been divided by a factor of three. It must have been an aim to accomplish the landing within daylight of the first day. While we know that the landing in AD 43 was unopposed, the sources are silent in terms of whether the landing was actually assisted. It is possible that, if the landing took place in areas where the Romans were actually welcomed, then significant assistance could have been rendered in providing pilotage through any coastal hazards, and physical assistance in unloading, securing the beach-heads and the space required for feeding and watering men and animals.

Plautius would therefore have required a harbour or harbours for landing, which were protected from the wind, a good knowledge of the local tides, currents and coastal hazards, and knowledge of the beach materials and gradient for beaching the ships. The harbour would need to give easy access to a large area, which could be secured easily by some sort of defensive perimeter, in order to hold men, horses (some of which would be seasick) and equipment. The next requirement would have been water and fodder, and the place would need to have a clear assembly point for the troops to marshal before marching. The documentary sources that have survived do not tell us exactly how the Roman landing took place, and are silent on the amount of local assistance provided,[17] but we can surmise that specialist troops would be employed first to secure the ships on the beach and to make the first footfalls. These might have been followed by auxiliary troops who were tasked with securing the perimeters of a defensible site, preparing the way for the disembarking of the legionary troops. We have no way of knowing how long Plautius would have stayed at the landing place. He may already have had in mind that the initial landing place would develop into a major supply base for the invasion and for the conquest in subsequent years, and surveys and instructions would need to be formulated for this to happen. Cavalry scouts would have been sent out for reconnaissance while Plautius remained on the coast. It may well be that a few days were taken in camp, in order to rest the men after the crossing and in preparation for the march ahead. Clearly our sources indicate that the enemy was not close at hand, and therefore an opportunity for a few days of familiarisation and organisation may have been taken.

If we compare the obvious candidates for the initial landing place (the Fishbourne/Solent area and Kent/Richborough) then some crude comparisons can be made between them.[18]

Fishbourne/Solent:

In Favour	Against
Four available harbours for simultaneously unloading maximum number of troops in the shortest possible time	Longer crossing, with embarkation points from the Seine or further to the west
Sheltered harbours	Harbours only have one entry and exit point, and are therefore cul-de-sacs; although this does not matter if there is adequate space anyway
Friendly locals e.g. local knowledge provided by supporters of Verica?	Beaches are gravel, sand and mud
Large coastal plain would be very useful for organisation, with the added bonus that the Chichester Entrenchments could have provided valuable protection	An army marching inland from this area cannot be re-supplied or supported by the fleet sailing along the coast
Water, food and fodder were available	Can be observed from the Downs by the Britons, although such observations may not have been of much help in ancient warfare
The chalk Downs gave a good perimeter[19] especially on the first day of operations	More difficult to force a decisive battle, since an obvious barrier (such as the Medway) was not so apparent

Kent/Richborough:

In Favour	Against
Visible from Gaul	Goodwin Sands – a clear hazard
Shorter crossing (with embarkation from the Boulogne area) and possibly good shelving sandy shoreline[20]	Landing in this area could be easily anticipated by local forces

Knowledge of this area may have been better (because of Caesar's invasions[21])	Route of march would have been predictable (although this may have made it easier to force a decisive battle!)
The Wantsum Channel enjoyed some shelter from the Isle of Thanet	Very limited space on the 'island' of Richborough would have made deployment and organisation difficult
Water within 4 miles (6.4km)	Ships could not be unloaded at same time due to space restrictions
Defensive site (i.e. the Richborough promontory or island)	Unfriendly locals?
Amphibious support and re-supply possible using the Rivers Stour, Swale, Thames and Medway, although there is no evidence for such support	Exit by land westwards from the Richborough 'island' was constrained physically
March has logical and clearly visual boundaries[22]	No certainty that even a third of the fleet (say 300 vessels) could be afforded sufficient anchorage in the Wantsum Channel (Fulford 2000, 43)

The British Opposition (by Ernest Black)[23]

What forces did the British princes Togodumnus and Caratacus have at their disposal? No definitive answer is possible, but it is certainly worth exploring some possibilities, using comparative figures from other campaigns and hints in Dio's account.

In 54 BC Cassivellaunus dismissed all his men except for 4,000 charioteers whom he retained to harry Caesar's army (Caesar BG 5, 19). Presumably these 8,000 men (each charioteer was accompanied by a warrior in his chariot) were his best trained and most effective troops. It is probable that they were drawn from the coalition of tribes that Cassivellaunus headed as inter-tribal war leader. The manpower resources he could call on were perhaps not very different from those available to Togodumnus and Caratacus in 43, essentially the Catuvellaunian-Trinovantian alliance and the tribes of Cantium south of the Thames.

What size would a full levy of Plautius' British opponents have represented? At the battle of Mons Graupius Agricola's army faced a force of over 30,000 Britons. The Romans' numbers can be estimated at *c.*19-22,000 men (8,000 auxiliary infantry and 3,000 cavalry attested in Tacitus' account and a legionary component of *c.*8,000-11,000, roughly equal to the auxiliaries) (Tacitus Agricola 29 & 35). Assuming that Plautius had an undivided force of *c.*40,000 men, less one fifth (*c.*8,000 men) for securing his disembarkation point with any ships left there and to protect the unloading of additional supplies or reinforcements, this left him an effective army of c.32,000 men,[24] approximately one and a half times the size of Agricola's army. Can we extrapolate from this that Plautius might have expected to face a full British inter-tribal levy of c.45-50,000 men?

Caesar certainly claims to have faced armies of this size in Gaul. He lists the tribal forces pledged to an anti-Roman coalition by the Belgae (Caesar BG 2, 4). The highest individual tribal totals (each 50,000 men) belonged to the Suessiones and the Nervii. The Atuatuci promised 19,000 men and the Eburones and three other tribes between them up to 40,000. Later, in the winter of 54 BC, Quintus Cicero and his legion were besieged in their camp by the Nervii, their client tribes and the Atuatuci and Eburones, in all a force estimated by Caesar at c.60,000 men (Caesar BG 5,49). These sets of figures are convincingly compatible and the inter-tribal coalition that besieged Cicero seems comparable to the sort of coalition that Plautius could have expected to face. This can therefore be estimated at c.45,000-60,000.

What proportion of this would have been militarily effective? Cassivellaunus' effective force of charioteers (and warriors) was c.8,000 and a similar size of force may have been the core of the British army in 43. Certainly the detail that the Batavians shot at the chariot horses in the first river battle (Dio 60.20.3) suggests that this element continued to be of prime importance in British military tactics.

However, it is doubtful if Plautius ever actually faced the full military complement of the Catuvellaunian coalition. The initial slowness of the British mobilisation, and the separate defeats of Caratacus and Togodumnus before the first river battle, suggest that Plautius may have faced only an incomplete levy of the Britons in that battle. The British belief that they were safe from attack beyond the river (Dio 60.20.2) shows that they had chosen it as a defensive position and did not yet feel strong enough to act aggressively. It may be that the British force at the river was smaller, or at least no more numerous, than the Roman force that attacked it. It may have had a higher proportion of trained warriors (the chariot crews) than most barbarian armies since these could have been easier to mobilise quickly then the lower-grade infantry.

Such reconstructions, based largely on analogy, are not provable, but the exercise does open up the question of how difficult the campaign really was for Plautius and his lieutenants.

The march to Colchester

Leaving aside Claudius' desire for military success, most commentators seem to be agreed that there were two main immediate aims for the invasion of Britain in AD 43 – one was to bring peace and stability to the southern Atrebatic kingdom ruled by the aged Verica and the second was to defeat the Catuvellaunian princes whose aggressive expansionist policies were beginning to threaten the stability of south-east Britain. The simple question is which of these objectives the Romans would have tackled first. The answer must surely have a great bearing on where we think the

Romans made their initial landing; however, the answer finds less agreement in contemporary commentators. Frere & Fulford (2001) imply that the restoration of Verica was indeed the primary objective, and taking Colchester was the secondary objective. However, since the former could not be definitively achieved without the latter, the latter became the primary objective and the restoration of Verica became secondary. While this sounds eminently sensible from the vantage point of the twenty-first century, did Plautius in AD 43 entertain quite the same logical calculations? Much might have depended on the contemporary situation in the southern Atrebatic kingdom. There is no evidence that the southern Atrebatic kingdom had recently been overrun by Catuvellaunian forces, nor that a landing near Chichester was bound to meet strong resistance (*pace* Frere & Fulford 2001).

Of the two possible lines of march to Colchester from a landing place, again most commentators, influenced by a combination of the ambush of Varus in AD 9 and the reports of eighteenth-century travellers, seem agreed that the Weald was best avoided by the invading army (Bird 2000, 95). Only two main routes (with individual variations) are therefore usually considered: from Richborough to Colchester via Rochester and London (about 116 miles or 187km) or from Chichester to Colchester via Silchester and Staines (about 135 miles or 218km). How long would it have taken the Roman army to march such a distance? Gilliver (2001, 32ff) provides some figures that give an insight into the realities of marching on campaign. The arrangement of an army on the march depended on the current tactical situation. If the column was marching through friendly territory with no danger of attack, then a long narrow column might be deployed. If, on the other hand, attack could be anticipated then the *triplex acies* (triple battle line) or *agmen quadratum* (squared column) might be utilised, resulting in a shorter, broader column. These latter types of marching formation were designed so that the army could wheel from line of march to battle lines facing the enemy without undue difficulty. The actual length of the columns could be considerable. An attempt to calculate Vespasian's line of march in Judaea, as described by Josephus, resulted in a marching column some 17–18.5 miles long (28 to 30km). So long indeed was it that it seems, rather implausibly, that the head of the column may have been entering its overnight camp before the last of the troops were leaving their previous night's camp. Approximate calculations on the column length deployed by Arrian marching against the Alans in the second century AD suggest a length of 3.5 miles (4.8 km) for an army about 13,000 strong (Gilliver 2000, 47–8). In terms of speed of march, Caesar managed up to 25 miles (40km) a day with his troops during the Gallic campaigns. However, evidence from marching camps in Scotland suggests that distances covered each day were of the order of 15 miles (24km) and sometimes much less. In particular, natural obstacles such as rivers clearly slowed progress down even further. Assuming an average distance of 10 miles (16km) per day, and allowing five days for overcoming rivers and other natural obstacles, the invading army could have reached Colchester within 17 days (via Richborough) and 19 days (via Chichester); in other words there is very little difference in the two routes in terms of practical marching time. Indeed, rivers were things to be avoided, especially wide rivers, since they, more than anything, would impede progress.

We have now looked at three of our four types of evidence. It is time to turn to the last, and perhaps the most emotive kind of evidence, that has a bearing on this issue. This is the evidence that is dug from the ground, in a very real attempt to find the first ditch dug by the invading army, and the first pot dropped or discarded. And there is no better, and perhaps no more emotive place to start, than by looking at the site of Richborough itself.

9 What did they really find at Richborough?

The Society of Antiquaries' excavations at Richborough

The excavations at Richborough were conceived as a project by the Research Committee of the Society of Antiquaries. The initial idea for the excavations was presumably formulated shortly after the end of the Great War in 1918. The undertaking was a considerable one and the publication of the excavations, ultimately in five volumes, was not without its difficulties. However, the excavations and subsequent publications, spanning almost a half century, record both changing techniques of excavation, and changes in form of publication, as well as having much to tell us about the contemporary perception of the events of AD 43. It is best at first to lay out in tabular form the excavation seasons and the respective publications.

Excavation seasons	When published	Excavators and authors
Summers of 1922 and 1923	1926 – First Report	J.P. Bushe-Fox FSA (both excavator and author)
Summers of 1924 and 1925	1928 – Second Report	J.P. Bushe-Fox FSA (both excavator and author)
Summers of 1926 and 1927	1932 – Third Report	J.P. Bushe-Fox FSA (both excavator and author)
Summers of 1928-30	1949 – Fourth Report	J.P. Bushe-Fox FSA (both excavator and author)
Summers of 1931-38	1968 – Fifth Report	J.P. Bushe-Fox (excavator); Mr B.W. Pearce (author); Barry Cunliffe (editor)

It can thus be appreciated that the excavations took place at Richborough every summer between 1922 and 1938 – a total of 17 consecutive seasons. Publication was admirably prompt initially, and the first three reports appeared with a speed that many archaeologists today would envy. However, the fourth report was greatly delayed not only by the outbreak of the Second World War, but also by a serious accident to Mr Bushe-Fox, then Chief Inspector of Ancient Monuments at the Ministry of Works, on an archaeological site in Colchester. The fifth report was further delayed by the deaths of Mr Bushe-Fox and subsequently Mr Pearce, with the publication finally being rescued by the intervention of a young Barry Cunliffe who in 1963 was commissioned to produce the final and fifth report.

The initial aim of the excavations seems to have been the exploration and better understanding of the surviving monumental concrete foundation. This is now known to be the base of a monumental arch, but at that time its purpose was a matter of speculation (I, 2).[1] However, it was clear also that work would be undertaken to elucidate the internal plan of the Saxon Shore Fort (I,10). The table below indicates what was achieved in each season of excavation,[2] and should be consulted in association with **15 & 18**. As will be seen the excavation methodologies changed considerably over the course of the 17 seasons.

Excavation season	Area excavated	Main results
1922-3	Site I – to the north-west of concrete foundation – site chosen because of parch marks in grass; Site II	Masonry building and first indication of the ditches around the mid-third-century smaller fort; hexagonal structure revealed at Site II
1924-5	Clearance of topsoil (some 3ft) had begun by workmen earlier in the year – so start was made in the north-east corner – Site III – later extended to the south to include site of Chapel	Masonry buildings, and discovery of three defensive ditches associated with the smaller fort
1926-7	Much exploratory work, mainly to west of concrete foundation	Discovery of the parallel Claudian ditches both within the Saxon Shore Fort, and to the north of it. Many sections excavated through Claudian ditches; mid-third-century fort ditches and ditches of Saxon Shore Fort; shaft sunk near to concrete platform; discovery of two temples in railway cutting south of the site
1928-30	Area X to the south of the concrete platform; area near the entrance to the Claudian ditches; tracing of Claudian ditches to the north and south of the Saxon Shore Fort	Discovery of Early Iron Age ditches; discovery of timber granaries in Area X; detailed exploration of the entrance through the Claudian ditches
1931-8	Areas XVII and XXIII, south of the main east-west road; areas XVIII, XIX and XXI north of the concrete platform; extensive clearance on the southern length of the mid-third-century fort ditches	Iron Age palisade trench to the north of the concrete platform; diagonal trench 1 in the south-west corner revealed Claudian ditches; more granaries to the south and east of the concrete platform; timber buildings to the north and east of the concrete platform
1933-5	Mid-third-century fort	Removal of fill of the three parallel ditches

18 *Detailed plan of Richborough showing location of some excavated and published sections across the Claudian ditches from the Society of Antiquaries' excavations.* Courtesy of the Society of Antiquaries

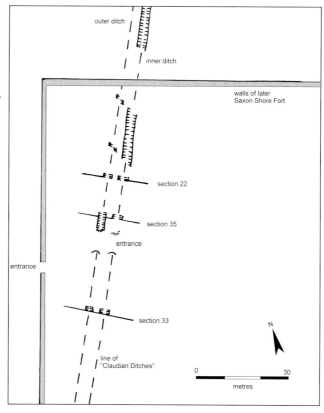

Having established the main sequence of excavations and the principal results obtained, it is relevant to outline briefly the personnel and techniques employed on the dig. It is clear that the workforce providing the main labour on the excavation, was drawn from the ranks of the unemployed and that the project thus provided welcome relief from unemployment. The clearance of the 3ft of topsoil from the interior of the Saxon Shore Fort, starting in the north-east corner in the winter of 1924-5, was carried out by some 40 to 60 unemployed, under the supervision of a Mr W.G. Klein, FSA. This clearance was effected by normal hand tools (picks, shovel, wheelbarrows) and an opportunity was taken to collect large amounts of pottery and considerable numbers of coins (e.g. 15,365 coins found in the surface clearing reported in II, 2). In the summer a number of scholars, most drawn from the ranks of the Society of Antiquaries, would supervise the excavations or undertake the cataloguing of the finds; scaled drawings were the work of staff of the Office of Works. In the later seasons in the 1930s, unemployed workmen were again utilised, and the Fourth Report details the activities of over 100 men who had been engaged on a variety of tasks: e.g. complete clearance of the ditches around the Saxon Shore Fort; moving of spoil heaps from the earlier excavations that had been dumped across the line of the Saxon Shore Fort ditches; clearing out of sections of the Claudian and mid-third-century fort ditches; examination of the ground to the south which was prepared for a car-park.

Some flavour of this enterprise can be gained from the following accounts (IV, 1):

> The supervision of this large body of sometimes over 100 men was under-
> taken by . . . Mr W.J. Klein, assisted by Mr B.W. Pearce . . . During the
> winter long stretches of the defensive ditches were cleared, and thousands of
> tons of soil were removed to various tips. The site is on rising ground near
> the east coast where there is little or no shelter from wind and rain. At times
> during bad weather the mud was over a foot deep. In spite of this these two
> enthusiasts carried on day after day, summer and winter, throughout the
> working hours of the men, directing them and collecting and noting the
> positions of the various numerous finds and coins. The latter from the
> ditches of the Saxon Shore Fort alone amounted to nearly 3000.

Such clearance work, of course, went beyond the strict needs of the research excavation.
However, it was a necessary part of the programme being developed by the Ministry of
Works to present the monument to the public. Clearly this work of clearance could only
be supervised on the macro-scale and the conditions were such that any structural detail,
and many finds, would not have been retrieved. There is also the implicit understanding
that such things as ditch clearance could only produce useful results in terms of the finds
in them, and the ultimate profile of the ditch; little attention seems to have been paid
to the stratigraphy within ditches. However, by the late 1920s there seems to have been
a growing realisation that evidence for timber buildings could be systematically
recovered, and this necessitated a different approach to excavation.

> During the summer months the Society's excavations were also undertaken
> upon areas where more intricate work was possible than during the unemploy-
> ment relief programme and where very close supervision was essential. (IV, 2).

> A large area to the south and south-west of the great foundation was laid
> bare to the surface of the undisturbed sand, and the layout of several early
> large wooden buildings obtained. (IV, 2).

The approach in the latter paragraph clearly refers to area excavation undertaken to
reveal the regular patterning of negative features (slots and post-holes) which made
up the ground plans of timber buildings, as opposed to the earlier concentration on
the sectioning of ditches and uncovering of the plans of masonry buildings. However,
despite the improvement in techniques, the overall standard of the excavation, judged
by Barry Cunliffe, was not satisfactory.

> . . . stratigraphy appears to have been discontinuous, frequently difficult
> to discern and seldom recorded . . . postholes and shallow pits could pass
> unrecognised . . . occasional references to hearth, clay floors and pebble
> layers are met with in the reports, but it is only in the north-east corner
> that these features were adequately planned. (V, 247-8).

Writing an introduction to the Fifth Report in 1967, Professor Frere set the Richborough excavations in context. The project was the first large-scale research excavation to be undertaken in the south of England since the uncovering of Silchester. Yet Frere acknowledged that during the 1930s Mortimer Wheeler was perfecting his methods for the better control and recording of excavations. Judged by Wheeler's criteria, the Richborough excavations were old-fashioned in terms of methodology. Not enough records were made, insufficient sections drawn and those made 'were often of a deplorable standard.' (V, iv). Wheeler, with his grid system of excavation, was the contemporary face of modern excavation technique, and just such techniques were being deployed by Barry Cunliffe in the excavation of a site whose popular fame would eclipse that of Richborough, the Roman Palace at Fishbourne.

A link with Silchester can be seen in the early seasons of excavation. As noted above, the choice of location for the very first excavation was determined by observations of parch-marks, indicating buried masonry wall-lines, north-west of the concrete platform. Some of the flint walls were located on the very first day of excavation and work then continued on uncovering the rest of the structure. This is similar to the situation at Silchester, where Roman wall-lines were revealed each summer in the ripening crop. Despite the well-preserved walls of the building in Site 1 at Richborough, which judging from the plates must have survived to at least 1m above foundation level, there seems to have been little attempt to record the location of finds according to the different room-fills excavated, nor any attempt to record sections through such room-fills at right-angles to the walls themselves. In addition, despite the depth of stratigraphy below the floor-levels of the masonry building (up to 2m) the complexity of the stratigraphy defeated the excavators; it was not that they didn't realise the potential importance of the stratigraphy; it was simply that they couldn't make sense of it (I,12). Recognition of timber buildings was also problematic. Post-holes were recognised underneath the masonry building, and some were planned, but not enough were revealed for the excavators to reconstruct a timber building (I, pl. xxxii). There is also a feeling in this first report that timber buildings, even if they could be recognised, might not be that important; they could have formed 'a series of shanties of a temporary character.' (I, 12). Following the exploration of the masonry building the excavators employed the Silchester technique of narrow trial trenches running away from the known masonry building, deliberately set at a diagonal to the presumed Roman street-grid, in order to reveal the location of further masonry structures.

There is no mention of the procedures for collecting a full range of finds, such as animal bones and broken tiles. Presumably in the winter, with a large number of men and one or two supervisors, only coins and exceptional pieces of metalwork or pottery were retained. In the summer seasons, rather more was retained, but the publications reveal an emphasis on coins, metalwork, decorated samian and coarse ware; most of the bulk finds were probably discarded, with just a representative sample of the finer objects or more complete pieces kept. The publication format of the First Report, published in 1926, illustrates the approach to finds recovery, and also highlights how the excavators treated the various kinds of evidence. Pages 1 to 35 describe the main results of the excavation: the excavators recognised masonry buildings, ditches, pits, wells and roads but were not proficient, as we have seen, at recording complex stratigraphy or features associated with timber buildings. On pages 35-173 were recorded the finds from the excavations: decorated samian (about 1000 sherds); stamps on decorated samian; stamps on plain samian; stamps on amphorae; stamps on mortaria; a vast quantity of coarse ware; some 3,133 coins (the latter being catalogued on pages 107-73 of the report). What can we deduce from these finds reports about the collecting policy? It appears that some attempts were made to record finds by location (I,88); this may have been more to find several sherds of the same vessel and therefore reconstruct the vessel form rather than to understand the significance of finds location for dating specific deposits and understanding the functions of discrete assemblages. For instance there are references in the report to objects being found in 'Site 1, room 6' (I,73); and some of the coarse ware is described according to the pit it was located in (I,96). However, other finds (e.g. the coarse ware described on page 97 and following) and most of the coins do not have recorded, or at least published, find-spots. In the case of the coins this was because many were located as surface finds in years before the excavations commenced (I,109). It is noteworthy that while decorated samian forms are mentioned, no plain samian forms are given. Is this because plain samian sherds were discarded, either at the excavation stage or during the washing and cataloguing processes?[23] Taking the report overall, while there is some attempt to integrate features with the finds found in them (e.g. in the description of the contents of pits – pit 13 – I,21), there seems to have been little attempt to do so for more complex areas of stratigraphy. Indeed, individual context or layer numbers were not used, the finds simply recorded on occasion by their depth in a particular feature. At the end of the report are plates showing the main excavated features, drawings of the key finds, and some basic plans and sections. The few sections drawn were through the ditch of the mid-third-century fort and sections through roadways.

By 1949, when the fourth report was published, very little had changed in terms of publication. The first 105 pages dealt with the main features found during the excavations, either area by area or phase by phase, with the following 214 pages devoted to finds, described in much the same categories as before: small objects (bone; glass; metal etc.); decorated samian, potters' marks, stamps, coarse ware and coins. There seems to have been a great desire to record any find that contained either evidence of artistry (like the decorated samian) or evidence of literacy (like the stamps and coins). Numbers were given to particular features (e.g. the pits) but not different layer numbers for the pit-fills, the finds simply being described by their depth in the pit (e.g. pit 131 – IV,93). Plates and pull-out plans appeared at the back of the volume, and a few more plans appeared in the body of the text. The publication of the Fifth Report in 1968 betrayed its hybrid character. The main description of the excavation was essentially the manuscript left by Mr Pearce, that followed the basic headings of the previous four reports. However there were significant additions: an opening summary of the results by Barry Cunliffe, and concluding sections in Part Two dealing with the physical geography of Richborough and the Wantsum, a comprehensive review of the various phases on the site itself, a history of the excavations at the site prior to 1922, a brief review of works involved with presenting the site to the public and a section on the Roman Fleet; pull-out plans by this time appeared integrated with the text and not at the back of the volume. In essence the 1968 publication spans two successive generations of archaeologists, those pre-Wheeler and the first generation post-Wheeler.

Before leaving the context of the history of excavations at Richborough it is worth reminding ourselves of contemporary world affairs, and also the developments within archaeology concerning the Roman Invasion of AD 43. Excavations began in 1922, four years after the ending of the Great War, a war that had been fought strategically by using fixed frontier lines, which were defended with great losses of life. Two years later, in 1924, *The Roman Occupation of Britain* by Haverfield was published posthumously. As we have already seen, in this book the author, *inter alia*, dismissed with some conviction any other landing place for the Romans in AD 43 than the north-east coast of Kent (Haverfield 1924, 102). During the 1930s the power of Hitler grew in Germany and the threat to the coasts of England, and especially Kent, became ever more menacing. Haverfield's views, and his domination of Roman studies in Britain, must have influenced Bushe-Fox to such an extent that archaeological evidence of the Roman beachhead in AD 43 was a discovery waiting to happen. It appears (see below) that the convincing archaeological evidence appeared during the excavations of 1928-30, when trenching to the south and north of the Saxon Shore Fort revealed that the Claudian ditches ran to the cliff-line at both ends. In 1957 the Bredgar coin hoard was found, crucial circumstantial evidence for the putative Battle of the Medway, and when Barry Cunliffe began to write up Richborough in 1963, he found no reason to disagree with the conclusion of his peers; indeed he felt no need to question it – by then it had become incontestable fact. So what exactly was the decisive archaeological evidence at Richborough for the Roman Invasion, evidence that had been so compelling?

The archaeological evidence of AD 43 at Richborough

The archaeological evidence which apparently confirmed the invasion bridgehead at Richborough consisted of two parallel ditches (the 'Claudian ditches' – some 640m in length and enclosing an extant area of some 4.5ha), a single excavated entrance through those ditches, the remains of two ovens within the enclosed area and the finds associated with these features. Detecting the earliest phase of Roman occupation on the site cannot have been easy, since features from this earliest phase seem to have been built over, at least in the central area examined, by timber buildings and granaries assumed to be part of a supply base established at the site during the Claudian period. It is not the intention in this section to query the military nature of the parallel ditches – their size, profile and contiguity do, I think, argue for a military origin. What I want to look at, however, is the nature of the deposits within the ditches, the finds in them, how they were interpreted at the time, what the ditches may have enclosed, the conclusions which can be drawn from them when comparisons with the similarly-sized ditch at Fishbourne are made, and, ultimately, whether the evidence justifies the certainty of the interpretation which has been placed on the features from Richborough.

Richborough III

The key reports for the early Roman features are III and IV, since it was in seasons 1926-7 that the Claudian ditches were discovered, while the entrance through them and their full extent was revealed in 1928-9 (**19**). The first published record of the find occurs early in III, in the summary (page 3):

> . . . evidence of a Claudian occupation . . . two parallel ditches of this date . . . it seems certain they formed part of a defensive work . . . a fortification of this date on the Kentish coast can hardly be associated with any other event than the invasion in AD 43.

In addition, on page 7, it is clear that the Claudian ditches were traced some way to the north of the Saxon Shore Fort. I suppose what is interesting here is the immediate leap from the discovery of what was then simply a length of parallel ditches to the clinching certainty that these features had to be associated with the invasion of AD 43. It seems clear that the excavators were working within a theoretical framework which had already hypothesised that the Romans landed in Kent in AD 43, and nowhere else.

Once we move on to the detailed description of the results, more details are forthcoming. A recurrent problem in the interpretation of the ditches, originally excavated into fairly sandy soil, was whether they had silted up by natural agencies or not. Bushe-Fox (III,11) states that this was difficult to tell, but on balance he presumed the upper part of the filling was the result of the deliberate slighting of the presumed inner bank on the inner east side. What convinces Bushe-Fox that this must be so is not direct observation of the stratigraphy in the ditch but the contingent argument that a) a bank must have existed on the inner east side of the ditches and b) that the logical thing to do when the bank was no longer needed would have been to push it back into the ditches. We have slightly more to go on when it comes to dating the filling of the ditches. The ditches were filled in before AD 60, since the overlying occupation contained many objects dating to the period AD 50-70. The small amount of pottery from the bottom of the ditches suggested brief occupation, and, notably the two samian bowls stamped with the potter's name SENICIO (and therefore of early Claudian date), found to the north of the Saxon Shore Fort, argued that the ditches were open in the period AD 40-50. Confirmatory evidence of an early date was provided by some Claudian coarseware and the fact that a pre-Flavian pit was excavated into one of the filled ditches.

By page 12 of report III, we find a more measured assessment of the Claudian ditches:

> The almost entire lack of finds from the site generally that can be assigned to the period immediately preceding the Claudian invasion eliminates a date prior to AD 43. The character of the ditches suggests that they formed part of a Roman military work, but whether this was constructed at the time of the invasion or shortly afterwards has yet to be proved.

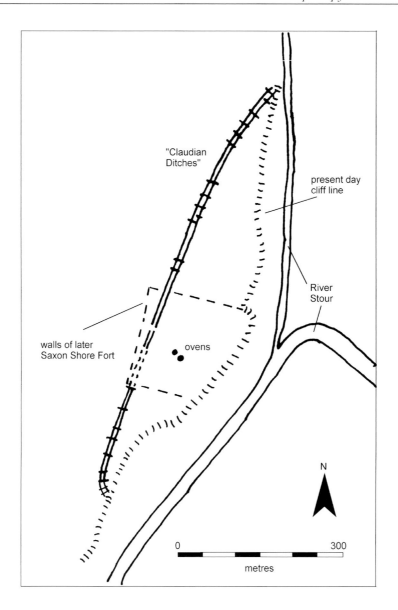

"Claudian
Ditches"

present day
cliff line

River
Stour

walls of later
Saxon Shore Fort

ovens

N

0   300

metres

*19   Plan of Richborough, illustrating the full extent of the Claudian ditches, and showing
locations of all excavated sections from the Society of Antiquaries' excavations.*
Courtesy of the Society of Antiquaries

It is now time to take a detailed look at what was found in the Claudian ditches.
Described in Report III were six separate excavations of one or both ditches, and it
seems preferable to summarise the main findings in tabular form. Please note that
italics are used in the Table to highlight my comments and suppositions; for the
location of some of these trenches see (**18**).

Location	Stratigraphy and finds	Comment by original excavators
North of the entrance: West Ditch	West ditch: filling of clean sand; small white lid type 318, skull of horse and bones of pig the only objects found at the bottom. Upper filling: fragments of samian forms 18 and 27 and coarse ware; portions of a cylindrical amphora. Stratum above contained two coins of Nero with Flavian and pre-Flavian artefacts	Upper filling certainly pre-Flavian and could well be Claudian
North of the entrance: East Ditch	East ditch: sand filling; three fragments of a samian bowl from 29 (*c.*AD 40-55) found, *presumably in the bottom.* Upper filling – fragments of pre-Flavian form 30 and early Flavian form 37	Ditches filled in pre-Flavian times; early Claudian samian ware in east ditch suggests Claudian date, *presumably for the digging of ditches*
East Claudian ditch, south of Site II	Bronze brooch and a samian cup form 24 (stamped OFI•O) from bottom. Sand filling above contained one sherd of samian dish form 18 of early type, another of form 27, portions of an incense cup and cylindrical amphora. Filling above this disturbed and contained sherds from pre-Flavian to end of the first century	Three pits dug through the ditch filling (dates for their filling in brackets): pit 10 (late first century); pit 31 (first century) and pit 64 (pre-Flavian)
Beyond North wall of Saxon Shore Fort ditches traced for *c.*190m	West ditch: greater part of two samian bowls, form 29, both stamped SENICIO (*c.*AD 45-60). A fragment of another form 29. Plain dish form 15, stamped SCOTNS (now dated *c.*AD 45-65), from slightly higher level; early coarse ware, including two grey Belgic plates	The ditches were open during the period AD 40-50.
Section 22 (**20**)	Filling of the ditches, with the exception of a layer of light clay near the bottom of the east ditch, was of practically clean sand. The lower portion had more the appearance of silt than the upper, but there was little difference between them . . . Only objects found . . . many fragments of a flagon and part of a lamp decorated with a cupid, the latter lying near the bottom of the west ditch	Ditches were filled in by 60 or earlier. Few objects in the filling suggests either that the ditches were in use for a very short time, and were purposely filled, or that there was little occupation in their vicinity while they gradually silted up
Section 33 (**20**)	Filling composed of sand, and difficulty experienced in dividing silt and filling above. No objects found in silt of either ditch. Mid- to late first-century pottery found in upper fills of both ditches.	Evidence, although inconclusive, suggests a pre-Flavian date for the filling of the ditches
Section 35 (**20**)	Both ditches filled with almost clean sand, not able to tell if this was intentional filling or a gradual deposit	Ditches open during the reign of Claudius
Section 35: West Ditch	In top of the silt: five fragments of a combed olla type 135-6; part of a cordoned bowl type 267; fragment of a jug type 186-7; and parts of a cylindrical amphora	All objects may well be Claudian
Section 35 East Ditch	At the bottom – a neck of a barrel-shaped urn type 277, and the rim of an early olla	Both probably Claudian in date

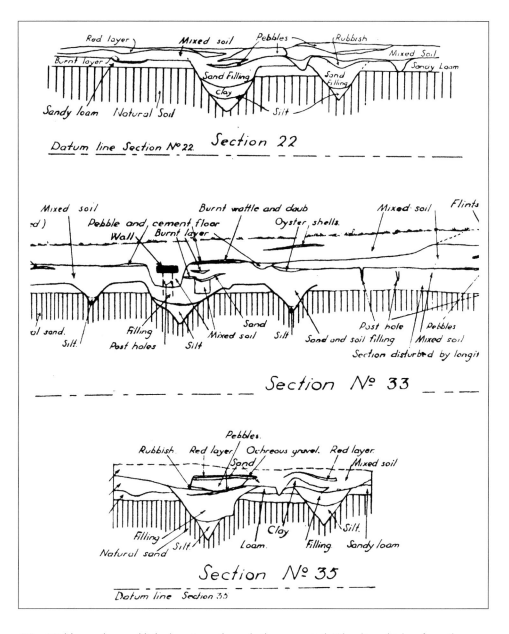

20   Richborough – published sections through the excavated Claudian ditches from the
Society of Antiquaries' excavations. Courtesy of the Society of Antiquaries

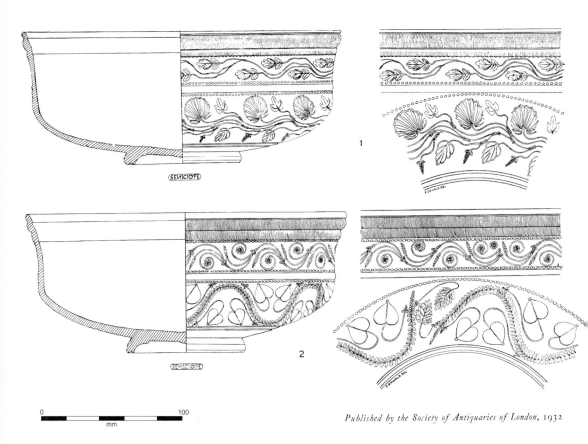

0   100
mm

Published by the Society of Antiquaries of London, 1932

21 Decorated samian, bearing the SENICIO stamp, from the Claudian ditches at Richborough from the Society of Antiquaries' excavations. Courtesy of the Society of Antiquaries

Some of the most dateable finds from the Claudian ditches were the bowls with the SENICIO stamp (**21**). Davies Pryce wrote on the samian (just the decorated samian[4]) in Richborough III. He reported that SENICIO was one of the earliest South-Gaulish potters and that his chief period of activity lay in the reigns of Tiberius, Caligula and Claudius, *c.*AD 25-54 (III, 94ff).[5] Typologically these bowls were not the early output of the potter, but instead could be dated approximately to late Tiberian to early Claudian, say roughly the period between AD 35-45. Form 29 found in the same deposit was dated to the Claudian period. Another form 29 came from the east Claudian ditch to the north of the entrance and was dated to the early Claudian period (III, 102). The OFI•O stamp on a plain cup form 24 is described as 'probably Claudian' (III, 141). SCOTNS was principally a Claudian potter whose output continued into the reign of Nero (III, 146). The overall impression, certainly from the samian pottery report, is that all of the samian found in the Claudian ditches was manufactured, at the very earliest, in the late Tiberian period. The great difficulty, of course, is knowing when that pottery was broken and subsequently ended up in the ditch fills.

Richborough IV

In seasons 1928-9 some of the work concentrated on trying to trace the full extent of the Claudian ditches. This was coupled with an exploration of the only entrance located through the ditches, and two ovens were discovered, which the excavators associated with the ditches. These two ovens were the only traces of 'occupation' in the area enclosed by the ditches. It is useful to note that the exploration of the entrance marked a different style of excavation, one which departed from the aim of exploring masonry structures to one which was based on medium-sized open areas, designed to reveal the fuller extent of negative features (i.e. those dug into the subsoil such as pits, post-holes and ditches); the change in technique greatly improved the chances of recognising timber buildings.

The full extent of the Claudian ditches was again described, and interpreted, in the first few pages of Richborough IV:

> This earthwork has now been shown to consist of a mound with two defensive ditches on its west side, stretching north and south from a central entrance to a total length at the present day of 2,176ft . . . it curved eastwards . . . the northern end resting on slightly rising ground above the marsh which was then the sea-shore . . . the southern end in all probability did the same . . . the area enclosed . . . is now approximately 11 acres (4.45ha), but it must formerly have been larger . . . the earthwork was built against attack from the west . . . its date can be definitely assigned to the reign of Claudius and its purpose was undoubtedly to cover the disembarkation of his legionaries . . . at the time of his invasion of Britain in AD 43 . . . the defences were levelled by throwing the mound into the already partly silted-up ditches. (IV,3-5).

The overall line of the Claudian ditches was determined by digging a series of narrow trenches at widely spaced intervals along their length; there is, therefore, a possibility that additional entrances were not discovered. The principal findings are again tabulated.

Location	Stratigraphy and finds	Comment by original excavators
Claudian entrance:		
Pebble causeway	One coin of Claudius embedded in the pebbles and one below them	Claudian date for entrance indicated by finds
Channels		Wooden barricades across the entrance
Four post-holes, A–D	Coins of Agrippa and Claudius came from B; shallow dish Rich. 9/10 from A	To support the ends of the inner bank
Two groups of three post-holes		Supports for a bridge or fighting platform linking the two ends of the inner bank
Inner ditch north of entrance	Greater part of filling by wind-drift. Coin of Caligula and one of Germanicus; two sherds of form 29 of Claudian date	
Outer ditch south of the causeway	Loose filling, intermixed with patches of soil containing slight occupation debris; sherd of Claudian mortarium in the bottom; above this a coin of Germanicus, a sherd of Claudian form 29 (*c.*AD 45-65), a sherd of grey Belgic plate; upper part of the fill: a coin of Germanicus (AD 37), an Aucissa fibula, a sherd of Claudian form 29 (the latter piece part of the same vessel as found near the bottom)	
Inner ditch south of causeway	Near the bottom – sherd of a cup Rich. 229-31; small sherd of samian form Ritterling 14. Near the top – coin each of Agrippa and Tiberius, four of Claudius, two Claudian jug necks, Rich. 347-8 and a sherd of a cylindrical amphora	
Ditches north of the Saxon Shore Fort	Practically nothing came from the filling of the ditches – only object 'worth recording' was a dish, Rich. 10, probably of Claudian date	
Ditches south of the Saxon Shore Fort	Ditches again 'singularly barren'; only find of note a portion of a Claudian mortarium	Concentration of finds around the only known entrance suggests either that defensive work not utilised for along, or that a skeleton garrison only remained behind
Two ovens	One contained 'fragments of early pottery', the other a coin of Claudius	

The finds and features outlined in the last two tables represented the full extent of the features that were to be associated with the Claudian invasion. The excavators remarked:

> Taking the Claudian finds as a whole . . . there was no heavy occupation during the early years of his reign . . . the scarcity of Belgic plates is significant in relation to this . . . and decorated samian of AD 40-50 is not found in large quantities . . . stratification of ditches suggests . . . lower part represents a gradual silting up while the levelling was accomplished by returning into them the soil used for the rampart . . . earthwork was without doubt . . . a temporary defence . . . at the time of the invasion . . . and . . . as a protection for ships drawn up on the shore during the initial stages of the campaign in AD 43 . . . only a small detachment may have been in garrison there: it may have even been left derelict for several years. (IV, 17-18).

Later timber buildings, associated with the earliest phase of the Claudian supply base, were erected on either side of the ditches, but not over them, indicating that the builders knew of the dangers of subsidence over filled-in ditches (IV, 18), or even that the ditches were still recognisable as a sunken feature. In a subsequent phase timber buildings were erected on top of the filled-in ditches (IV, 21). To the south of the Saxon Shore Fort, and seemingly near the point where the Claudian ditches ran out into the cliff-face a 'fair quantity of pottery and coins of the Claudian period was found' to the east of the parallel ditches (IV, 77). As a precautionary point the samian report comments on two sherds from a form 11, one of which was found in the filling of the outer ditch, the other was found in the make-up of the main east-west road laid across the ditches before AD 85 (IV, 161), indicating how sherds from the same vessel could be deposited in different places (and differently dated contexts) on the site.

Richborough V

The excavations at Richborough in the 1930s were reported in Richborough V, but add little information to the data possibly pertinent to AD 43. The Claudian ditches were sectioned by a diagonal trench in the south-west quarter of the Saxon Shore Fort, and lengths of the ditches to the north of the main later east-west road were emptied, 'the results being entirely consistent with what has been recorded in previous years' (V, 4). In his summary of the Richborough excavations Barry Cunliffe provided additional analysis of the features recovered. The two parallel defensive ditches ran for a total length of 640m[6]; the outer, or western ditch, averaged 2.13m wide by 1.2m deep while the inner ditch was 3m wide by 1.8m deep with an interval between them of 1.8m. The entrance passage was some 3.3m wide by 3.3m deep and flanked on each side by three squared timbers set in large pits. The wooden entrance comprised timber gates, a tower and a walkway through the tower. The two groups of three post-holes were reinterpreted as door-stops, while the channels were also reinterpreted as drainage gullies across the causeway. Additional features and deposits were potentially added to this earliest Claudian phase: some of the pits and wells north of the main east–west road, and a heavily burnt layer containing pottery to the south of the Saxon Shore Fort (V, 232-2).

The dating evidence left 'little doubt that the first phase of occupation falls within the earliest days of the invasion of AD 43 . . . Bushe-Fox has drawn attention to the absence of Gallo-Belgic platters and the relative scarcity of decorated samian pottery from the earliest levels, facts which are in complete agreement with a transient military occupation in a hostile territory' (V, 233). The silts in the bottom of the ditches might have derived from a single winter's weathering before deliberate re-filling began (V, 234). 'Archaeological evidence makes its virtually certain that Richborough played a vital part in the early stages of the campaign, first as a bridge-head and later as a vast supply depot in the rear of the campaigning armies.' (V, 255).

Discussion

So what can we deduce from the Richborough excavations, now 60 years and more have passed since the final season? I suppose, looking back on it, it was quite natural for the excavators to link the Claudian ditches with the invasion of AD 43. After all, Haverfield's publications had indicated that a Kent landing was the only serious contender, and a modern German army had threatened the Kentish coast just years before the programme of excavation began. In addition, of course, Fishbourne Roman Palace, and the features around and under it, had not yet been discovered. There really was no other archaeological contender once the Richborough ditches had been found.

The ditches themselves were not that easy to excavate. There were difficulties in locating the bottoms of the ditches on occasion, and there were consistent difficul-ties in terms of interpreting whether the ditches had been filled by the natural agencies of wind and rain, or whether the defences had been slighted by the delib-erate dumping of the inner eastern bank back into the ditches. In part, these diffi-culties were caused by the nature of the underlying soils, which were sandy in consistency. The bank itself, of course, must have been made of the same sandy soil and would have required some sort of revetment to stabilise it, perhaps one of turf. The size, profile and contiguity of the ditches do suggest their military origin.

The surviving area enclosed, as we have seen, was approximately 11 acres or about 4.45ha. If we assume, as indicated above, that at least 100m could have been eroded to the east in the central area of the site, that would indicate that the enclosed area could have been another 6.5ha in extent, making a total of 11ha. However, the coastline has not eroded evenly, and in fact more land has been lost both to the north and south of the Saxon Shore Fort. I am tempted, therefore, to add a further 6.5ha to account for these losses, making a grand total of 17.5ha. Trying to estimate what the forces of nature might have done over the last 2000 years is a very inexact science, but until further work[7] is done at the site this rough estimate is probably about as good as we can get. We can assume that the soldiers were accommodated in tents, heating food on open fires, which might have left features like the ovens discovered at Richborough. A text probably written by a military surveyor (the so-called Pseudo-Hyginus) in the late first or early second century AD provides some insight into what area an army of some 40,000 men would have required. Extrapolating from this work some 1174 men could have been accommodated in 1ha. Therefore, 17.5ha would have provided protection for around 20,500 men. The marching camp of Durno, 32km north-west of Aberdeen, is some 58ha in size, and, following the formula contained in Pseudo-Hyginus could have contained an army of 53,500 men. Such a camp was extraordinarily large; most legionary fortresses tended to be between 16 and 25ha in size. Pseudo-Hyginus' camp of 34.9ha was designed for an army of 41,000 soldiers (Gilliver 1999, 86-7). However generous we make the possible area that the Richborough ditches enclosed it seems to fall short of what would be required to protect an invasion force of 40,000 men.

Two other points can be made before we turn to the finds from the site. An interesting argument has been put forward by Black (2000) who suggests, after allowing about 12.2m width or beam per ship, that only about 62 tightly-packed transport ships could have been unloaded at any given time within the 762m (*c.*2,500ft) of shoreline at Richborough that was protected by the Claudian ditches. Given the numbers quoted elsewhere in this book regarding the number of vessels involved in the invasion, this protected area at Richborough seems far too small. The second point concerns the 'Fleet Causeway', a very well-made stretch of Roman road to the west of the site which connected the 'island' of Richborough to the mainland, or at least allowed dry passage across the marsh that separated the site from the mainland. The road itself was solidly constructed, and its foundation comprised a double layer of flints, of remarkably uniform size, laid on a layer of blue clay (V, 39). Of course, there is no dating for the roadway, but the solidity and regularity of its construction suggests a military origin, although whether an invading army would have wanted, or been able to construct, such a work at the start of a major campaign is, of course, another matter.

Turning to the finds from the earliest Roman phase of the occupation at Richborough, they seem to be equally problematic; however, at least there is no Late Iron Age, or Belgic, occupation to complicate the story. The pottery from the Claudian ditches that is most dateable, is, of course, the samian ware (Dickinson *et al.* 1968), and that seems exclusively Claudio-Neronian in date. Yet as has been rehearsed already, the date of manufacture of the pottery is not the real indicator for the date of digging the ditches, but the dates that the discarded pottery found its way into the ditch-fills. In other words, just how quickly was the samian found in the ditches, discarded? This, to an extent, can be approached by thinking about the nature of activities that would have taken place behind the ditches. If we assume that at least part of the invading army landed at Richborough, then they would have been stationed in tents within the defended area for a few days at most before the majority departed. Clearly, some pots would have been broken, some refuse would have accumulated, and some of it might have been collected and thrown into the ditches. An obvious place to throw the pottery might have been near the entrances, since this was where the ditches could be easily approached. Indeed, there does seem to have been some concentration of pottery near the entrance, and much less in the ditch sections to the north and south of the Saxon Shore Fort. But there are at least two problems. One is that the site was built over by a whole series of timber buildings associated with the Claudian supply depot, and the earliest phase of the timber buildings did not cover the Claudian ditches near the entrance. Much more Claudian samian will have been broken in the years of the supply base than in a transitory military occupation, and some of this supply-base samian could have found its way into the Claudian ditches. Secondly, samian itself could certainly be kept for a number of years after its date of manufacture. Willis provides studies of Dragendorff 15/17, which was becoming residual[8] around AD 100, continuing to be found in deposits 30 years later, while Dragendorff 29, becoming residual around AD 85, continues to be found in deposits dated to AD 120 and later (Willis 1998, 104).

Two further points can be made about the samian from Richborough. Judging from the quantities of samian stamps reported, decorated samian would have been in the minority. This would be consistent with early military occupation. Willis (1998, 106) reports percentages of 13.7% (Fishbourne Period I), 24.7% (Longthorpe I) and 13.8% (Kingsholm, Periods I to III), all early military occupations. The second point concerns the fact that in the first century the supply of samian to Richborough was almost exclusively from south Gaul (V, 147), and, most striking, that the trade fell to relatively few south Gaulish factories; 17 potters produced almost half the stamped samian.

Little can be gleaned relevant to our specific enquiry from the remaining finds. There is not a great deal of military material (particularly in terms of copper-alloy small finds), but perhaps that is not surprising given that the nature of military occupation might have been, initially, transitory, followed by a garrison for the supply depot that was quickly left some way behind the active campaigning troops. There are an enormous number of coins (56,084) and there is certainly a relative abundance of coins in the Claudian period (V, 209), but much of that abundance derives from losses at the supply depot. Intriguingly there are a number of ships' nails and other ship fittings from Richborough, including two unused copper spikes from the Claudian defensive ditches (Lyne 1999, 147), and other contexts spanning the first four centuries AD. The arrival of ships, their maintenance, and perhaps the construction of some ships and the breaking up of others would have been part of the annual routine at the site.

New studies on the ground at Richborough will no doubt alter our understanding of the site, and possibly its relevance to the events of AD 43. For the time being I hope I have demonstrated that there is a raft of assumptions and analytical difficulties, arising from the previous excavations, that underpin any unqualified remark that the Romans landed at Richborough in AD 43. I want to turn now to a site I am more familiar with, Fishbourne Roman Palace, and particularly to the deposits underneath and near the Flavian Palace. There are no certainties at Fishbourne, anymore than there are at Richborough, but the comparisons may be revealing.

10 And what did they (and we) really find at Fishbourne?

Excavations by Barry Cunliffe (1960s)

In April 1960 a water main was being laid across fields to the north of the village of Fishbourne when substantial Roman walling was disturbed. Barry Cunliffe, then aged 20, was invited to conduct exploratory excavations, which commenced in Easter 1961. The rest, as they say, is history, or to be a little more accurate, archaeology. The nine seasons of work brought to light the remains of an unique building in Roman Britain, a veritable palace, with parallels in Rome itself. The splendid series of mosaic floors, and the generosity of Ivan Margary of the Sussex Archaeological Society, guaranteed that the discoveries would be put on permanent display. At the same time as the excavations at Fishbourne were taking place, Barry was working on the final Richborough report, published in 1968. With commendable speed, not equalled often today, the results of the Fishbourne dig were published in two volumes in 1971. Barry Cunliffe, therefore, throughout the 1960s, became very familiar with the interpretations of the archaeological evidence at these two key sites. The difference in excavation technique was readily apparent. The diagonal trenching to locate major archaeological features, so apparent at Richborough and Silchester, had given way to a new form of excavation by gridded squares, inspired by the system championed by Mortimer Wheeler. Since the 1960s other archaeologists have continued to work at Fishbourne from time to time: chiefly Alec Down (1980s); David Rudkin (1980s); staff from the now-defunct Southern Archaeology (1990s) and, of course, David Rudkin and myself (1995-9). I very much doubt that we will be the last. In order to gain an appreciation of the data which are relevant to our story I think it is best we summarise the various campaigns of excavations in chronological order; at the end we can try and pull the evidence together.

The first-century periods at Fishbourne were defined by Barry Cunliffe as follows:

Period	Main features	Occupation
1a – AD 43-5	Timber buildings 1 (granary) and 2 (store)	Military
1b – AD 45-65	Timber buildings 4 (workshop) and 5 (house); ditched enclosure	Civilian
1c – AD 65-80	Two masonry buildings; one identified as the 'proto-palace'	Civilian
2 – AD 75/80+	Main Palace	Civilian

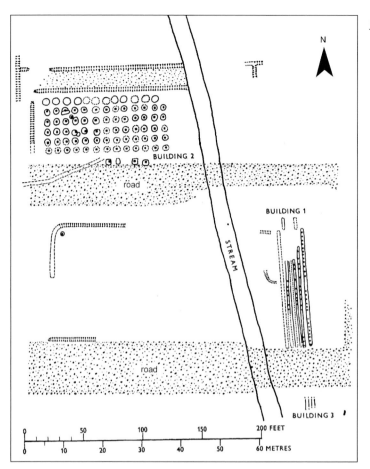

22 Plan of the earliest buildings – Phase 1a – from Fishbourne. After Cunliffe 1998

These divisions have stood the test of time and it is common, for archaeologists writing about the Palace, to refer to these periods. That does not imply that everyone has been in agreement with the chronology and Black (1993), in particular, has argued for a later date for the construction of the Palace itself. The overall understanding of the Ia structures was provided in the second paragraph of volume I of the 1971 report:

> During the first period of occupation, *c*.AD 43-4, the site was developed as a military supply base used in conjunction with the main camp thought to be in Chichester. A likely context for these installations is the campaign fought by the Legio II Augusta under Vespasian, which in 43-4 swept across south-west Britain. Fishbourne and Chichester were at this time well within the pro-Roman territory ruled by the client king Tiberius Claudius Cogidubnus: as such the area would have been suitable for a rearward supply camp in the initial stages of the advance.
> (Cunliffe, 1971, I, xxv).

How did Barry Cunliffe arrive at this interpretation? To answer this question we have to look at the excavated detail. The principal remains of 1a were two timber buildings, (T1 & T2) separated by a shallow stream (**22**). Six roughly parallel foundation trenches defined the incomplete footprint of T1, which measured at least 6.71m east-west by 30.5m north-south. Its proportions were closely comparable to the timber buildings at Richborough and, that, together with the method of construction, argued compellingly for a military building (Cunliffe, 1971, I, 40), with a probable function as a granary. Timber building 2, west of the stream, measured some 29.56m east-west by some 15.85m north-south, and was defined by a grid of 78 post-pits. Possible inter-pretations as either a pair of military barrack blocks or a military store were debated, with a preference for the latter. Support for a military interpretation came from a small number of copper-alloy military fittings and a high proportion of Claudian coin copies.[1] The military significance of the buildings was perhaps further reinforced by the realisation that their orientations, with the associated road-system, indicated that they formed (part of[2]) a larger orthogonal layout; their rather curious topographic siting, either side of a small stream, was not commented upon.

To my knowledge no-one has seriously questioned the fact that these timber buildings were built by the Roman military, or that they probably functioned as storage buildings. However, dating them is more problematic, and, as we shall see, their attribution to AD 43 is not so much derived from evidence gained from the site itself, as from the wider historical framework in which they were interpreted at the time. Put simplistically the Fishbourne interpretation had to fit in with the orthodoxy of the day: 1) that the main Roman invasion had landed at Richborough, and therefore whatever was at Fishbourne was secondary and 2) that Roman military buildings did not exist in Britain before AD 43.

I present the dating evidence of the timber buildings and 1a in tabular form for ease of reference:

Feature	Context	Dating evidence
Timber Building 1	To the north-east of the building a thin occupation layer was found, sealed beneath a 1b floor	Sherds of Claudian girth and butt beakers and a few sherds of Claudian samian; a little coarse ware consistent with a date of AD 43-50 (evidence post-dates construction of building)
Timber Building 2	Material thrown back into the post-pits when timbers were removed	Pottery recovered was all Claudian-Neronian (evidence post-dates construction of building)
Not clear	Not clear from published report	One rim sherd of decorated Arretine, *c*.AD 30-40
Not clear	Not clear from published report	Three decorated samian sherds *c*.AD 40-55

While the stratigraphic sequence of the early phases of activity at Fishbourne was clear, in the sense of what buildings and features lay on top of, and which were later than, others, the dating evidence for these phases, as will be appreciated from the number of sherds indicated in the above Table, was minimal; there were simply not enough undisturbed and sealed contexts or layers. In addition there was one anomaly that did not fit the perceived interpretation. A number of fine-ware sherds made by potters near Arezzo in northern Italy had been found during the excavations. There were sherds from 33 vessels: 15 of the sherds had been found in Period I contexts, with one from a 1a context (see Table above), three from 1b floor-levels and 11 from 1b occupation; the other 22 sherds presumably came from later contexts but were deemed residual and assigned to a Period 1 origin (Dannell in Cunliffe 1971, II, 262). Of the sherds, 19 were attributed to the workshops of Ateius, who was thought to have ceased business around AD 30.

How was this Arretine pottery, conventionally seen as pre-AD 43 in date, to be explained? Dannell, in his report, indicated that Arretine ware at Camulodunum belonged almost exclusively to the pre-conquest period. It was being hypothesised at Colchester that civilian markets post-AD 43 at that city were prepared to buy forms of samian that were out-of-date, and could not be sold so readily on the Continent. Dannell countered this idea by stating that the Arretine from Fishbourne must surely have come with the army, and if the army arrived in AD 43, then the army was provisioned with out-of-date stock. Sheppard Frere was later to take Dannell to task on his statement, arguing that Arretine ware was only found on high-status Late Iron Age indigenous sites, such as Canterbury, Silchester and Leicester, and was not imported with an invading army. I think Geoff Dannell was swayed by Frere's arguments but his doubts still remained, not least because there was no significant Late Iron Age occupation at Fishbourne, which the Arretine could have been derived from. Clearly, there were alternative hypotheses that would have dispensed with the anomaly – 1) that the dating for the retirement of Ateius was incorrect and that he continued to work for another 15 years or so or 2) that the timber buildings were earlier than AD 43.

More recent work on samian pottery has confirmed that samian was imported in vast quantities during the first century and a half of Roman rule, that it was used on a wide variety of sites, both 'Roman' and indigenous, and that it is found at military sites of all types (Willis 1998, 87). In particular, more up-to-date ceramics are likely to be associated with military sites (Willis, 1998, 101 & 104). Arretine ware is still dated pre-AD 43 and is still considered to be associated with larger, indigenous complexes of the Late Iron Age. Writing about Roman pottery in West Sussex, Millett noted that Arretine was only found at Fishbourne and Chichester, and, while acknowledging the claims of others that Arretine could have been imported pre-AD 43, the absence of other pre-conquest material suggested to him that it had arrived with the invading Claudian armies (Millett 1980, 62).

Before leaving the 1971 publication three other points are worth noting from its contents. The connection between Tiberius Claudius Cogidubnus (or as we now know him, Togidubnus) and Fishbourne was indicated early (Cunliffe 1971, I, 13). Togidubnus was seen as potentially fleeing to Augustus with Tincomarus as a child before AD 14, and perhaps returning with the invading Claudian army 'to stabilise the Southern Atrebatic area on the left flank of the advance for sufficient time to allow for the military consolidation of the east'. In addition, through the surveys of Richard Bradley (in Cunliffe 1971, I, 17-36), attention was rightly drawn to the significance of the assumed Late Iron Age system of dykes enclosing Fishbourne and this part of the coastal plain, their similarity in part to some of the dykes around Camulodunum, and their importance for an understanding of the wider topographical context for Fishbourne. And finally, it was noted that Togidubnus 'romanised' Chichester within a generation of AD 43, the evidence being dedications to Nero and to the Imperial household, at least one temple, guilds of craftsmen organised on a Roman basis and stone-workers capable of cutting good quality Roman lettering.

Excavation by Alec Down (1980s)

Alec Down can justifiably be described as the founder of modern archaeology in Chichester. Over a period of 30 years he devoted himself to the challenge of investigating and recording the archaeology of Chichester and its surrounding district, the results of which were published in nine monographs (the Chichester Excavation series) between 1971 and 1996. I owe a special debt to him for our excavations of 1995-9 were based on initial results he had obtained from three trial trenches he dug to the east of the Palace in 1983; and I had the great pleasure of showing him around our 1995 excavations a few months before he died. Alec had the great foresight to realise that the road, now known as the A27, which sweeps in front of and around the Palace to the north, would probably encounter significant archaeology during its construction and he set out to organise a campaign of excavations in advance of the line of the road. These excavations took place from 1983-6, with little proper funding and often in very difficult weather conditions. The results were published in 1996, and it is these excavations to which I now turn (Cunliffe, Down & Rudkin 1996).

There are three aspects of these excavations that may be relevant to the arguments presented in this book: the basic interpretation of many of the features; the pottery; and the interpretation of Ditches 4A and 11. Most archaeologists, often unconsciously, bring to any excavation a set of ideas which to a large extent govern how they excavate the site and the conclusions they seek to draw from the evidence. These ideas may be general ones about the specific historical period in question or more specific ones to do with the nature of the particular locality and site they are about to excavate. They have gathered up these ideas largely through their studies of other people's work and writings throughout their own careers. There is a tendency among most archaeologists to work within the orthodox views of their time, so much so that their findings often 'fit in', more or less, with the prevailing orthodoxy. Not every archaeologist works in this way. There are those who, acknowledging the orthodoxy of the day, set out to disprove it; some do this successfully, others less so. Of course, such outlooks are not confined to archaeologists, or academics; this sort of polarisation of attitudes may be common to many of us, whatever we do. But to return to Alec Down; I think he was someone who worked within the orthodoxy of his day.

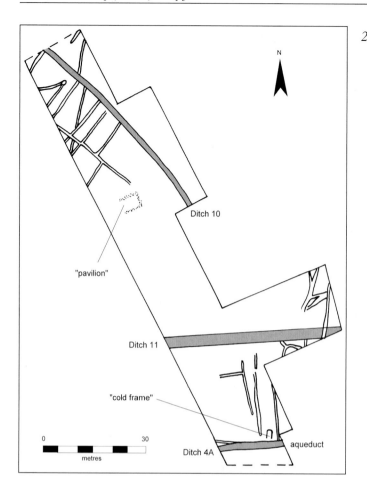

23 *Simplified plan of Alec Down's 1985-6 A27 excavations; for location see **24**.*
After Cunliffe *et al.* 1996

In the 1980s excavations Alec found a whole series of negative features, post-holes, ditches, slots or gullies and pits (**23**). These features were found in a linear excavated strip that ran in front of the Palace and to the north of it, separated from the Palace by about 80m. Alec had witnessed the impressive excavations of the 1960s, the discovery of the Palace, the publicity that surrounded the excavations at the time, and the discovery of an unique feature, the formal Palace garden with its curvilinear bedding trenches filled with different coloured soil. There is little doubt in my mind that he imagined that one of the things he would find in front of the Palace would be a range of bedding trenches that would form part of a formal garden in front of the Palace. This is completely unsurprising; most of us would have expected the same at that time. And it was completely unsurprising that he claimed to have found bedding trenches in the excavations. Throughout the excavation report many of the gullies are described as 'bedding trenches'; ditches were often interpreted as 'drainage channels'; groups or lines of post-holes were interpreted as 'trellis supports'; some pits were described as tree or shrub holes, and a small, rectangular structure was interpreted as 'a small potting or tool shed, or possibly even the base of a cold-frame' (Cunliffe *et al.* 1996, 37).

But there are some distinctly anomalous aspects to the archaeology that Alec uncovered. Looking at the distribution of features overall, it is clear that most of the supposed 'bedding trenches' lie not in front of the Palace but to the north-east of the building. In addition, many of the bedding trenches in the northern part of the excavation lie in a south-west:north-east alignment, and do not echo the east-west alignment of the Palace itself. Furthermore, there is an apparent complete lack of features in the area immediately to the east of Building 3, a structure I will comment on below. One of the principal east-west ditches that Alec uncovered was 4A/4B. Alec stated that the ditch was 'deep', that it had been re-cut on at least one occasion, and that a gravel path lay on its south side. Correctly he assumed that it was the same ditch that he had observed much closer to the Palace in the 1983 trial excavations, and the same ditch was to be discovered in excavations by Southern Archaeology in the 1990s to the east of the A27. We now know that this ditch functioned as an aqueduct, and probably contained a timber conduit, leading water towards the area occupied by the later Palace. I say later, because evidence from our own excavations indicates that the aqueduct ditch was excavated at an early date, possibly around AD 50. There is an immediate stratigraphic problem here. Alec indicated that Ditch 4B cut the arrangement of linear bedding trenches. Therefore, if our dating of the aqueduct is correct, at least some of the bedding trenches would have to be earlier than AD 50. The difficulty here is that the Palace was not constructed until AD 75/80. So if this particular group of bedding trenches were not, in fact, such, what could they be? I suppose an alternative interpretation would be to see them as the ephemeral remains of the foundations of timber buildings, aligned north-south.[3]

Another feature I want to consider briefly is Ditch 11. The first thing you notice about the reproduced plan of Ditch 11 (Cunliffe et al. 1996, 43, fig 2.18) is that the sides of the ditch are very straight, indeed I would bet a large amount of money on the surmise that the alignment of the ditch had been drawn with a ruler; it is orientated east-west. Alec records several interesting aspects of this ditch: it was large and deep, and had partially silted up before being backfilled with clay; brushwood lay on the south side of the ditch which Alec interpreted as some form of revetting; Alec thought, from the presence of ceramic water-pipes in the back-fill, that the ditch may have carried a piped-water supply to the Palace. A north-south ditch (Ditch 5) cut through the top of the back-filled Ditch 11. Alec surmised, I think correctly, that Ditch 5 would join up with Ditch 4 to the south, and I think Ditch 5 is a feeder channel leading water down from the north into the east-west aqueduct represented by Ditch 4. But there is another stratigraphic and phasing problem here. Alec, working within the phasing framework from the Palace excavations, placed Ditch 11 in Period 2, phase 1 (i.e. post-AD 75) and Ditch 5 slightly later. However, Ditch 5 contained mainly pre-Flavian fine wares and included fine and coarse wares from the Neronian kilns in Chapel Street, Chichester, together with a few sherds of pre-conquest Arretine (Cunliffe *et al.* 1996, 42). It would seem that Ditch 5 might have been dug in pre-Flavian times, and Ditch 11 earlier still. Before turning to the finds, it is worth noting in passing that, underneath the main approach road to the Palace, Alec uncovered two parallel lines of post-holes, 12m apart, and aligned east-west.

These clearly formed part of a larger structure which Alec assigned to the early Roman period and interpreted as stockades, possibly for cattle. Two large square-cut post-holes along the south side could have represented an entrance about 2m wide.

When we turn to the pottery finds from Alec's excavations, and particularly to the specialist reports on those finds, we discover some equally fascinating and equally problematic evidence; this concerns the pottery found which can be dated to pre-AD 43. Dannell records a number of plain Arretine sherds dated to the Augustan-Tiberian period (Cunliffe *et al.* 1996, 110); they all were found in the northern part of the excavations, and some of the sherds are clearly residual (e.g. number 9 from D1002, Ditch 5). When Valery Rigby commented on the fine wares she indicated that a number of small sherds had been imported to the site pre-AD 43; again there was a concentration in the north of the excavations. Significantly she went on to suggest that the late Augustan vessels were of particular importance because they complemented similar vessels found by Barry Cunliffe in the 1960s excavations underneath the Palace. She differed from the earlier interpretations, claiming that these early sherds did 'not have to be explained away as heirlooms from Roman officer's baggage, or out-of-date stock unloaded upon unsuspecting natives in the immediate post-Conquest period' (Cunliffe *et al.* 1996, 117). Instead she saw these sherds as evidence of trade and exchange in the early first century AD, by the native elites within late Iron Age oppida, such as those demarcated by dyke systems around Chichester and Fishbourne, and similarly at Camulodunum. The quantity of pre-AD 43 material from the Fishbourne area was clearly increasing, and, in a discussion of Terra Nigra and Terra Rubra, Gallo-Belgic imported finewares dating from 15 BC to AD 85, Rigby pointed out that the early material now came from three separate excavations: those in the 1960s under the Palace, those along the route of the A27 east of the Palace, and from excavations in Chichester itself. All this evidence was very conveniently summarised in the 1996 excavation report. A map (fig 2.4) and a Table (2a) summarised the information; some 286 pre-Conquest vessels had now been found at Fishbourne and Chichester. The only difficulty remained a lack of Late Iron Age indigenous features to associate with this pottery.

Excavation by Southern Archaeology (1990s)

One of the major developments in British Archaeology in the late twentieth century was the privatisation of archaeological organisations and the introduction of competitive tendering; in effect, excavating sites before they were destroyed became a commercial business. Like any businesses, some have proven more financially secure than others; sadly, Southern Archaeology was not amongst those and it no longer exists; only the briefest of interim reports record the important series of excavations it conducted east of the Palace.[4] The excavations east of the A27 (**24**) indicated that the area, especially the northern part of the area, was heavily utilised in the Roman period. The principal results of the excavations are presented in the Table on p.120:

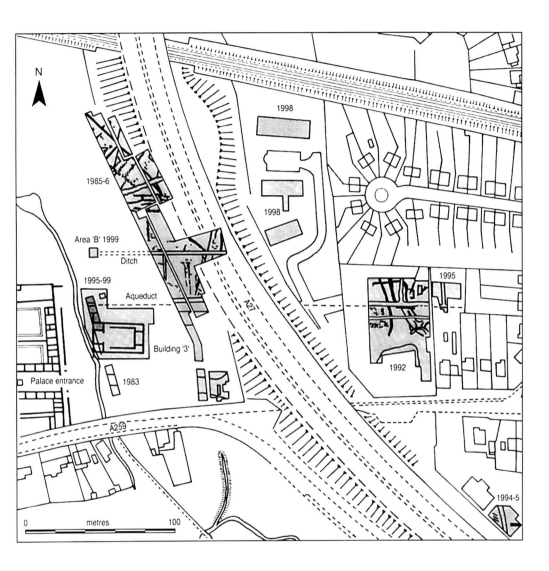

24 Location of excavations, mostly by Southern Archaeology, east of Fishbourne Roman Palace; the years refer to years when the excavations took place; Building 3 and Area B were excavated by the Sussex Archaeological Society. Courtesy John Magilton, James Kenny and Derek Turner; drawn by Sue Rowland

Excavation year/name	Main results (relevant to this book)	Main finds	Reference
1992 – Westward House	Phase 2: a number of pits, including cremation burial, a butt-beaker; two timber buildings aligned east-west; three gullies	Quantities of Arretine and early imported wares	ACD⁵ 1992
	Phase 3: further sections of the aqueduct recorded by Alec Down	Ceramic pipe in the north-south feeder channel	ACD 1992
1994-5 – 51 Fishbourne Road East	Two large ditches, aligned north-south, were filled with clay early in the Roman period	Feeder channel contained large quantities of first-century	ACD 1995
1995 – 36 Fishbourne Road East	Part of a ring gully that could mark site of a round house; maybe Iron Age; later aqueduct and north-south feeder channel	AD domestic refuse including high-status pottery, and a gold signet ring – Tiberius Claudius Catuarus	ACD 1995
1998 – Glebe Meadow	East-west aqueduct again observed on the same line; considerable number of post-holes, pits and ditches	Military belt-buckle of first century AD	ACD 1995

Without full publication it would be unwise to place too much interpretation on these preliminary reports. However, the presence of a possible round-house, the rectangular timber buildings and the Arretine add significant elements to the archaeology east of the Palace. In addition, the discovery of the signet ring, with a Celtic cognomen, Catuarus, implies the owner was a British chief enfranchised by Claudius or Nero (Tomlin 1997) (**25**).

Excavations east of the Palace by the Sussex Archaeological Society (1995-9)

I excavated, along with co-director David Rudkin, just to the east of Fishbourne Roman Palace between 1995 and 1999. The excavation is currently being written up and will be published in due course. We started off with a written Research Design that indicated that we intended to investigate more of the early military phase at Fishbourne. In 1983 Alec Down, in three small trenches (A,B,C) had uncovered some masonry foundations apparently overlying a series of post-holes that he thought

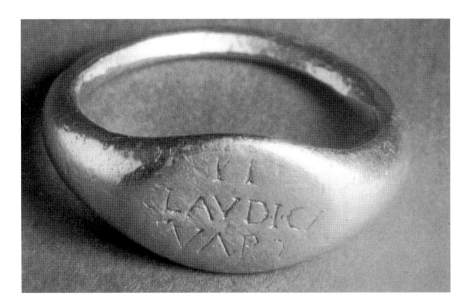

25 A first-century gold ring found in 1995 to the east of Fishbourne Roman Palace. Its mirror image inscription TI CLAVDI CATVARI identifies it as the signet ring of one Tiberius Claudius Catuarus. By wearing the ring he claimed to belong to the Roman upper class, but his name indicates that he was a new Roman citizen of Celtic origin. So it is probable that, like his contemporary and perhaps his kinsman, Togidubnus, he was a local chieftain honoured by the Romans. Photograph courtesy of the British Museum

might belong to the earliest military phase at Fishbourne. Unfortunately, it turned out that the post-holes did not relate to a timber building, nor were they earlier than the masonry structure. However, we did make some discoveries which, I think, fulfilled our Research Design.

Our overall discovery was the footprint, formed by masonry foundations, of a rectangular courtyard building whose long axis was aligned east-west (**26-8**). Interpretation of the date and function of the building, known as Building 3, is problematic. To the south and north of the west face of Building 3 ran, for a yet unknown length, flanking walls. One of the best pieces of evidence for the dating of Building 3 (**29**) comes from the fact that the aqueduct (previously located by Alec and Southern Archaeology) smashed through the flanking wall to the north; we have already seen that pottery[6] indicated that the aqueduct could have been constructed as early as AD 50; logically, our building must be earlier than the aqueduct. In functional terms the footprint of the building seems to be paralleled to a certain extent by the ground-plans of military *principiae*. However, there are anomalies. No *principia* in Roman Britain, to my knowledge, has 'flanking walls'; it would be very early for a *principia* to be constructed at least partly in stone; there is not a great abundance of military small finds from our excavation. I am convinced, however, that it is some sort of public administrative building; it

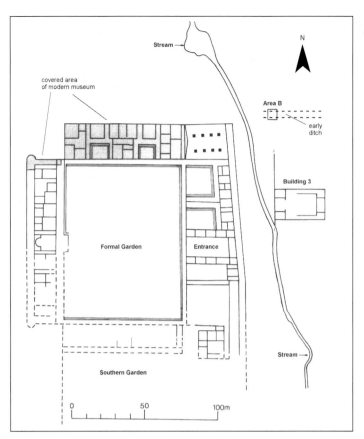

26 Plan of Fishbourne Roman Palace, showing location of Building 3 and Area B, through which the 'early' ditch passed

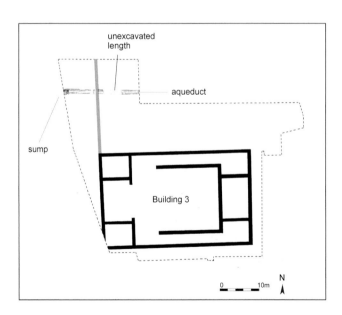

27 Simplified plan of Building 3, showing the position of the aqueduct to the north

*28 A possible reconstruction
  of Building 3.* After
  David Taylor

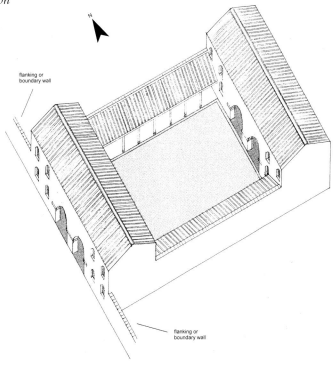

flanking or
boundary wall

flanking or
boundary wall

certainly was not a building people lived in; the standardised sizes of the individual rooms, for instance, are clearly different from the more varied room sizes in the adjacent Palace which were used for accommodation.

In 1998 we excavated a section of the northern flanking wall, finding that, although at its northern extremity all the foundations had been robbed out, the wall continued on to the north and disappeared out of the trench. In 1999, therefore, we opened up a small area some way to the north of our main trench, to ascertain whether the flanking wall could be traced that far north. We positioned this trench, known as Area B (**26**), also in line with the possible continuation of Ditch 11, which had been found to the east by Alec Down. Something had to give, and, indeed, it did.

On top of the clay brickearth in Area B was a surviving Roman ground surface, comprising a dark yellowish-brown sandy clay. This context produced 19 sherds of Atrebatic overlap, Terra Rubra and early Roman pottery. These fragments included an Italian Arretine sherd stamped ATEIXANTHI and dated 5 BC to AD 20. It became apparent that the northern flanking wall was not going to continue into Area B; something had clearly happened to it between the north edge of Area A, our main excavation, and Area B. However, running straight across the trench was the large ditch excavated by Alec. The ditch went straight across, from east to west, and disappeared under the western side of the trench. Its dimensions were some 3.5m N–S, by about 1.5m deep at its deepest point. It was essentially V-shaped in profile with a

29 The north-west corner of Building 3 at Fishbourne, looking south; scales are 2m.
Photograph John Manley

possible 'cleaning slot' at the bottom (**30-2**). The filling of the ditch was very distinctive with a light grey silt (937; 919) in the cleaning slot and adhering to the sides of the ditch, a charcoal spread (919.2) observed over the south side of the ditch (the latter had been observed also on the south side by Alec Down (Cunliffe *et al.* 1996, 42), and then a deliberate filling of red clay (913).

I must confess that when we positioned Area B we initially thought that Ditch 11, which Alec had found, might have been the robber trench for a masonry foundation that would have formed the north side of a masonry enclosure around Building 3. That was disproved and, as we began to excavate the ditch in Area B, we became persuaded that it might have been dug by the Roman military. This conviction, I suppose, came from three factors: 1) it was clearly very straight,[7] 2) its shape and size were right for a military ditch and 3) it had been deliberately filled in, slighted if you like, with red clay. The ditch was excavated into the underlying Reading Beds clay. The clay is particularly homogeneous at this point and digging by hand would have been a laborious activity. It was noticeable how unstable the clay sides were, and summer contrasts of sun and scattered showers indicated how easily the sides would have slumped into the ditch bottom. The ditch, when open, must therefore have demanded quite regular maintenance.

The surprise came from the finds in silts in the bottom of the ditch. They included large, freshly-broken sherds from some Arretine vessels, including two cups, the bottom of one bearing the owner's initials, TV, and sherds from a large platter. One of the cups was Conspectus form 12.3 and had no sign of wear on it. However, it carried the potter's stamp: MENA (*c.*10 BC – AD 10). In all, the silt contexts produced 111 sherds (1425 gm) of Atrebatic 'overlap'[8] pottery and early imports. Unfortunately this key assemblage was unsuitable for any kind of meaningful quantification, as it was largely made up of a number of fresh sherds from just a handful of vessels. It seems likely that this ditch was excavated in the first decades of the first century AD, and certainly before AD 43.

30 (right) Fishbourne, Area B – plan of the 'early' ditch, cut by two later pits

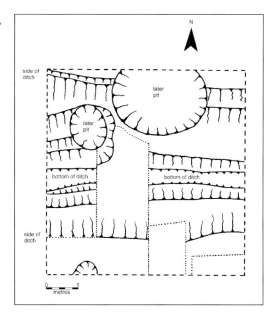

31 (below) Fishbourne, Area B – the eastern section across the 'early' ditch, illustrating the silts in the bottom sealed by the red-clay backfill; the numbers refer to the individual layers or contexts

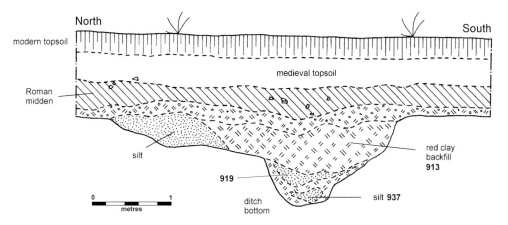

32 (right) The 'early' ditch in Area B at Fishbourne, looking north-east. The ditch runs from left to right and the upright scale (2m) on the right-hand side of the image lies against the eastern section of the ditch. The line of the bottom of the ditch is marked by the small scale. The two other vertical scales mark the positions of later pits cut into the back-filled ditch. Photograph John Manley

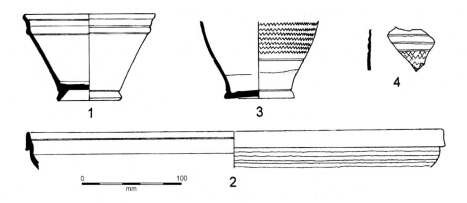

33 Arretine ware from the 'early' ditch at Fishbourne. After Malcolm Lyne

Due to the importance of this assemblage it is worth presenting it in tabular form; comments are drawn from the reports supplied to me by Geoff Dannell and Malcolm Lyne:

Context number (latest at top)	Finds
919 (33 & 34)	52 sherds, including large, fresh fragments from two Arretine vessels; a large Loeschke 1A/Conspectus 12.3 platter (late Augustan-Tiberian) and a Loeschke 8A/Conspectus 22 cup, stamped MENA and dated 10 BC – AD 10; large sherds from an ovoid AVILI beaker of Verulamium type GB24A in Gallo-Belgic Terra Rubra fabric (late Augustan-Tiberian). The coarse pottery includes grey Rowlands Castle fabric sherds and a black Southern Atrebatic Gallo-Belgic platter copy. A body sherd from an amphora in Baetican fabric and a small fragment from a salt container of East Kent cup type
919.2	9 sherds, all pre-AD 60 and quite possibly Late Iron Age in date
919.3	32 sherds including fragments from the same Arretine platter (late Augustan-Tiberian) and amphora as occurred in 919 and 3 fragments from a beaker of unspecified form in Terra Rubra 3 fabric. Coarse pottery includes a bead rim of certainly Late Iron Age date
937	18 sherds, all but one sherd coming from a handmade/tournetted jar paralleled in Late Iron Age assemblages nearby from North Bersted

This assemblage of 111 sherds is extremely interesting, even though they come from a small number of vessels. The sherds are large, freshly broken and some of the biggest that we found in five seasons of excavation. It does not appear that they were

34 A general view of some of the Arretine ware from the 'early' ditch at Fishbourne; the platter is over 400mm (16in) in diameter; note the initials TV on the base of the cup top left. Photograph David Rudkin

'old' vessels when they were thrown into the ditch. There is a mixture of imported wares from Italy and Gaul and locally-produced vessels. The dilemma is this: should we be swayed by the appearance of the ditch itself, very straight and a military-style profile, and therefore assume that the local pottery was requisitioned by a resident Roman garrison,[9] or should we instead see the ditch as the work of Late Iron Age elites with good contacts abroad?

Since the width of the ditch nearly filled the whole of the trench there was no indication of whether the ditch was associated with any bank (but see below). The current interpretation of this ditch is that it represents a feature excavated by the Roman military for demarcation, if not defensive, reasons. As such it represents the first definitive military earthworks from the pre-Palace landscape. Clearly much work needs to be done to answer some of the basic questions regarding this feature – such as whether it is associated with a bank, where the feature goes (both to the east and west), whether there are any buildings north or south of it that can be stratigraphically linked to it and, crucially, whether the feature turns a corner at any point and therefore forms part of an enclosure.

In addition, since the flanking wall running northwards from Building 3 did not appear in Area B the question of where the flanking wall terminates or turns remains unanswered. It is possible that the flanking wall turns to the east before it reaches the ditch and runs eastwards, parallel and to the south of the ditch. This begs questions concerning the relationship, functionally and chronologically, between ditch and wall.

There is no doubt the ditch was deliberately backfilled with material resembling redeposited natural buff-to-red clay (913) when its purpose was no longer required. There is little doubt how the red-clay capping was formed. It looks like material that was initially dug out of the ditch and may have once formed the core of material in a bank (yet to be located) associated with the ditch. After the ditch was no longer required, the remains of the bank were presumably shovelled back into the ditch to fill it up flush with the extant ground surface. One piece of Arretine ware from the backfill was a sherd from an Augustan or Tiberian dish. A total of 141 sherds came from the red clay comprising a mixture of imported and local wares. This pottery suggests that the red clay was dumped back into the ditch sometime between AD 50 and 60. This is confirmed by the finding of a Nauheim derivative brooch in the backfill, which can be dated to pre-AD 60.

The current interpretation of this ditch is that it represents a feature excavated by the Roman military for demarcation, if not defensive, reasons, before AD 43.[10] The deliberate slighting, represented by the red clay capping, suggests that the need for a military ditch (and presence?) was less compelling after AD 50. At this point I must confess to being conscious of one of the great maxims of archaeology: that interpretation stops at the trench edge. We have only excavated 5m of this ditch; I don't think Alec, because of adverse weather conditions, managed to 'bottom' his Ditch 11. If we excavated another 10m of it, as well we might, the finds and conclusions drawn here could be different. And as for Building 3, the fact that it might have been contemporary with at least the later life of our east-west ditch, suggests that it may well be a military building; that is, of course, if it was indeed a military ditch!

11 Is there archaeological evidence for the Romans' route to the Thames?

Today is a Sunday 2 September, just after 9am; I sit on my settee, about to start the penultimate chapter of this book. I know you are interested so let me tell you that the weather is ever so slightly autumnal; there is a hint of a chill coming through the open window which persuaded me to wear socks this morning and not go barefoot. I type these words really to get my brain and fingers working together. Of course, some of you will have realised that this is not the penultimate chapter – the next one is – but that chapter is already written. I have not always followed the order of chapters in writing this book; but the last chapter, the Discussion, I have saved to last and it is still to write.

That in itself is just as well. I say that because my ideas have changed during the writing of this book. I have a reasonable idea of what I will now write for the Discussion at the end, but I have no doubt it will be a different Discussion from the one I vaguely thought about last April when I started writing. I know this because I have the rough outline of this book beside me. It was drafted on 20 May 1999 on a train between East Croydon and London Victoria. Of course, it didn't come to me in a flash. The basic outline structure had been going around in my head for some time. And for all of 2000 I never got near the writing of this book since I had to write the report from our recent excavations at Fishbourne Roman Palace. But the basic outline structure is significantly different from the book I have written. My perception is that my initial idea has been altered by the things I have read in the last few months, to such an extent that the end product will be unanticipated, and unforeseen, at least by me. I am aware of the possibility of subtle biases of mine creeping in during this process. Some of us, me certainly, from time to time tend to read, say in our newspapers, those stories where we have some affinity with the writer's viewpoint, and ignore those columnists whom we imagine hold contrary views to our own. I am aware I approach archaeological texts in roughly the same manner, unconsciously sifting out those authors I find stimulating and tending to skip those whose views I don't agree with, and at a more detailed level, homing in on the bits of data that support my argument and discounting the bits that don't. I am therefore aware that another researcher, starting out in April with the aim of writing another book on this subject, would come up with different conclusions; and if I had written this book in 2000 or in 2002 my conclusions might have altered.

Time to return to the main argument of this book. In debating whether in AD 43 the Romans landed at Richborough or anywhere else, archaeologists have naturally looked for evidence of the passage of the army up to the Thames crossing, in the form

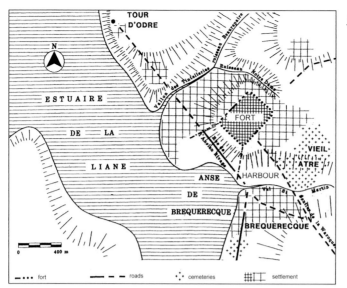

35 *The location of the early second century AD* Classis Britannica *fort at Boulogne.* After Seillier 1996

of forts or finds associated with the soldiers. But it is worth asking, at the outset, whether there is any evidence on the other side of the English Channel for the harbours from which the Romans sailed. The short answer is no. Boulogne has always been the favourite, but French archaeologists readily admit that the town is very much under-studied, that few excavations have examined the earliest Roman levels and that the earliest date for the *Classis Britannica* fort is in the early second century AD (Seillier 1996). A rough calculation of the length of the shoreline below the fort between the two tributaries suggests a total length of 1500m, capable of harbouring only about 120 ships; this suggests that the estuary of the Liane was only large enough to accommodate a fraction of the invasion fleet. Even Caligula's famous lighthouse, identified traditionally with the Tour d'Ordre north-west of the fort (**35**), seems more likely to have been constructed in the second century AD. The actual lighthouse built by Caligula, therefore, remains to be discovered. Sailing to the Solent area the Roman army would have embarked from the mouth of the Seine or further to the west; but there is little archaeological evidence, as yet, for large mid-first century Roman ports in these areas.

On this side of the Channel a convincing line of marching camps from disembarkation point to the Thames could settle the debate once and for all. However, that sort of evidence is always going to be difficult to find. If we take Cassius Dio at his word, there were only ever four military engagements south of the Thames during the invasion; those being the separate defeats of Caratacus and Togodumnus, and the two river battles. The only things marching legionaries might have left behind as evidence in the south-east of Britain would be the remains of marching camps, where they camped overnight, and a very few finds associated with those camps. Assuming a march speed of about 10 miles (16km) per day then we might expect four or five overnight camps before reaching the Thames. However, this assumes that the army would have acted in the same campaigning manner in the south-east as they later did, say, in Wales. The distinct lack of military evidence from the south-east in terms of fortifications (**11**) strongly suggests that, rather than a native population being overrun and cowed into submission by force of arms, the army may simply have passed through a territory in which communities, if not overtly pro-Roman, felt at least unthreatened by the presence of a lot of soldiers. The army may simply have been searching out Togodumnus, Caratacus and the Catuvellaunian forces and this aim may have been reasonably well understood by indigenous leaders in the south-east, who may have even perceived the incoming army, to use a contemporary analogy, as peace-keepers. David Bird (pers comm) has reminded me that the Romans initially fought against enemy forces and their leaders, rather than trying to annex territory. The enemies of Rome lay north of the Thames (the Catuvellauni) and west into Dorset (the Durotriges). Assuming that these enemies did not move into the south-east with a view to controlling large areas, earthwork barriers around all the marching camps in the south-east may not have been so necessary,[1] and even if they were and we could find them, the difficulties of dating the precise year (and month) of occupation, and the direction a military force was heading in, are beyond the limits of current archaeological techniques. However, there are a few potential indicators of early Roman military activity approximately along the lines of the possible marches from either Richborough or Chichester to the Thames and now is the time to review them. For ease of reference they are laid out in the Table below.

Possible support for march from Richborough	Possible support for march from Chichester
Early military remains below Canterbury	Early military remains below Chichester
Bredgar Hoard	Chichester legionary helmet
Watling Street	Stane Street
Possible fort at Syndale	Forts west of Solent
Ditch at Eccles[2]	Fort at Alchester

Canterbury

Webster, in his arguments in support of a Roman advance from Richborough, assumed that the first attempt at indigenous resistance to the invading army would have been at the crossing of the river Stour, and he surmised the construction of a fort underneath modern Canterbury, superseding the large Gallo-Belgic oppidum in that area (Webster 1980, 98). The only indication of any defensive perimeter for such a fort was found in excavations near Canterbury Castle in the late 1970s. A ditch of military design, and possibly of two phases, aligned roughly north-east/south-west was uncovered (Bennett *et al.* 1982, 21). The ditch was traced for a length of 55m; its fills contained large quantities of early Roman coarse wares, including stamped and decorated samian dating from AD 50 to 70 (**36**). In the conclusion the excavator suggested that the military presence might have been in two phases. However, uncertainty surrounds the date of

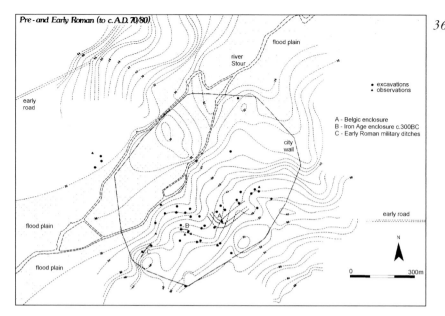

36 Plan of Late Iron Age and early Roman Canterbury. Courtesy of Canterbury Archaeological Trust

these two phases: Frere (in Bennett 1982, 30, fn) thought that the first phase might have been in AD 43, with evacuation and reoccupation during and after the Boudiccan revolt; alternatively the first occupation could have been during the Boudiccan revolt, with the reoccupation during the 60s AD. Canterbury was certainly seen as the nodal point in the road communication network, linking Richborough, Reculver, Lympne and Dover to Watling Street and London beyond.

Frere (1967, 47-8) – an early excavator of this site – described a large pre-Roman Belgic oppidum at Canterbury, with as yet unknown defences but circular and rectangular huts, with drainage gullies, over a wide area. Crudely baked slabs of clay were used for the hearths, and plentiful supplies of oysters attested the emergence of a resource that was to become a focus for trade in the Roman period. The site appears to be the residence of an important chief in the first decades of the first century AD. This basic information was added to considerably by the results of the excavations in the Marlowe area of the city during the late 1970s and early 1980s. These excavations revealed part of a Belgic enclosure. Within the enclosure were two timber roundhouses, a sunken-floored building and a stake-built structure. One of the roundhouses was built in the later first century BC, and underwent two rebuilds before being demolished *c*.AD 70-80. Belgic occupation at Canterbury has now been located over some 150ha on both sides of the river Stour. The events of AD 43 appear to have had little effect on the town, and the Belgic settlement was only levelled a generation after the conquest (Blockley *et al.* 1995, 458).

It is interesting to note at this point the report on the samian from the Marlowe sites by Joanna Bird. She commented (in Blockley *et al.* 1995, 772) that some 68 sherds of Arretine ware were located, although all of these were very fragmentary and much was redeposited in later levels. All of the Arretine sherds came from presumed rubbish filling, mostly of pits.

Chichester

Chichester is something of a contrast to Canterbury. There is very little evidence of indigenous, Iron Age, structures. On the so-called Cattle Market site, by the East Gate of the later Roman town, the remains of two sub-rectangular huts and one circular hut were located, the former having sunken floors. Associated finds included a hand-made platter in black ware, a wheel-turned small globular beaker, sherds of Dressel 1B amphorae, three Roman Republican coins and five pre-conquest denarii. Traces of a 7m wide ditch were also located nearby, quite possibly part of the north-south section of the Chichester Dykes (Down 1989, 59-61). Further to the north-east, and to the north of Stane Street, a possible military ditch (some 4.5m wide and 2.14m deep), with a possible palisade trench to the east, was found. The ditch was not open for very long and its fill contained pre-Flavian samian and imitation Gallo-Belgic wares; the ditch was deliberately filled in. Alec Down surmised that the ditch might have been part of a defensive work associated with a detachment of the invading army in AD 43 (Down & Rule 1971, 67). Another section of ditch was located underneath the Needlemakers site, south of Stane Street. Here the ditch measured some 5.2m wide by 2m deep, with three sherds of samian (one pre-Flavian) above the silt in the bottom of the ditch. Down (1981, 84) hypothe-sised that these two ditches might be sides of the marching camp of the Second Legion in AD 43.[3] The final early ditch section was excavated on the site of the Theological College outside the West Gate of the Roman town (**37**). Here, a V-shaped ditch ran north-south across the site; it appears to have been about 3m wide and 1.4m deep. The ditch was back-filled with brickearth and the finds included a number of sherds of *Terra Nigra*, all pre-Flavian, the majority being pre-Claudian (Down & Magilton, 1993, 54). In the same volume Dannell (p 149) lists 12 sherds of Augustan-Tiberian Arretine from

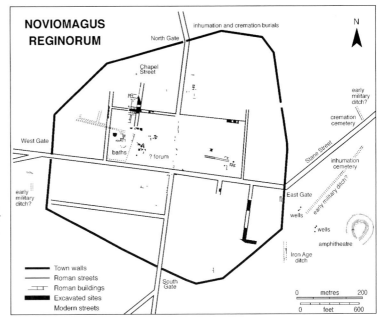

37 Simplified plan of Roman Chichester, showing location of 'early' ditches, and the Chapel Street excavations.
Drawn by Sue Rowland

38 The gold coins from the Bredgar Hoard. Courtesy of the British Museum

the site, describing the majority of finely-slipped, well-moulded pieces as similar to the range from the fort at Haltern in Germany, which was abandoned in AD 9.

Military finds that were deemed to date to AD 43 or later were found in the north-west quadrant of the later Roman town, and have subsequently been located in other areas. On the County Hall site sherds of Tiberian samian, and early Gallo-Belgic wares associated with a number of fragments of legionary[4] equipment, including a ballista bolt, pieces of lorica and a belt buckle were located (Down 1989, 2). On the west side of Chapel Street a number of rectangular buildings was located, of which one phase, and probably two others, was constructed by the Roman military. The regularity of the plan suggested to Down that they were part of barrack blocks, and the quantity of first-century legionary equipment led him to claim, beyond doubt,[5] this area as part of the Second Legion's base camp in AD 43 (Down, 1978, 43). Some of these structures were clearly associated with Arretine wares, Tiberian-Claudian samian and Gallo-Belgic fine wares (Down 1978, 52, 54), summarised by Dannell as amounting to some 206 sherds (Dannell in Down 1978, 227). Later excavations in the same area in the late 1970s again produced evidence of military timber buildings, and a quantity of Augustan-Tiberian Arretine from the ATEIUS workshops. There was also a collection of Italian and Gaulish vessels from pit X 165, which Dannell estimated to be of the period AD 25-40 (Dannell in Down 1981, 263-4).

The Bredgar Hoard

On 30 July 1957, when a trench was being dug for the foundations of a bungalow, 33 gold aurei (**38**) were found and a subsequent search produced one further coin (Carson 1960). There was no sign of a container but since some of the coins were still stacked together the implication was that they had been packed in rolls and wrapped in cloth, which had rotted. The coins ranged in date from Julius Caesar to Claudius, with the four latest issued in the reign of Claudius in AD 41-2. The latest coins were in mint condition but the earlier coins were worn. Since no native coins were found with the hoard the find was associated with Roman as opposed to indigenous ownership. Pay for an ordinary centurion was about 150 aurei per year, and it was concluded that the 34 aurei could well have represented the personal savings of someone of the rank of centurion or upwards in the legions which invaded Britain in AD 43. Of course the location of the village of Bredgar, on the Downs some 10 miles (16km) to the east of the Medway, and just before the line of the hills begins to descend towards the Medway, raised the obvious possibility that an official might have concealed these savings at the army's last halting place before the battle of the Medway.

Superficially the argument is plausible, but underlying it are numerous assumptions: for instance that the hoard was concealed in the summer of AD 43, that it did belong to a Roman officer, that it was hidden by him and not stolen from him, that the officer was part of an invading unit heading for the Medway – all these things are unknowable. In addition, it seems debateable whether a campaigning officer fighting in a contested invasion would carry with him his personal savings. What did Roman soldiers do with their pay when they were on the march? Surely pay, or any savings accrued, were kept in safely guarded stores, capable of being redeemed by an individual when the progress of the campaign allowed some leisure time. In addition, it again seems unlikely that an officer would deliberately conceal a personal fortune, knowing that his army was on the march and would stay at a particular location for only a brief period of time. In reality the Bredgar Hoard may imply the presence nearby of the Roman military, but it tells us nothing of the size of the force, the year in which it was present, the direction it was taking, and least of all is it proof for the battle of the Medway.[6]

The Chichester Helmet

On the ground floor of the museum in Barbican House, Lewes is displayed a bronze legionary helmet (**39**) with, rather emotively, the remains of an oyster shell attached to its crown. In *Sussex Archaeological Collections* 39 (1894) it is recorded as a purchase and, although not attributed to the Bateman Collection there, other items listed are. In an Accession Register of the museum started in 1928 it is listed on page 82 as:

> No. 196 Bronze helmet of the Roman Foot Soldiery (Legionary Helmet) from the Bateman Collection and previously from the Collection of George Lane Fox, Esq. Bramham (Bateman Cat. No.159). This helmet has lain in the seas for some time as an oyster has attached its shell to the crown. Found near Chichester.

39 The Roman helmet from Chichester harbour. Note the oyster shell at the top of the helmet and the ?modern visor bottom left.
Photograph Barbara Alcock

Visual inspection of the helmet confirms that it had indeed been recovered from a salt-water environment. It lacks cheek pieces. However, Emma O'Connor, Museums Officer for the Sussex Archaeological Society, has pointed out that the thin, curving strip of metal meant to protect the eyes of the wearer, has a different patina from the rest of the object, and looks very much less worn. The suggestion is, therefore, that the visor is possibly a twentieth-century addition.

The helmet is typologically one that could have been worn (and lost overboard) by a legionary arriving in Chichester harbour in AD 43; it is a Coolus type 'F' helmet (Bishop & Coulston, 1993, 93). It was significantly damaged in antiquity as evidenced by the slightly displaced crest fitting and the substantial damage to the helmet bowl. But as with the Bredgar Hoard, using a single find as proof for the presence of an invasion force some 40,000 strong is not advisable.

The Syndale Fort

In autumn 1999 a new publication from the recently formed Kent Archaeological Field School announced the discovery of a possible 4 acre (1.6ha) Roman fort at Syndale, near Faversham in Kent. Two trenches were excavated through the bank and ditch of the fortification, which was roughly rectangular in shape, and a small area was opened in the interior. The excavators argued that the fort was constructed before Watling Street, the main Roman road between Canterbury and London, which lay alongside the north side of the fortification, and that the fort would have housed about 1000 men.[7] The excavators concluded that the pottery found in the ditches was 'consistent with the period of the Claudian invasion of AD 43' and the implication was that this new find was additional proof of the Richborough landings.

A proper consideration of this discovery must await full publication of the results. However, the excavator, Paul Wilkinson, was kind enough to allow me access to the pottery report, which was compiled by Malcolm Lyne (2000). His results are tabulated below.

Assemblage location	Dating and comment
Assemblage 1 – from the primary silting of the ditch in Trenches 1 and 2	Lack of rims and other diagnostic sherds; any closer dating than AD 43 to 70 difficult
Assemblage 2 – from rubbish dumped in the partially silted up ditch in Trench 1	70 sherds of Late Iron Age to pre-Flavian character; none of the dateable forms has an inception date later than AD 50; assemblage accumulated between AD 43 and 50/60
Assemblage 3 – from rubbish dumped in the partially silted-up ditch in Trench 2	Pre-Flavian sherds present, but large quantities of late first- to late second-century material indicates that rubbish continued to be dumped in the ditch until *c*.AD 200
Assemblage 4 – from the interior of the fort	Pottery spans first and second centuries

As has been remarked elsewhere in this book, it is not possible to date the digging of a ditch to any particular calendar year from pottery alone, and the assemblages described above make it impossible to assign this possible fortification to AD 43. It is also slightly odd that there is clear evidence of second-century activity. This implies some other functions for this site, which are unlikely to be military.

Forts west of the Solent

Graham Webster's lattice-work of postulated Roman forts over southern and eastern Britain is well known (Webster 1980, 112, Map II). While the logical regularity of the system is appealing it is surmised, from other areas, that networks of occupation fortifications could be very different. For instance, after Caesar's campaigns, some of Gallia Belgica seems to have been held by a mixture of chiefs loyal to Rome and military units established at native oppida. In terms of Webster's model for southern Britain, the bulk of his forts were unknown then and they remain so now. The absence of early military forts in the south-east is still very evident (**11**). Nevertheless, Bird (pers comm) has drawn attention to early known forts just to the west of the Solent (Lake Farm, Wimborne, and the famous fort inside the Iron Age hillfort of Hod Hill). Although these have been claimed as Claudian forts, Bird has commented on the fact that their proximity to one another is inappropriate for a campaign in progress, but rather has the appearance of a temporary frontier, perhaps designed to control the eastern Durotriges while actions were being pursued elsewhere. This is an interesting idea, and it might be leant on to support the idea of a Chichester invasion, but any support offered is rather fragile. A further fragmentary piece of evidence is the partial remains of an east-west orientated military style timber building discovered at Bitterne (Clausentum) in 1998. Closely-spaced parallel foundation trenches suggested a warehouse or granary with parallels at Fishbourne and Richborough. Dating evidence, however, was sparse and a mid-first century AD date is all that can be suggested (Russel 2001, 18).

Watling Street and Stane Street

It is interesting to ask whether the two main Roman roads (Watling Street from Richborough and Stane Street from Chichester) can tell us anything about the conquest of AD 43. Watling Street would appear to be later than AD 43 on the grounds that it leads to Southwark, on the south side of the Thames in London, and current knowledge of Roman London suggests that a settlement does not emerge there until AD 50 or later (Bird 2000, 101). There is nothing to suggest that the roads which served it, which required considerable engineering across the marshes, were constructed before this. In addition, we have seen the suggested stratigraphic relationship between a supposed fort at Syndale and Watling Street, which apparently lies over it.

Stane Street, on the other hand, is a little more helpful. John Magilton has summarised some recent thoughts on the southern end of Stane Street and the following paragraph is taken from his discussion (Magilton 1995). Stane Street cuts diagonally across the south-east corner of the Roman town of Chichester, entering by the East Gate and exiting near the South Gate (**37 & 42**). It is clearly earlier than the orthogonal street pattern of the town, but later than the possible 'military' ditches that were excavated outside the East Gate. The road heads towards Fishbourne creek, and Magilton claims the ultimate destination is a place on the east side of the creek, now known as Copperas Point. Although there are tile kilns near Copperas Point, there are few other indications of Roman activity; however, it does appear plausible that a main Roman harbourage on Fishbourne creek lay at Copperas Point. Taking Stane Street north-east of Chichester, Magilton argues that the road was not surveyed to link Chichester with London, but rather to link the Fishbourne creek with the Pulborough area. From the latter area a considerable quantity of Dressel 1A and 1B amphora has been located (more sherds than any other site in southern Britain apart from Hengistbury Head – Barry Cunliffe pers comm) and it seems plausible that the line of Stane Street, at least at its southern end, could be very early in the Roman period, if not pre-AD 43.

Alchester

The last piece of evidence I want to discuss briefly is the recent excavations at the Roman fort of Alchester, north of Oxford. This has been reported as potentially a 8-9ha fort with a garrison of perhaps 3,500 to 4,000 men (Sauer 2000, 22). The excavator makes the intriguing suggestion that, as Alchester lay on the boundary between the Dobunni and the Catuvellauni, this might have been the fort that Cassius Dio implies Plautius garrisoned, instead of one postulated at Cirencester, for which there is little evidence to date. This, as you can imagine, would cause some complications to our story, since Plautius would therefore be at Alchester, and north of the Thames, and would then have to cross to the south side of the Thames in order to pursue the fleeing indigenous forces to the Thames and attempt to follow them northwards across it. Sauer (2000, 41) wonders whether this crossing of the Thames from north to south might have been the famous two-day battle described by Dio. Fortunately, two dendrochronological dates from timber gateposts (one of October AD 44, the other of March AD 45) in the western gateway of the annexe at Alchester are conclusive in indicating that the annexe was built, probably to house troops, in AD 44/45, and not AD 43, so a conquest-year garrison at Alchester can likely be ruled out.[8] Nevertheless, Sauer comments, I think quite rightly, that the alliance indicated by Dio between Plautius and a section of the Dobunni favours those proponents who champion an AD 43 landing in the Chichester region.

Sometimes, the more one looks for supporting evidence for a Richborough or a Chichester landing for the main Roman force, the less there really seems to be that is incontestable; everything begins to be hedged with 'ifs and buts, possiblys and probablys'. Excavation reports and academic tomes can really take the edge off excitement or contro-versy. If you want passion, organise a conference, or, better still, organise two.

12 Does talking lead to the 'truth'?

The two conferences that I was involved with which debated this issue were great fun, and both were well attended, with in excess of 300 people at each. The Sussex Archaeological Society held a conference on *The Roman Invasion of Britain* in Chichester on 23 October 1999 while the Council for Kentish Archaeology held a conference at Faversham on the 7 April 2001 on *The Roman Invasion AD 43: Kent or Sussex?* My involvement in each was different: I organised the first and spoke at the second. The Sussex conference was problematic to organise because a lot of people wanted to speak at it and there were a limited number of places. And, as organiser and therefore selector of who was to be invited, I was always open to the accusation that I had somehow influenced the outcome of the day by the speakers I had chosen. Barry Cunliffe, as President of the Sussex Archaeological Society, excavator at Fishbourne and editor of the fifth report of the Richborough excavations, was an obvious candidate for Chair. Ernest Black seemed to offer the most original interpretations of the historical evidence. David Bird was about to publish a paper on the subject and was invited. I wanted someone to talk about the naval and maritime side of things and I approached Sean McGrail, who was unavailable. However, he put me in touch with a PhD student of his, Gerald Grainge, who admirably filled the bill. I wanted someone to talk about things military, and again Mark Hassall of UCL seemed an obvious candidate. To counter David Bird's views I wanted someone to champion the Kentish cause. Brian Philp offered, but I did not accept; not, I hasten to add, out of any disrespect, but because I sensed that he had little novel to say in favour of Kent that had not been rehearsed in print. In the end I asked Mike Fulford, who I surmised would provide an unbiased account of the Kentish cause. I also invited Andy Russel, from Southampton, who had recently made some military discoveries at Clausentum. That was the chosen line-up. Two late entrants I managed to squeeze in: Nigel Nicolson (of Medway Monument fame) and Martin Henig, a proponent of the Fishbourne-landings theory; time constraints restricted the latter two to about 10 minutes apiece. The one person whom I had wanted to speak, but who declined to do so, was someone who had already played a pivotal role, and who was in the audience: John Hind; his presence was a great benefit to us all.

Summaries of the two conferences can still be found on our website – www.sussexpast.co.uk – so I will only outline here the major conclusions and talking points. Barry Cunliffe opened the conference, indicating that the day's proceedings would comprise a deconstruction of the Claudian invasion, a close look at the evidence and then a re-assembly of those pieces of evidence that could be put back together. Ernest Black examined the historical evidence, unafraid at times to stray into matters archaeological with the statement that only about 10% of Plautius' ships could have been unloaded at Richborough at any one time. Mike Fulford gave a cautious appraisal of the evidence from Kent, commenting on the fact that the invasion beachhead would not be the context for erecting elaborate defences or the discarding of masses of material. David Bird stated his views in advance of his paper in the *Oxford Journal of Archaeology*, favouring three landings in the Solent area for the main army. He also indicated that what we knew of subsequent events made a better fit with Hind's model than a landing in Kent. Mark Hassall suggested that the dykes around Chichester might have been erected at the time Verica was ejected from Calleva, and Chichester itself was settled as Noviomagus; this could be paralleled by the construction of dykes at Camulodunum in response to the Trinovantian threat. I remember Mark being put on the spot towards the end of the day. He was asked directly which landing site he preferred. He answered saying that if the Bodunni (of Dio) and the Dobunni were one and the same that would be compelling evidence for a south-coast landing. However, he was also persuaded by the details of tides and current to support the traditional view. Barry Cunliffe summed up the day, suggesting that there was something cyclical to this debate and that tradition had no god-given right to be correct. In the 1880s Clausentum was suggested as the landing place for AD 43, while in the twentieth century the discoveries at Richborough had brought that site into prominence. Perhaps Hind's article had pushed the pendulum back towards Sussex?

In retrospect, while the day was successful and I am sure enjoyed by many, I felt that we had not really examined the details of the archaeological evidence, particularly for Fishbourne and Richborough. I have tried to remedy this here. In addition, rather unwisely, I suggested to a journalist post-conference that I thought that about 75% of the audience at the Chichester conference would now favour the Sussex landing. Of course, I was only guessing and the tactic rebounded on me in due course, as did the title of an article I wrote for the newsletter of the Sussex Archaeological Society. I think it was called *Medway Muddle*, and it drew attention to the difficulties of erecting a permanent monument to an event for which no archaeological or historical evidence existed.

Tables were duly turned at the conference 18 months later at Faversham in Kent. David Bird opened the afternoon's proceedings with a restatement of the case he had given at the Chichester conference. He suggested, *inter alia*, that the granaries at Richborough might have been used to store locally produced grain that was then shipped out for army use probably elsewhere in Britain. I then gave my views, most of which you will now be familiar with. Nigel Nicolson then addressed the audience, I think sensing that at last he had the opportunity to put the case for Kent properly. He agreed, however, that the issue was a matter of discussing probabilities rather than incontestable facts. He suggested, quite correctly, that we were all guilty of selecting pieces of this jigsaw that fitted our picture of the events. He demonstrated this again by emphasising the difficulties that a Roman army would have had in crossing the Weald, notwithstanding David Bird's assertions that the army might have gone around the western end of the Weald and not through it. Instead, he favoured a crossing of the Roman army at Snodland since he claimed there was evidence of a

Roman ford there, which the army would have required since it had not brought any bridging equipment[1] with it. In attacking the Sussex case, Nigel Nicolson claimed that the Arun at Pulborough was too insignificant for a major two-day battle, although I have visited both the Medway at Snodland and the Arun at Pulborough and the rivers both now seem to be about 15 to 20m wide. Brian Philp then spoke, countering the *Medway Muddle* story with a quip about *Chichester Confusion* and arguing that the Kent conference was better balanced than the Sussex one had been – which was probably right! Most of his lecture attempted to deconstruct the Hind article, and I sensed also he was having a bit of a swipe at the editorial board of *Britannia* for some reason, perhaps because the journal had truncated or even refused an article from him in the past. He also had a bit of fun at Verica's expense, dismissing him as 'some man from Worthing'. John Smith, a military historian, then spoke, with some fascinating detail about the practicalities of planning an invasion, from intelligence gathering, mustering the invading army at the embarkation point, the organisation of shipping and the landing. It was all entertaining and valuable material and conducted, I must say, in a spirit free from antipathy. I remember at the end of the day in Kent they did actually take a vote, which was overwhelmingly in favour of a Kentish landing. David Bird blamed me for starting the idea of a vote, even if the verdict was not surprising. No-one mentioned the claims by Paul Wilkinson of a possible Claudian fort at Syndale, near Sittingbourne, which was surprising.

Overall, I suppose that honours were even across the two conferences. It was entirely right that a 'return leg' had been organised in Kent and that Kent had had 'its say'. I suppose now it is time I had 'my say'.

13 What conclusions can I draw (if any)?

It's Sunday 7 October at 8.30 in the morning on the other side of the Roman Empire; modern and ancient Jerash, in Jordan, to be precise. Off in the distance I can hear not the evocative echoes of the Islamic call for prayer, but the repeated strains of 'Nick Nack Paddywhack', played from the pick-up of the mobile gas-bottle seller who uses the tune to alert householders to his presence in their street. It seems an incongruous location to write the final words of this book, but distance may help in achieving some sort of balance.

If this book were about prehistory, the conclusions would be easier to draw. Prehistorians are used to metaphors of 'alternative readings' or 'parallel texts' in their interpretations of archaeological evidence; in other words material culture can be used to support a variety of interpretations, with no single interpretation being the 'right' one. The different interpretations stem largely from the writer's theoretical viewpoint. For instance, some people assume Iron Age hillforts in south-east Britain were largely functional and defensive, others see more evidence for their symbolic role in the landscape; neither viewpoint is necessarily incorrect or indeed incompatible with the other. The problem about AD 43, of course, is that we view it as a single, historical event happening at a precise place in a specific moment in time; and such things demand a certainty, and a 'right' interpretation.

At present, unfortunately, there does not seem to be a 'right' interpretation for the events of AD 43. We have seen, elsewhere in this book, how the sources used by ancient authors, and their own biases, have bequeathed us a few pages of text for this event that are full of ambiguities and lack geographic and temporal precision. The archaeological evidence, likewise, while fixed geographically is again ambiguous and chronologically imprecise. It can be argued that the timber buildings discovered by Barry Cunliffe at Fishbourne, seemingly part of a larger, orthogonal layout, look too 'planned' to have formed part of an invasion beachhead. On the other hand, surely too much weight has been placed on the Claudian ditches at Richborough, resulting in a premature finality to the debate. In addition, I have already commented upon the inherent dangers of linking archaeological to historical evidence, and the variety of different theoretical viewpoints that modern archaeologists and historians bring to the events of AD 43. Finally, of course, I would argue that the different 'world views' of the Romans and ourselves form a further considerable barrier. The last thing I think we need at present is another 'grand narrative' for the events of AD 43, which presents concluding arguments (*pace* Frere & Fulford 2001).

40   *The wall-footings of House 1 in Insula IX at Silchester. This structure is not aligned with the Roman street grid in the town (established c.AD 100) and should pre-date it. House 1 and associated buildings sharing the same alignment may respect the Late Iron Age street grid.* Photograph John Manley

An alternative understanding of AD 43 is to consider the events of that year as the culmination of a process over the preceding century, which effectively had subjugated at least the south-east of Britain and brought that area within the complete control of the Roman Empire some time before AD 43. Viewed in this light the events of AD 43, with its unopposed landings, were less a military invasion than a political annexation of an already 'romanised' region.

What evidence is there to back up this suggestion? There are several strands that can be used to support this hypothesis, although, even collectively, they do not offer definitive proof. First, I think, is the archaeological evidence for the increasing multiculturalism of social groups in south-east Britain between Caesar and Claudius. I know multi-culturalism is a distinctly modern term with contemporary meaning in political discussion in Britain. It can be used, however, to describe a kaleidoscopic pattern of different communities that were resident in the south-east in the century prior to AD 43, each perhaps drawing on different ethnic identities and speaking a variety of languages. I have in mind here specific examples such as the Belgae, the colonists at Silchester (**40**) and the newcomers to the Chichester area evidenced by the coin distributions. Cutting across such cultural ties would have been allegiances which were political and/or military in character.

Second, analogous evidence, brought together by Creighton (2000; 2001), persuasively supports the theory that local dynasties in south-east Britain, friendly to Rome, were effectively controlled by the Romans between Caesar and Claudius. Such controls were effected by the mechanism of *obsides*, children and other close relatives of indigenous chiefs who were educated in Rome, and by the growing practice of indigenous rulers first seeking recognition from Rome when coming to power, and then, from Augustus onwards, being actually appointed by the princeps. It is an unrewarding exercise to consider whether such friendly kingdoms with their local chiefs were part of the Empire or not. It is largely a matter of semantics. At times, these chiefs could be viewed as imperial administrators (Creighton, 2001, 5)

Thirdly, there are increasing hints concerning the presence of Roman soldiers (**41**) in Britain before AD 43. In particular Creighton (2001, 7ff) has drawn attention to the Roman fort in the Gosbecks region at Colchester, close to the enclosure known as 'Cunobelin's farmstead'. The fort is only known from aerial photography and is therefore undated, but its west side is formed by the Late Iron Age dykes, known as Kidman's Dyke Middle and Heath Farm Dyke Middle. There are alternative interpretations for this fort other than the orthodox view that it dates to AD 43 and the Roman occupation of Camulodunum. If Cunobelin had been trained in the Roman army, then, like other friendly chiefs, he may have organised his own forces along similar lines to Roman *auxilia*, and constructed a fort to Roman design. Alternatively, the fort may have been garrisoned with genuine Roman *auxilia* before Roman annexation.

Creighton has also drawn attention to the orthodox reading of the evidence from Fishbourne itself. He suggests that the chronological sequence of building in AD 43 and after at that site is very compressed, and instead considers that the timber buildings of phase 1a, and the orthogonal road layout, could have been constructed pre-AD 43. Again, if true, the interpretation might invoke a pro-Roman Verica organising his own forces in Roman style military buildings, or a detachment of Roman *auxilia* stationed at Fishbourne to assist Verica. In addition, it has been suggested that the Chichester dykes, problematic to date but generally assumed to be very Late Iron Age, are very straight in some sections, possibly due to Roman influence or land-surveying expertise.[1] There is probably military metalwork from pre-Claudian contexts at Silchester, too (Creighton, pers comm).

What historical evidence do we possess for the practice of stationing Roman troops beyond the formal frontier of Roman rule? There are several instances which include

41   The Ermine Street Guard take a break at Fishbourne Roman Palace.
Photograph Andy Freeman

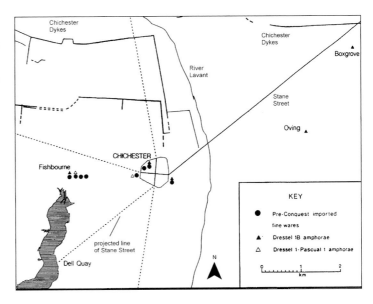

42 Simplified plan of Chichester and Fishbourne area, illustrating the distribution of Arretine and pre-conquest imported wares and early pre-AD 43 amphorae; note the location of the Chichester Dykes or Entrenchments

Caesar's stationing of three or four legions with Cleopatra VII and Ptolemy XIV in Egypt when he left the country; Herod's arrival in Jerusalem in 37 BC with the support of a Roman legion; the accession of Cotys I in the Bosphorus aided by Roman forces led by Aulus Didius Gallus; the presence of an auxiliary unit in Armenia in AD 31 under a Roman commander, Caelius Pollio; the gift by the Emperor Hadrian to King Pharasmanes of Iberia of 'an elephant and a quingenary cohort'; an inscription dated to a little after AD 84 which records a detachment of the Legio XII Fulminata in Albania[2]; and finally the arguments that the Romans maintained garrisons in each of the Caucasian client kingdoms (Colchis, Iberia and Albania) to help secure their control of three Caucasus passes through which the Alani might penetrate, as they had done in the past.[3]

Nearer to home, there is some tantalising archaeological evidence to complement the historical examples quoted above. Creighton (2001, 9) has already inferred a possible connection between pre-AD 43 Arretine pottery and a military presence. While some of this Arretine may well have arrived through conventional mechanisms such as diplomatic gifts to Late Iron Age elites, and trade, some of the distribution may suggest a Roman military presence. The fairly ubiquitous distribution of Arretine in the Fishbourne and Chichester areas (**42**), and particularly its association with ditches of potentially Roman military profile at Chichester, and now at Fishbourne itself, coupled with the absence of Late Iron Age settlement[4] activity, may argue for the presence of Roman soldiers in this area of the south-east in the decades prior to AD 43. In contrast, places like Canterbury have produced substantial amounts of Late Iron Age settlement activity, but very little Arretine pottery (Joanna Bird in Blockley *et al.*, 1995). There is a clear contrast here between these two areas. Late Iron Age elites in Canterbury, importing substantial quantities of Belgic pottery, may have continued in power for a generation after AD 43.[5] By contrast, whether through the actual presence of Roman soldiers pre-AD 43 or not, influential figures in the Chichester and Fishbourne areas seem to have had contacts

43 Aerial photo of the Chichester harbour. The location of Fishbourne Roman Palace is right at the top of the channel; the image also shows sailing ships moored off Dell Quay (right-hand side of the channel), and Chichester itself at top right. Photograph John Manley

with Italy and Rome in the period pre-AD 43. Such contacts paved the way for a much quicker transformation of the area post-AD 43, with public buildings in Chichester and, of course, ultimately the Palace at Fishbourne. However, like Canterbury, indigenous leaders (e.g. Togidubnus) remained in power.[6] In relation to the possibly military ditches at Chichester and Fishbourne, it is useful to remember that we should not necessarily anticipate, before, or in AD 43, Roman military installations of classic 'playing-card' shape. David Bird (2001) has pointed out that early imperial fortification did not always follow a standard design,[7] and Wightman (1985) has also drawn attention to the establishment of Roman forces within native oppida in Gallia Belgica following Caesar's conquests.

In conclusion, I do not wish to suggest a new orthodoxy of an increasing number of Roman soldiers in the south-east prior to AD 43 (**43**), and therefore force an interpretation of the events of AD 43 as political annexation rather than military invasion. Certainly, political annexation of the south-east would help to explain some of the 'few facts' we possess, such as the unopposed landings; the 'stage-management' of Claudius' arrival and departure, and the lack of significant military forts in the south-east.[8] Annexation of south-east Britain remains a possibility, but only that. It seems best to wait patiently for future archaeological discoveries to provide further information and suggest alternative and better informed interpretations.[9]

John Manley, Jerash, 7 October 2001, 10.50a.m.

Appendix 1

Dates of Emperors, and Governors of Roman Britain

Dates	Emperor	Dates	Governor of Roman Britain
Julio-Claudians			
27BC–AD14	Augustus		
14–37	Tiberius		
37–41	Gaius (Caligula)		
41–54	Claudius	43–47	Aulus Plautius
		47–52	Publius Ostorius Scapula
		52–57	Aulus Didius Gallus
54–68	Nero	57/8	Quintus Veranius
		58–61★	Gaius Suetonius Paulinus
		61/2–63	Publius Petronius Turpilianus
		63–69	Marcus Trebellius Maximus
68–69	Galba	69–71	Marcus Vettius Bolanus
69	Otho		
69–70	Vitellius		
Flavians			
69–79	Vespasian	71–73/4	Quintus Petillius Cerialis
		73/4–77/8	Sextus Julius Frontinus
79–81	Titus	78–84	Gnaeus Julius Agricola
81–96	Domitian	83/4–96	Sallustius Lucullus
96–98	Nerva	96?	Publius Metilius Nepos?
98–117	Trajan	97/8–100/1	Titus Avidius Quietus
		100/1–103?	Lucius Neratius Marcellus
		115–8	Marcus Appius Bradua
117–138	Hadrian	118–122	Quintus Pompeius Falco
		122–125?	Aulus Platorius Nepos
		131–132/3	Sextus Julius Severus
		132/3–135?	Publius Mummius Sisenna

★AD 61 was the year of the Boudiccan rebellion.
★★The Antonine Emperors began with Antoninus Pius in AD 138 and ended with Didius Julianus in AD 193.

Appendix 2

Early Roman military sites

For location see **11**

Number and site name

1	Malton	43	Walltown	85	Sea Mills
2	Stamford Bridge	44	Greensforge	86	Cirencester
3	York	45	Metchley	87	Wanborough
4	Hayton	46	Lunt	88	Dorchester-on-Thames
5	Brough-on-Humber	47	Irchester	89	Alchester
6	Castleford	48	Godmanchester	90	Cow Roast
7	Winteringham	49	Saham Toney	91	Verulamium
8	Doncaster	50	Scole	92	Chelmsford
9	Rossington Bridge	51	Ixworth	93	Colchester
10	Templeborough	52	Coddenham	94	Fingringhoe Wick
11	Littleborough	53	Cambridge	95	Silchester
12	Newton-on-Trent	54	Great Chesterford	96	Reculver
13	Lincoln	55	Towcester	97	Canterbury
14	Chesterfield	56	Alcester	98	Richborough
15	Chester	57	Droitwich	99	Martinhoe
16	Rhyn Park	58	Leintwardine	100	Old Barrow
17	Whitchurch	59	Brandon Camp	101	Wiveliscombe
18	Chesterton	60	Caer Gaer	102	South Cadbury
19	Trent Vale	61	Trawscoed	103	Ilchester
20	Rocester	62	Llanio	104	Ham Hill
21	Strutts Park	63	Castell Collen	105	Waddon Hill
22	Littlechester	64	Walton	106	Hod Hill
23	Broxtowe	65	Pen-min-caer	107	Spettisbury Rings
24	Osmanthorpe	66	Beulah	108	Lake Farm
25	Thorpe by Newark	67	Pumsaint	109	Hamworthy
26	Margidunum	68	Llandovery	110	Maiden Castle
27	Ancaster	69	Y Pigwn	111	Winchester
28	Wroxeter	70	Brecon Gaer	112	Bitterne
29	Leighton	71	Clyro-on-Wye	113	Fishbourne
30	Stretton Mill	72	Clifford	114	Chichester
31	Kinvaston	73	Pen y Gaer	115	Hembury
32	Wall	74	Abergavenny	116	Tiverton
33	Leicester	75	Gloucester	117	Cullompton
34	Great Casterton	76	Kingsholm	118	Topsham
35	Longthorpe	77	Coelbren	119	Exeter
36	Water Newton	78	Hirfynydd	120	Bury Barton
37	Mancetter	79	Neath	121	Taw
38	Wigston Parva	80	Loughor	122	Okehampton
39	High Cross	81	Penydarren	123	Nanstallon
40	Forden Gaer	82	Gelligaer	124	Staines
41	Caersws	83	Caerphilly		
42	Usk	84	Cardiff		

Notes and references

A personal preamble

1 'Roman Invasion of Britain' issues, at least currently, seem to be a peculiar obsession of males.

1 It was a long time ago: does it really matter?

1 For the dates of various Emperors mentioned in the text see Appendix 1.
2 I am conscious in this paragraph of using words such as 'invasion' and 'conquest' rather automatically. Practically all the mainstream discussions in the last century use such terms. However, it is possible, particularly in some areas of southern Britain, that the Roman soldiers were either invited into regions as 'liberators' or, when truces were concluded, they were seen as 'peace-keepers'.
3 It is easy to use such shorthand as 'factions' to summarise what local tribes and communities might have thought about an invading Roman army. However, the shorthand masks difficult questions. It cannot be known to what extent all the individuals living in discrete areas associated themselves with a particular tribe, or whether they acted in concert. It is entirely possible that the 'pro-Roman and anti-Roman factions' may have been confined to the sympathies of the political leaders, rather than the general populace.
4 The stone states: 'This stone commemorates the battle of the Medway in A.D.43 when a Roman army crossed the river and defeated the British tribes under Caractacus'. I understand from personal sources that there was a good deal of debate about the exact wording. Nigel Nicolson wanted it to be more precise, stating that the stone marked the site of the actual crossing, but more cautious views in the end prevailed. The monument was also sponsored by Kent Archaeological Society and Maidstone Museum.
5 Claire Ryley, former Senior Education Officer at Fishbourne Roman Palace, has kindly provided the following insight:

> children at even 7 years old (the earliest age at which they would study the Romans) would learn about archaeological uncertainties, as long as the teachers were aware that there are other possible interpretations. Many of the children who visit us at Fishbourne are aged 9 to 15, and at this stage they would be expected to weigh up evidence from written sources. The important task therefore is for archaeologists to take the debate into the public arena, as Sussex Archaeological Society and Kent Archaeological Society have done, and get school publishers to include alternative interpretations in their text. I have been working with an A-level class and the teacher is delighted that there are disagreements and alternative interpretations for the invasion, as this gives his pupils much more reason for studying and debating the evidence, and realising that it is partial, and possibly biased.

6 Frere, S, (1967), *Britannia – a history of Roman Britain*, Routledge and Kegan Paul, London.
7 For example, see the map in Scarre, C, 1995
8 For instance, displays in the Museum of London, the Yorkshire Museum (York) and, indeed, at Fishbourne itself cite Richborough without qualification.

2 Were the Romans really like us?

1 The commander of the Roman invasion of Britain in AD 43 and the first governor of the province (see Appendix 1).
2 By *ourselves* I mean those who subscribe to a 'western' world view.
3 But is this another way of saying that what was really desirable was to be a landholder?
4 For instance, the Roman system of orders, of patricians, equites and plebs runs counter to the western concept of individualism.

3 What kinds of evidence do we have for the Roman invasion of Britain?

1 You need also to isolate and discard those sherds, which are known by archaeologists as either 'intrusive' or 'residual'. The former are deemed to be later sherds that have somehow entered an earlier deposit, post-deposition; the latter are earlier sherds that have entered a later deposit, post-deposition. There are no objective procedures for isolating such unwanted material, and the exercise is usually undertaken by the excavator applying his or her knowledge of the site, and taking an informed view. However, the dangers of circular arguments, and of ignoring the sherds that don't 'fit' the current interpretation of the site, are obvious.
2 Recent research suggests that these Italian wares were made more widely than just in the Arezzo region (Joanna Bird pers comm), but the term is retained in this book.
3 More precisely the date after which the ditch was filled.
4 More precisely the date before which the ditch was dug.
5 Sauer, pers comm.
6 In *theory*, of course, it is possible that the annexe was constructed at a later date using stock-piled timber, or indeed that the annexe was constructed earlier and the gateposts were being renewed.
7 For instance, some members of a post-Vietnam generation of British archaeologists downplayed warfare in prehistory; a new generation may now be putting warfare (and slavery) back into prehistory – see Armit 2001.
8 I am grateful to Ernest Black for the use of this term in relation to the writings of ancient historians.
9 Francis Haverfield (1924,101) was correct when he described Dio's text as 'brief and vague'; Frere and Fulford (2001, 46), however, 'see no certain justification in rejecting any part of Dio's account of the campaign.'
10 I stress I am not trying to patronise any audience by these remarks. I sit with them in as much as I, too, am a product of the same cultural system; I share the same world-views. Indeed, it is an irony that because of this I can never reach a position of objectivity or neutrality, since I write within the system, not outside it.
11 Quote from FM Viscount Montgomery of Alamein, in Peddie 1987, v.

4 Why was Richborough eventually chosen by modern historians?

1 Richard Bradley's happy phrase.
2 There were some exceptions – see Eddy, M., 1995, 122-3.
3 I do not know whether this book will be just another statement in the debate, or indeed whether it will be damned by silence or critical peer review. Whatever the reaction to it, I do not want it to be viewed as the 'last word'. I foresee the debate, of interest perhaps to a minority, continuing for many years.

5 What happened between Caesar and Claudius?

1 Black (1990, 10) argues that Caesar says that these immigrants came from Belgica, but were not necessarily Belgae.
2 Remember, however, that accounts by ancient historians of numbers of opposing forces could be exaggerated for emphasis and propaganda, and were always likely to be prone to considerable error.

3   It should be noted that the location of *Portus Itius* has not been identified with certainty, although there is a consensus that it refers to Boulogne (Seillier 1996, 212).

4   Grainge estimates that each transport ship in 55 BC contained about 150 men; in 54 BC the average loading could have been as low as 60 to 70 men per transport, since the second expedition carried much more equipment.

5   It is important to note that our terms 'dynasty' and 'kingdom' may conjure up more modern analogies involving rules of succession, and fixed territories with demarcated borders. In the Late Iron Age there were rulers who claimed descent from earlier rulers, and there were territories associated with certain communities, but the rules and customs governing rights to rule and rights to land were probably very different than later periods.

6   'Exotic' here means coinage that originates in more distant areas, other than the geographically closer regions of Armorica and Belgic Gaul.

7   How was news of Caligula's farce received in Britain? Perhaps the 'internal disturbances' recorded by Cassius Dio were exacerbated by Caligula's perceived failure.

8   What exactly those 'preparations' were that might have survived for three years is, of course, debatable. They might have ranged from strategic plans of the invasion, to more tangible assets such as harbour works, ships and supplies in stores. However, three years is a long time for some of these things to lie idle.

6 What can Roman historians tell us?

1   It is important to note the amount of conjecture in this paragraph. In reality we do not know what Cluvius Rufus wrote, or to what extent Dio made use of his writings.

2   This translation is taken from that appearing in Hind 1989.

3   Despite the similarities in their names, there is no known connection between the anti-Roman Togodumnus of Dio, and the pro-Roman Togidubnus of Tacitus.

4   Was the episode described really a serious mutiny? Or is this passage just a literary device to add a bit of drama to the occasion? Despite the notion that Narcissus was sent out by Claudius I find it incredible that the army would wait for Narcissus to journey from Rome and it seems more likely that Narcissus, as advisor to Claudius, was already with the army.

5   In some translations this is rendered as 'hindered'; there are similar debates concerning the alternative readings of words or phrases in other places in Dio's text (e.g. the debate concerning whether Dio meant 'there' or 'thereupon' in relation to the possible construction of a fort after the surrender of a part of the Dobunni – see Frere & Fulford 2001, 48 and below).

6   This statement partly contrasts with that of Diodorus Siculus, who stated that the chiefs of Britain for the most part 'live at peace amongst themselves' (Siculus, World History, 5.21.4). He may, however, have been using a much earlier source.

7   The auxiliaries who swam across rivers in full armour are normally designated by translators and historians as Batavians, because of their reputation of crossing rivers in the way described. Dio actually calls them Celts.

8   They would also have been aware of the dangers of being lured into a trap, however.

9   According to London Zoo (pers. comm.) elephants can walk at 4-6km an hour over long distances.

10   The issue of timing is further complicated by the discovery of a coin struck at the mint of Alexandria in the third regnal year of Claudius (i.e. on 28 August 43 at the very latest), which carries the title Bretannikos. This was an honorific title awarded to Claudius and his son by the senate on receipt of the official news of the Emperor's victories in Britain. If the coin was really struck *after* Claudius had won a victory in Britain, Claudius must have departed from Rome by June at the latest (see Sauer 2000, 38-9 for this argument), and Dio must have been wrong about Claudius returning to Rome in AD 44. However, it is possible that the coin anticipated the victory of Claudius, and may have even been struck after the victories of Aulus Plautius which guaranteed the subsequent triumph of Claudius.

11   Plautius would thus have had a month with little to do. How did he and his army spend their summer? There are two possible scenarios, depending on whether you believe that the main thrust of the invasion was along the north Kent coast, or you prefer to see invasion through the Chichester area. If the former,

now would be the time for Vespasian and the II Augusta to strike towards the south-west and into the territory of the Durotriges. If the latter, in addition to the departure of Vespasian, one legion could have been sent eastwards to secure Kent and Richborough itself for the arrival of Claudius. Alternatively, Claudius could have set off from Rome as soon as news of a successful embarkation or landing had reached him, shortening Plautius' wait.

12 This timetable, however, looks very compressed. It is possible that Claudius, rather than waiting to leave Rome as soon as he heard that Plautius had reached the Thames, actually set out from Rome once news reached him that the fleet had sailed from Gaul. In this scenario Claudius would leave Rome in mid-July and be in Britain by early to mid-August. Such a scenario would also have the merit of reducing the length of the wait at the Thames for Plautius and his troops.

13 A Roman triumph was a procession through the streets of Rome by a returning victorious military leader, accompanied by some of his soldiers, by captives and booty taken from a defeated enemy.

14 Claudius Britannicus was born, to Claudius and Messalina, on 12 February AD 41, and was awarded the title Britannicus after the invasion of Britain.

15 Messalina would have been about 18 or 19 years old at the time, and the reference to Livia (the deified wife of Augustus) was meant to suggest that Messalina was as worthy as Livia.

16 The arches are interesting in that, since Claudius is assumed to have departed from Boulogne, the arch must have been constructed there. The arch at Richborough, erected over the remains of earlier Claudian occupation, was constructed around AD 80, however, and signalled, at that time, the most frequented entry point to Britain from the Continent. The Richborough arch, as known, has no relevance for the events of AD 43.

17 Agricola was governor of Roman Britain from *c.*AD 78 to 84.

18 I think this point is important. Roman historians used secondary sources, but uncritically. There was no concept of the necessity of referring to the sources a writer had used, or of examining critically a sequence of events where the accounts provided by two different secondary sources were at odds with one another. The onus on the contemporary historian was therefore to 'make sense' of the contrasting accounts, either by conflation, repetition or omission.

19 Tacitus' text has Cogidubnus, but see Tomlin 1997 for the justification of Togidubnus.

20 Observant readers will have noted that I now have Vespasian carrying out three elements of the invasion almost simultaneously (i.e. the march from the Thames to Richborough; accompanying Claudius to Colchester; the campaign in the south-west – see note 11). These are some of the imponderables caused by the ambiguities of the historical evidence. Successful though he was it seems unlikely that Vespasian could have done all three, although they could have been carried out in rapid succession.

21 Claudius needed to relieve Plautius of his command and take overall control in order to qualify for a full Triumph.

22 It is probable that, during the wait for Claudius, some essential infrastructure for the south-east was put in place. Some elements of the major road system, including Stane Street and Watling Street, might have been surveyed by military engineers.

23 Such an argument, however, is based on several imponderables (eg oversight, antipathy, 'garbled sources' and the greater accuracy of Eutropius, who did not 'garble his sources'). As such, it is not entirely convincing.

7 What do we know about the environment in AD 43?

1 Pers. comm. Mike Allen.

2 Although such a statement implies that the north-south parallel ditches, which ran across the *middle* of the island (see 2 below), might have performed other roles than a functional defensive barrier.

8 What else can we deduce from our own experiences about the events of AD 43?

1 I don't wish to sound patronising about 'enthusiasts'. After all, there are no professional Roman soldiers around and the wearing of replica armour, and firing of replica ancient weapons has told

us a great deal about the practical problems a Roman soldier would have faced; such activities are part and parcel of experimental archaeology.

2   Derek Turner has kindly pointed out that a mid-first century strengthening of the legion resulted in the nominal addition of some 320 men, taking the total closer to 5500. However, it is unclear whether such a reform had occurred before AD 43.

3   Roughly modern Croatia and Bosnia-Herzegovina.

4   Plautius was therefore probably chosen because he was a 'safe pair of hands' and someone Claudius could trust, not necessarily because of outstanding military experience or ability.

5   Adminius probably fled from Kent so an embarkation point at Boulogne would make sense for Gaius.

6   Approximately equated with modern Hungary.

7   There are brief summaries of the origin and history of each of these legions, and accompanying auxiliary units, in Peddie 1987, 180ff; see also Keppie 1984.

8   Thrace can be broadly equated with modern Bulgaria.

9   Raised in Gaul in AD 21 (Peddie 1987, 181).

10 Raised from the Vettones of Central Spain.

11 Vespasian was the only one attested as a legionary legate, so they may not have all been of equal status.

12 A knot is a nautical mile per hour.

13 A UK nautical mile is 6080ft, or 1.85km.

14 Gerald Grainge has kindly pointed out that if departure is from some way up a river then sailing just as the tide turns is correct. If the embarkation is from the coast, however, then paramount significance is given to the direction of tidal streams off-shore. Care needed to be taken to ensure that vessels, if loaded at high water, did not ground with their deeper draughts once the tide ebbed.

15 His log records an estimation of the wind strength at Beaufort Force 5 (page 123).

16 One of my staff has had that experience, and I still sense the fright in his voice when he describes lobster pots racing past his boat.

17 The lack of knowledge on the degree of local assistance inevitably leads to the supposition that Plautius and his troops were landing on *potentially* hostile shores, and acted accordingly.

18 I am grateful to John Smith for some of this information.

19 This sounds a little like modern army jargon, and may not be applicable to ancient warfare.

20 Tony Wilmott (pers comm) has indicated that the land south of the Saxon Shore Fort at Richborough shelves gradually towards the presumed Roman coast-line, and was not, as today, a moderate cliff.

21 There is nothing in Caesar about Richborough. However, the Romans must have gained some knowledge of the general coast of southern Britain from a century of maritime trade.

22 The visual boundary may have been psychologically comforting to the soldiers, but I doubt whether logic mattered much to them.

23 Ernest Black very kindly wrote this section on the potential size of the British forces.

24 Note that Fulford 2000, 45 argues that only half of the Roman army would have been active as a fighting force.

9   What did they really find at Richborough?

1   References in this format refer to the Richborough Report number, followed by the page number.

2   I should point out that it is not my intention to describe in any detail the multi-phase results of the excavations at Richborough. Readers are directed to the five volumes of the excavation report, or to the English Heritage guidebook.

3   A more accurate statement on the discard policy at Richborough would result from a detailed study of the archive from the site, including unpublished finds, now stored in Dover Museum.

4   The plain samian is not described and it is impossible to gauge the proportions of decorated to plain samian on the site. Stamps are described, both for decorated (22 examples) and plain (171 examples) forms (III, 123).

5   But note that this potter's work has now been dated to a slightly later period, beginning around AD 45 (Joanna Bird pers comm).

6   Note the slight discrepancy in overall length to that quoted in Richborough IV.

7   The Richborough 'Island' could have been much larger in antiquity than I have allowed for. Modern rates of coastal erosion in south-east Britain can be alarmingly high, althogh they were not constant in the past. Incidentally, I am writing this in August 2001, just a month before a new programme of work begins on the site under the auspices of Martin Millett, Tony Wilmott and English Heritage. Their work promises to provide more specific answers to these questions, and indeed, much more data about Richborough.

8   i.e. being used after the main period of production of this vessel was over.

10 And what did they (and we) really find at Fishbourne?

1   Sauer (2000, 49) notes the small number of Caligula coins from Fishbourne and suggests that the deposits at Fishbourne are slightly younger than those underneath Chichester. Claudian coin copies were bronze issues made in Britain, possibly by the army, because of a shortage of coin.

2   For example, to the north of the North Wing of the Palace, in trial trenches, the excavators noted traces of 'first-century timber buildings' (Cunliffe 1971, I, 55).

3   Interestingly, a reassessment of the coins from Alec's excavations by David Rudling indicates a higher number of Claudian and Neronian issues than stated in the published report (Cunliffe *et al.* 1996, 193).

4   Chichester District Council is planning to fund the outstanding publications, although this may mean considerable delays before the final reports appear.

5   ACD indicates the annual publication *Archaeology of Chichester and District*.

6   The pottery comprised 468 sherds (over 10kg in weight) from the bottom of the aqueduct, including a number of part-complete vessels and was probably dumped on top of a wooden conduit soon after the digging of the feature. A large percentage (46%) of Atrebatic 'Overlap' wares (indigenous coarse wares that cannot be closely dated to either pre- or post-AD 43) is in keeping with a date of *c.*AD 50 (pers comm Malcolm Lyne).

7   There is a 'progressive normative' view in this statement; i.e. that Romans could dig straight whereas 'natives' were not quite so adept at keeping to a straight line, which of course is nonsense. Sections of the Chichester Dykes or Entrenchments are pretty straight, but, as conventionally interpreted, were the work of Late Iron Age communities.

8   'Overlap' means here indigenous pottery that cannot be precisely dated to pre- or post-AD 43.

9   Or maybe by an encampment of Roman *negotiatores* or traders?

10 Malcolm Lyne very kindly looked again recently at the pottery (in Dover Museum) from the lower silts of the Claudian ditches at Richborough. The dating of the South Gaulish samian is still far too imprecise to fix a date of AD 43 for the material. However he pointed out that the SENICIO stamped bowls are now dated to AD 45-70 (Polak, M, 2000). In addition he noted the dominance of flagons and mortaria in the North Gallic fabric NFSE-2667, a fabric otherwise rare in Roman Britain. The assemblages of material from the Richborough and Fishbourne ditches are quite dissimilar, with no Arretine, or Terra Rubra and only insignificant amounts of local coarse pottery from the Richborough ditches. Malcolm concludes that the Fishbourne assemblage is the earlier of the two.

11 Is there archaeological evidence for the Romans' route to the Thames?

1   Although admittedly it would be unusual for a Roman army not to 'dig in' overnight, if only to follow established training procedures. The ditches might have been shallower in perceived friendly territories.

2   A military-style ditch, deliberately back-filled, was located beneath the later villa at Eccles in the mid-1970s, just to the east of the Medway and reasonably close to the Medway Monument. The ditch was traced east-west for a length of 92.65m; no corners were located and the ditch contained pottery apparently earlier than AD 65. However the full report is yet to be published (Detsicas 1977, 56).

3   Subsequent work, by Southern Archaeology, suggests that these ditches do not relate to one another.

James Kenny, Chichester District Council Archaeologist, reports that the lowest fill of the ditch on the Needlemakers site contained an assemblage of large sherds of *terra nigra* and *terra rubra*, probably of early first-century AD date.

4   However, for the difficulties of distinguishing legionary equipment from that of non-legionaries see Sauer 2000, 22-9.

5   In this context, as in others in this book, it is sometimes difficult to separate the archaeologist from the archaeology. James Kenny, Chichester District Archaeologist, who knew and worked with Alec Down, has supplied the following qualification: 'It must be acknowledged that Alec had been a professional soldier and was, I think at least partly as a result, almost obsessed with a need to identify a military phase at Chichester (and Barry finding just such a phase at Fishbourne can't have helped!). Alec's first thought when presented with a particularly early Roman phase or a particularly V-shaped ditch was always "this must be military".'

6   The hoard could just as easily represent, however, payment to a British chief who collaborated with the invasion force. (I am grateful to Alan Ward and others for this suggestion.)

7   500 would, however, be more likely.

8   Eberhard Sauer has also suggested to me, however, that in the light of the 2001 season of excavations it seems increasingly likely that AD 44 is the date of the annexe rather than that of the main fortress. The latter might thus still date to AD 43 or AD 44.

12   Does talking lead to the 'truth'?

1   There is no evidence that the army lacked bridging equipment and I am surprised that an invading force, knowing that a Thames crossing was planned, would have come without such equipment. However, the historical sources provide no evidence of the invading army constructing bridges.

13   What concluions can I draw (if any)?

1   I am grateful to James Kenny for this suggestion.

2   The Roman Albania (land adjacent to the western Caspian), not modern Albania.

3   I am grateful to Creighton (2001) and to David Kennedy and Brian Bosworth for these examples.

4   Of course, when we invoke the model of a pre-AD 43 military presence at Fishbourne and Chichester, 'advising' or at the very least 'assisting' local leaders, our arguments would be stronger if we knew where the main settlement of those Late Iron Age leaders was. Apart from the remains of three timber structures under Chichester, and a partial round-house east of Fishbourne, and the suggestion that the Chichester Dykes defend some kind of native oppidum, our knowledge is scanty. It is also plausible that a Roman military presence might have been stationed deliberately away from the main centres of Late Iron Age settlement.

5   It's worth repeating that such interpretations are based on the current data available. Major excavations currently in progress in the Whitefriars area of Canterbury (late 2001) may alter our understanding considerably.

6   Another major site where a small quantity of Arretine (63 sherds) has been located is, of course, Silchester. This site also has a small quantity of first century AD military metalwork. The Arretine ware is not so well stratified as the Fishbourne material, so its association with a military presence is more problematic (Joanna Bird in Fulford & Timby 2000, 184).

7   See also von Schnurbein in Brewer (2000).

8   Clearly, other areas of Britain, such as Wales and southern Scotland, do seem to have been conquered and subsequently patrolled in orthodox military manner.

9   A case in point is the recently discovered fort at Shapwick Road, on the western promontory overlooking the aproaches to Poole harbour. Excavations in 2000 revealed a fort at least 6ha in size, dating to the AD 40s (Bellamy & Pearce 2001). Note that this site does not appear on **11**.

Bibliography

Classical Authors

Augustus *Res Gestae Divi Augusti* (RG) – written by the Emperor Augustus, as a record of his achievements, shortly before he died in AD 14

Cornelius Tacitus *De Vita Agricolae* (Agric) – born *c.*AD 56, of Gallic or north Italian parentage, historian and politician who married Agricola's daughter in AD 77

Cornelius Tacitus *Annales* (Ann) – born *c.*AD 56, historian and politician who married Agricola's daughter in AD 77

Cassius Dio *Roman History* (RH) – a native of Bithynia (modern north-western Turkey), Roman senator and historian who died post-AD 229

Diodorus Siculus (WH) – wrote a World History between 60 and 30 BC in 40 books, from the earliest times to Caesar's Gallic Wars

Eutropius *Breviarium* (B) – historian who took part in Julian's Persian campaign (AD 363)

Flavius Josephus *Bellum Judaicum* (BJ) – born *c.*AD 37/8, a Jewish priest of aristocratic descent

Julius Caesar *De Bello Gallico* (BG) – statesman and general – 100-44 BC

Strabo *Geography* (Geog) – an historian and geographer of Greek descent – 64/3 BC to AD 21 at least

Suetonius *De Vita Caesarum* (VC) – born *c.*AD 69/70, a native of north Africa, lawyer and biographer

Vegetius *Epitome of Military Science* (EMS) – a professional bureaucrat who compiled the book from a variety of sources between AD 383 and AD 450

Secondary References

Akeroyd A.V., 1972, Archaeological and historical evidence for subsidence in southern Britain. *Philosophical Transactions of the Royal Society of London*, Series A 272, 151-69

Armit, I., 2001, Warfare, Violence and Slavery in Prehistory and Protohistory, *Past* (the newsletter of the Prehistoric Society), 37, 10-11

Barrett, J.C., Freeman, P.W.M., & Woodward, A., 2000, *Cadbury Castle Somerset*, English Heritage, Archaeological Report 20

Bellamy, P. and Pearce, P., 2001, *Shapwick Road, Hamworthy, Poole.* Report no. 5050.4, Terrain Archaeology

Bennett, P., Frere, S.S. & Stow, S., 1982, *Excavations at Canterbury Castle*, I, Canterbury Archaeological Trust

Bird, D.G., 2000, The Claudian Invasion Campaign Reconsidered, *Oxford Journal of Archaeology*, 19 (1), 91-104

Bird, D.G., 2001, *The Claudian Invasion Campaign Reconsidered*, unpublished transcript from lecture delivered at Faversham (Kent) on 7 April 2001

Birley, A.R., 1981, *The Fasti of Roman Britain*, Oxford

Bishop, M. & Coulston, J.C., 1993, *Roman Military Equipment*, Batsford, London

Black, E.W., Caesar's second invasion on Britain, Cassivellaunus, and the Trinobantes, *Essex Archaeology and History* 21, 6-10

Black, E.W., 1993, The period IC bath-building at Fishbourne and the problem of the 'proto-palace', *Journal of Roman Archaeology*, 6, 233-7

Black, E.W., 1998, How many rivers to cross? *Britannia* 29, 306-7

Black, E.W., 2000, Sentius Saturninus and the Roman Invasion of Britain, *Britannia*, 31, 1-10

Black, E.W., 2001, The first century historians of Roman Britain, *Oxford Journal of Archaeology*, 20 (4), 415-28

Blockley, K., Blockley, M., Blockley, P., Frere, S., & Stow, S., 1995, V, *Excavations in the Marlowe Car Parks and surrounding areas*, Canterbury Archaeological Trust

Brewer, R., (ed), 2000, *Roman Fortresses and their Legions*, Society of Antiquaries and National Museums and Galleries of Wales, London and Cardiff

Brown, A.E., (ed), 1995, *Roman small towns in Eastern England and beyond*, Oxbow Monograph, 52, Oxford

Bushe-Fox, J.P., 1926, *First Report on the excavations of the Roman Fort at Richborough, Kent*, Res Rep 6 of the Society of Antiquaries of London

Bushe-Fox, J.P., 1928, *Second Report on the excavations of the Roman Fort at Richborough, Kent*, Res Rep 7 of the Society of Antiquaries of London

Bushe-Fox, J.P., 1932, *Third Report on the excavations of the Roman Fort at Richborough, Kent*, Res Rep 10 of the Society of Antiquaries of London

Bushe-Fox, J.P., 1949, *Fourth Report on the excavations of the Roman Fort at Richborough, Kent*, Res Rep 16 of the Society of Antiquaries of London

Carson, R.A.G., 1960, The Bredgar Treasure of Roman Coins, *Numismatic Chronicle*, 19, 17-22

Clarke, S., 2000, In Search of a Different Roman Period: The Finds Assemblage at the Newstead Military Complex, *Proceedings of the Ninth Annual Theoretical Roman Archaeology Conference*, Durham 1999, 22-9, Oxbow Books, Oxford

Collis, J.R., 1968, Excavations at Owslebury, Hants: an interim report, *Antiquaries Journal*, 48, 18-31

Creighton, J., 2000, *Coins and Power in Late Iron Age Britain*, CUP, Cambridge

Creighton, J., 2001, The Iron Age-Roman transition, in James & Millett (eds) 4-11

Crummy, P., 1997, *City of Victory: the story of Colchester – Britain's first Roman town*, Colchester Archaeological Trust, Colchester

Cunliffe, B.W., 1968, *Fifth Report on the excavations of the Roman Fort at Richborough, Kent*, Res Rep 23 of the Society of Antiquaries of London

Cunliffe, B., 1971, *Excavations at Fishbourne 1961-1969*, Res Report of the Soc of Ant, London, No 26, vols I & II

Cunliffe, B.W., 1987, *Hengistbury Head, Dorset, I: The Prehistoric and Roman Settlement, 3500 BC-AD 500*, Oxford University Committee for Archaeology, Monograph 13

Cunliffe, B.W., Down, A., & Rudkin, D., 1996, *Chichester Excavations*, 9, Chichester District Council

Cunliffe, B.W., & de Jersey, P., 1997, *Armorica and Britain: Cross-Channel Relationships in the late first millennium BC*, Oxford University Committee for Archaeology, Monograph 45

Cunliffe, B., 1998, *Fishbourne Roman Palace*, Tempus, Stroud

Dark, K. & P., 1977, *The Landscape of Roman Britain*, Sutton Publishing Ltd, Gloucester

Denison, S., 2001, Roman Fort, *British Archaeology*, 58, 6

Detsicas, A.P., 1977, Excavations at Eccles, 1976, *Arch Cantiana*, 93, 55-9

De Jersey, P., 1993, The early chronology of Alet, and its implications for Hengistbury Head and cross-channel trade in the Late Iron Age, *Oxford Journal of Archaeology*, 12, 321-35

De Jersey, P., 1999, Exotic Celtic Coinage in Britain, *Oxford Journal of Archaeology*, 18, 189-216

Dickinson, B., Hartley, B.R. & Pearce, F., 1968, Maker's Stamps on Plain samian, in Cunliffe, 1968, 125-48

Dimbleby, G.W. & Bradley, R., 1975, Evidence of Pedogenesis from a Neolithic site at Rackham, Sussex, *Jnl. Arch. Sci.* 2, 179-86

Down, A. & Rule, M., 1971, *Chichester Excavations,* 1, Phillimore, Chichester

Down, A., 1978, *Chichester Excavations,* 3, Phillimore, Chichester

Down, A., 1981, *Chichester Excavations,* 5, Phillimore, Chichester

Down, A., 1989, *Chichester Excavations,* 6, Phillimore, Chichester

Down, A. & Magilton, J., 1993, *Chichester Excavations,* 8, Chichester District Council

Drewett, P., Rudling, D. & Gardiner, M., 1988, *The South-East to AD 1000*, Longman, London

Dungworth, D., 1998, Mystifying Roman Nails: *clavus annalis, defixiones* and *minkisi, Proceedings of the Seventh Annual Theoretical Roman Archaeology Conference* Nottingham 1997, 148-59, Oxbow Books, Oxford

Dupont, F., 1989, *Daily Life in Ancient Rome*, Blackwell, Oxford

Eddy, M., 1995, Kelvedon and the fort myth in the development of Roman small towns in Essex, in Brown, AE, (ed), 119-28

Fitzpatrick, A., 1997, *Archaeological excavations on the Route of the A27 Westhampnett Bypass, West Sussex, 1992. II: the Cemeteries*, Wessex Archaeology Report 12, Salisbury

Frere, S.S., 1967, *Britannia – a history of Roman Britain*, Routledge and Kegan Paul, London

Frere, S. & Fulford, M., 2001, The Roman Invasion of AD 43, *Britannia*, 32, 45-55

Fulford, M., 2000, The organization of legionary supply: the Claudian invasion of Britain, in Brewer, R. (ed), 41-50

Fulford, M., & Timby, J., 2000, *Late Iron Age and Roman Silchester: Excavations on the site of the forum-basilica 1977, 1980-86*, Britannia Monograph No 15, 2000

Gardiner, M., 1990, The Archaeology of the Weald – a survey and a review, *Sussex Archaeological Collections*, 128, 33-53

Gilliver, C.M., 2001, *The Roman Art of War*, Tempus, Stroud

Gough, R., 1789, *Camden's Britannia: Kent*, Hutchinson, London

Grainge, G., 2001, The Roman Channel crossing of AD 43: the constraints on Claudius's naval strategy, unpublished PhD thesis, University of Southampton

Hamilton, S., & Manley, J., 1999, The end of prehistory *c.*100 BC-AD 43, in Leslie & Short (eds), *An Historical Atlas of Sussex*, 22-3

Hammond, N.G.L. & Scullard, H.H., 1970, *The Oxford Classical Dictionary*, second edition, Clarendon Press, Oxford

Haverfield, F., 1923, *The Romanization of Roman Britain*, fourth edition, revised by G. Macdonald, Clarendon Press, Oxford

Haverfield, F., 1924, *The Roman Occupation of Britain*, revised by G. Macdonald, Clarendon Press, Oxford

Hawkes, C.F.C., 1961, The Western Third C Culture and the Belgic Dobunni, in E.M. Clifford, *Bagendon: A Belgic Oppidum*, Cambridge, 43-74

Helms, M.W., 1993, *Craft and the Kingly Ideal: art, trade and power*, University of Texas, Texas

Hind, J.G.F., 1989, The Invasion of Britain in AD 43 – an alternative strategy for Aulus Plautius, *Britannia*, 20, 1-21

Hingley, R., 1994, Britannia, origin myths and the British Empire, *Proceedings of the Fourth Annual Theoretical Roman Archaeology Conference* Durham 1994, 11-23, Oxbow Books, Oxford

Hingley, R., 2000, *Roman Officers and English Gentlemen*, Routledge, London

Höckmann, O., 1986, Römische Schiffsverbände auf dem Ober- und Mittelrhein und die Verteidigung der Rheingrenze in der Spätantike, *Jahrbuch des Romanisch-Germanischen Zentral Museums Mainz,* 33, 369-415

Hodder, I., 1999, *The Archaeological Process*, Blackwell, Oxford

Holman, D., 2000, Iron Age coinage in Kent: a review of current knowledge, *Arch Cantiana*, 120, 205-33

Ingold, T., 2000, *The perception of the environment. Essays in livelihood, dwelling and skill*, Routledge

James, S., & Millett, M., 2001, *Britons and Romans: advancing an archaeological agenda*, CBA Research Report 125, Council for British Archaeology

James, S., 2001, Soldiers and civilians: identity and interaction in Roman Britain, in James & Millett (eds), 77-89

Johnson, J.S., 1999, *Richborough and Reculver*, English Heritage site guidebook

Keppie, L., 1984, *The Making of the Roman Army*, Batsford, London

Leslie, K., & Short, B. (eds), 1999, *An Historical Atlas of Sussex*, Phillimore, Chichester

Lewis, N. & Reinhold, M., 1966, Roman Civilization. Sourcebook I: The Republic, Harper & Row, New York

Lyne, M., 1999, Roman ships' fittings from Richborough, *Journ. Roman Military Equipment Studies,* 7, 147-9

Lyne, M., 2000, A Roman Fort near Faversham, Kent, *Practical Archaeology*, 2, 8-10

Magilton, J., 1995, Roman Roads in the Manhood Peninsula, *The Archaeology of Chichester and District*, 31-4

Marsden, P., 1994, *Ships of the Port of London: First to Eleventh Centuries AD*, English Heritage, London

Mattingly, H., 1970, *The Agricola and The Germania*, Penguin, Harmondsworth

McGrail, S., 1987, *Ancient Boats in N.W. Europe,* Longman, Essex

McGrail, S., 1997, *Studies in Maritime Archaeology*, BAR British Series 256, Oxford

Millett, M., 1988, Aspects of Romano-British pottery in West Sussex, *Sussex Archaeological Collections*, 118, 57-68

Millett, M., 1990, *The Romanization of Britain*, Cambridge University Press, Cambridge

Nash, D., 1984, The Basis of contact between Britain and Gaul in the late pre-Roman Iron Age, in Macready S. & Thompson F.H. (eds), *Cross-Channel Trade between Gaul and Britain in the pre-Roman Iron Age*, Society of Antiquaries of London

Needham, S., 2000, Power Pulses Across a Cultural Divide: Cosmologically Driven Acquisition Between Armorica and Wessex, *Proc. Prehist. Soc.*, 66, 151-207

O'Neil, B.H.St., & O'Neil, H.E., 1952, The Roman Conquest of the Cotswolds, *Arch Journal*, 109, 23-38

Peddie, J., 1987, *Invasion – the Roman Conquest of Britain*, Guild Publishing, London

Polak, M., 2000, South Gaulish Terra Sigillata with potters' stamps from Vechten, *Rei Cretarie Romanae Fautorum Acta Supplementum 9*

Reddé, M., 1996, *L'armée romaine en Gaule*, Editions Errance, Paris

Robinson, D., 1999, The coast and coastal changes, in Leslie & Short (eds), *An Historical Atlas of Sussex* 1999, 8-9

Russel, J.I., 2001, *Archaeological report on the Watching Brief and Excavation for the new Parts Centre at Hawkeswood Road, Bitterne Manor, Southampton*, Report 409, Southampton City Council Archaeology Unit

Salway, P., 1982, *Roman Britain*, BCA, London

Sauer, E.W., 2000, Alchester, a Claudian 'Vexillation Fortress' near the western boundary of the Catuvellauni: New Light on the Roman Invasion of Britain, *The Archaeological Journal*, 157, 1-78

Scaife, R.G. & Burrin, P.J., 1983, Floodplain Development in and the Vegetational History of the Sussex High Weald and some Archaeological Implications, *Sussex Archaeological Collections*, 121, 1-10

Scarre, C., 1995, *The Penguin Historical Atlas of Ancient Rome*, Penguin, Harmondsworth

Sellar, W.C., & Yeatman, R.J., 1974, *1066 and All That*, Penguin, Harmondsworth

Seillier, C., 1996, Le camp de la flotte de Bretagne à Boulogne-Sur-Mer (*Gesoriacum*) in Reddé M, 1996, 212-19

Sharples, N., 1991, *Maiden Castle* London

Shirley, E., 2001, *Building a Roman Legionary Fortress*, Tempus, Stroud

Tomlin, R.S.O., 1997, Reading a 1st-century Roman gold signet ring from Fishbourne, *Sussex Archaeological Collections* 135, 127-30

Von Schnurbein, S., 2000, The organization of fortresses in Augustan Germany, in Brewer, R (ed), 29-39

Webster, G. & Dudley, D.R., 1973, *The Roman Conquest of Britain*, Pan Books, London

Webster, G., 1980, *The Roman Invasion of Britain*, BCA, London

Wheeler, R.E.M., 1943, *Maiden Castle, Dorset*, Res Rep Comm Soc Antiq, 12, London

Wightman, E., 1985, *Gallia Belgica*, Batsford, London

Willis, S., 1998, Samian pottery in Britain: exploring its distribution and archaeological potential, *The Archaeological Journal*, 155, 82-133

Woodcock, G., 1967, *William Cobbett. Rural rides*, Penguin, Harmondsworth

Index

Numbers in **bold** refer to illustrations, or captions to illustrations